Kingsholm

Castle Grim

Home of Gloucester Rugby

The Official History

MALC KING

GLOUCESTER RUGBY
HERITAGE

First published in 2016
for Gloucester Rugby Heritage
www.gloucesterrugbyheritage.org.uk

by The Hobnob Press, 30c Deverill Road Trading Estate, Sutton Veny, Warminster BA12 7BZ
www.hobnobpress.co.uk

British Library Cataloguing in Publication Data
A catalogue record for this book is available from the British Library

ISBN 978-1-906978-39-6

Typeset in Octavian 10/11.5 pt. Typesetting and origination by John Chandler
Printed by Lightning Source

The cover illustration is reproduced by kind permission of Martin Bennett

Contents

Appendices

Forewords

Mike Tindall
Rugby World Cup Winner, former Gloucester player and coach

Kingsholm is a very special place. It was an intimidating place when I played for Bath. It was like walking into a cauldron of noise. I used to love running a lap in front of the Shed and absorbing the friendly banter I heard. It immediately made the hairs on the back of your neck stand up and put you straight in the mental place you needed to be when Bath played Gloucester.

When I started to play for Gloucester it genuinely became the 16th man. When things weren't quite going right it was the team member who lifted your spirits and got your head back in the game. Kingsholm is steeped in history and always has the feel of an old school ground. Teams coming to play here knew they were in for a game and if they didn't bring their best game it could be a long day at the office.

Perhaps my most treasured memory at Kingsholm is Sinbad's try against Wasps, when he ended up going 80 yards and putting James Bailey over in the corner. Just a fantastic turnover try after about 20 phases of defence.

The Shed is world famous for the reason that they help their Gloucester team and make it mentally tough for the opposition, especially if you slice a kick or drop a high ball! They appreciate good play no matter which side it comes from and are always on song. I used to love listening to what was said during breaks in the game.

I have always been aware of the heritage at Kingsholm, which runs through Gloucester as a club. It is an old school ground with old school values, as long as you leave 100% of yourself on the pitch it will always look after you. This heritage is to be seen all around the ground thanks to the displays which the Heritage team have mounted. And now we have to thank them too for all the work they have put into this book. Hopefully it will serve to keep the ethics and values of Kingsholm and the Club alive and kicking for everyone to see.

Martine Walkinshaw
Former Owner, Gloucester Rugby

Kingsholm is a unique place. One that I feel privileged to have been part of. With my husband, I have stood and celebrated in times of triumph, and endured in times of defeat. We have supported the team through joy and heartache, both personal and professional. But whenever I returned after the summer break, it was always magical to breathe the smoky, autumn air as another season got underway. It was as if the ground was reawakening from its slumber.

We talk about Kingsholm as a fortress — a place to protect our rugby pride and passion, but it required a sturdy defence long before that first rugby game was played here in 1891. In Old Norse, a language spoken in Middle England, a "holm" was an island, a piece of land found in the midst of a river. A Kings Holm would have belonged to the monarch. So I've always believed that not only was this a noble place, but one that has always been defended to the very last man.

Over the years that the Walkinshaw family was involved with Gloucester Rugby, we saw the stadium grow and flourish. The trophy cabinet was extended too! With the 2015 World Cup our place is assured in the World Rugby gazetteer, with four pool games played here. So whatever may be written in history books about Kingsholm in the future — rest assured that the cherry and white shall always defend this island of green and I look forward to many more years of majestic competition here.

Heather Forbes,
Head of Information Management & Archives, Gloucestershire County Council

I am very pleased to write a foreword for a book focused on Kingsholm. As the current custodian of the Rugby Club's archives I have especially enjoyed reading the human stories, amusing incidents and interesting local facts extracted from the documents.

Kingsholm is well known as the home of Gloucester Rugby. Since the 1970s Kingsholm has also been the home of Gloucestershire Archives (formerly known as Gloucestershire Record Office). Based in Alvin Street, just round the corner from the rugby ground, this treasure house contains Gloucestershire's unique and irreplaceable archives from the 12th century onwards. Thus I was particularly delighted when the Rugby Club's own precious archive was transferred to the Archives for safekeeping. Gloucester Rugby Club's enormous contribution to the life of our city and county is now being fully documented for current and future generations.

Promoting and sharing the heritage of Gloucester Rugby is just as important as preserving it. Readers of this book will benefit from the encyclopaedic knowledge of the history of the Club and its Kingsholm home built up by Malc King and the other volunteers from Gloucester Rugby Heritage. As part of the Heritage Lottery Funded project, Malc and his team of dedicated volunteers collectively spent thousands of hours cataloguing the Club's archives, developing an interactive community website, and creating new oral history recordings with key people in the Club's history. Although the HLF project has been completed, the sharing and promotion of Gloucester Rugby Heritage continues. Many more hours of meticulous research have been undertaken and the best bits are being distilled into five volumes documenting the history of the club. I commend this first volume and look forward to reading the next four.

Martin St Quinton
Owner, Gloucester Rugby

I first visited Kingsholm in 1995 and was immediately struck by the special atmosphere of the place. Sporting crowds are often passionate and sometimes knowledgeable. At Kingsholm they are both.

So taken was I with Gloucester Rugby I approached the then Chairman, Tom Walkinshaw, and asked if I might buy a stake in the Club and join him on the Board. At first he declined but a number of years later he asked me if I was still prepared to invest in the Club, which of course I was. Consequently I acquired a 40% stake in Gloucester Rugby in 2007/8 and then 7 years later bought the remaining 60%.

I feel very honoured to be the Chairman of such a wonderful Club but as far as 'ownership' is concerned I don't really feel I own the Club. I may have a share certificate that says as much but the Club really belongs to the people of Gloucester. It is a community asset. I am merely the current caretaker. Following as I do a long line of dedicated caretakers starting with Jimmy Boughton and 'Commodore' Vears who took the initiative to buy the ground back in 1891. Brave men indeed, they were succeeded by generations of club stalwarts who gave their all to safeguard and develop the ground and the Club into what it is today. That's why a move from Kingsholm would be unthinkable. It is one of the country's most iconic and atmospheric stadiums and long may it remain.

This beautiful book detailing the history of Kingsholm is overdue and therefore all the more welcome. Heartfelt thanks go to the original trio of volunteers Malc King, John Theyers and John Cowen, who had the enthusiasm and vision to get this project underway. They were soon joined by Dick Williams, Chris Collier and Dave Smith who respectively contributed to the website, playing records and video productions. Current and future generations of Gloucester fans are greatly indebted to them all for their foresight and dedication.

Introduction

When people are asked to think of Gloucester, and to say what the City means to them, answers usually revolve around the cathedral, the docks and rugby, but not necessarily in that order. Gloucester became a rugby city in the nineteenth century, and it has remained that way ever since. In its early days the Club played on the Spa, a public park in Gloucester, but moved to its own ground at Kingsholm in 1891, and there it has remained. This book is being published in 2016, the 125th anniversary of rugby at Kingsholm, and, although the bulk of the book is about the history of the Kingsholm ground, there are some introductory chapters covering those early years at the Spa and one on Kingsholm before rugby.

The land purchased in 1891 for the new rugby ground was part of the Castle Grim estate, but this splendidly forbidding name, which so accurately reflects the feelings of many a visiting player after a typical Gloucester welcome on the pitch, was not retained. Rather the name of the district in which the ground is situated was adopted, and it was as Kingsholm that the ground has become famous as one of the world's most revered rugby venues. Many generations of players have regarded it as an honour to play on the hallowed turf, and many watching the games only wish that they had been able to, but players and spectators alike have delighted in the very special Kingsholm atmosphere of big match days.

In 2007, the main grandstand, a largely wooden structure which had been constructed in 1933, was demolished to make way for the magnificent new stadium which graces the ground today. Over the course of the previous 74 years, the bowels of the old grandstand had proved to be a convenient, and at least dry, place in which to store boxes of "stuff", which were cluttering up the Club offices, but which a succession of Club officials thought should not be destroyed. This treasure-trove only came to light when the stand was being demolished. All was headed for the skip, but fortunately this was queried by one of the demolition contractors, and Gary Little, then the Club's Community Manager, stepped in. Gary recognised that the Club's history was in danger of being thrown away. He asked Gloucestershire Archives if they might be interested, and 31 large boxes of material were hastily transported into the Archive's safe keeping.

The contents of these boxes were listed and assessed, and found to contain a wealth of documents and photographs, some of them going back to the early days of the Club in the nineteenth century. Given the high standing of Gloucester Rugby in the City, and indeed across the County, it was decided that this material should be preserved for future generations, that it should form the basis for an archive devoted to Gloucester Rugby, and that it should be used to educate and entertain. So, the Gloucester Rugby Football Club Community Heritage Project, as it was first known, was born. As the planning of this Project progressed, so ambitions expanded from not only establishing a physical archive, but also putting as much material as possible on-line. In addition it was decided that the archive should include not just documents and photographs, but also artefacts such as jerseys, caps and programmes, as well as audio and video recordings of Gloucester Rugby people and events.

Other objectives were to promote active community involvement in the project and to capture and preserve material from a wide range of sources. This is a two-way process – taking the archive out into the community by promoting its use through on-line access, interactive and static displays, events, and educational packages for schools; and bringing material into the archive by inviting contributions from members of the community through donations of physical memorabilia and by recording their memories.

The initial 3 partners in the Project – the Gloucestershire Archives, the Friends of the Gloucestershire Archives and Gloucester Rugby were very supportive, but if the objectives of the Project were to be met fully, more substantial funding was required. An application was made to the National Heritage Lottery Fund, and was successful to the tune of nearly £50,000. As a result the Project got underway with a vengeance towards the end of 2008, with a total commitment of money and manpower from all sources to a value of £88,000. The Lottery money had to be spent within three years, and the success of the Project was heavily dependent on volunteers, but all the initial objectives were met or exceeded by 2011. Thereafter the Project was able to expand further thanks to sponsorship by Ecclesiastical Insurance, a company which has been a part of Gloucester life for almost as long as the Rugby Club.

The Project volunteers have catalogued all of the material from Kingsholm, as well as the material donated by individuals. Many of these donors are former players, who have been delighted to find people interested in the boxes of rugby memorabilia which had been gathering dust in their attics. Indeed the large turnout by former players at events organised by the Project resulted in the Club setting up a Players' Association, which is now flourishing and organising its own events.

The Project has a website, www.gloucesterrugbyheritage. org.uk, which contains the digital archive, populated with all manner of things relating to the history of Gloucester Rugby, as well as educational materials. It has been a real success if measured in terms of the number of people accessing it every day from all around the world.

Throughout the Kingsholm stadium the Project has mounted interpretative displays, including a mural the length of the first floor summarising the entire history of the Club. Elsewhere there are exhibits recording the contributions which individual players and administrators have made to the success of the Club. There are also display cases containing historical artefacts. In the Lions' Den are the Club's honours boards and photographs of the teams through the ages. These displays of the Club's heritage form an important part of the Kingsholm experience for visitors to the ground.

Education has been perhaps the most important part of the Heritage Project, and has consumed more than half of the Project's expenditure. There are more than a hundred lesson plans on the website, together with supporting materials, aimed at both primary and secondary schools, and tied into Key Stages of the National Curriculum. Many schools are using these educational materials and tens of thousands of local schoolchildren have been to Kingsholm and the Archives, visits which are subsidised by the Project.

Two previous books have been produced by the Project. The first is a richly illustrated but brief account of the history of the Club, entitled "Gloucester Rugby Heritage". The second is a more substantial book by Martin and Teresa Davies detailing the wartime exploits of Gloucester rugby players, entitled "They Played for Gloucester and Fought for their Country".

The book you are now reading is the first in a series of five planned to chart the history of the Gloucester Rugby Club. This one concentrates on the Kingsholm ground, its acquisition and development, and those who have lovingly nurtured it over the years. A second volume will recount the many representative matches which have been staged at Kingsholm, and a third will give an account of the Club's exploits in European competitions and against other foreign opposition. The fourth will record the history of the Gloucester Club, covering the ups and downs of the team in every season since the Club was founded in 1873, and providing a comprehensive record of Club matches, both home and away. The fifth will focus on the players who have represented Gloucester, and their deeds of derring-do.

The enthusiastic commitment to the cause of Gloucester Rugby by so many people in the City and its environs is illustrated by those they have elected:

Richard Graham, Member of Parliament for Gloucester, says of Kingsholm: "This is the home of Kings, full of Kings of the sport and home of the Shed: where dreams are made, and sometimes lost. This is the beating heart of our city and beyond, whose psalms are timeless (and tuneless), where police are only for traffic, and all ages and kinds come together for the best two hours of the week. This is Kingsholm, Gloucester; and there is simply nothing, nowhere, quite like it."

Paul James, Leader of Gloucester City Council, reminisces: "My grandfather was born in the shadows of the Kingsholm stadium. He was a lifelong fan and I enjoyed watching the matches with him as a young boy. For twenty years I lived right opposite the ground in the aptly-named Pitch View block next to The White Hart / Teague's Bar. I've been a season ticket holder for around thirty years but a visit to Kingsholm to watch Gloucester play is still as special as it was the first time I went. It brings people from the City and beyond together to unite behind a common cause. Many people say the Cathedral is the soul of Gloucester but Kingsholm is the heart."

It is almost fifty years since your author came to live in Gloucestershire and first experienced the delights of rugby at Kingsholm. I joined the thousands of fans who pour through the turnstiles, who revel in the tingling excitement of a match day, and who are enthused by that heady mix of thrills and spills, pride and passion, elation and despair, and witty and wicked comment, which is the very essence of Kingsholm. What a wonderful and unique experience that has been. But I recognise that, not being born and bred in Gloucester, I did not grow up with the cherry and white bones of those who cannot remember a day when Gloucester Rugby did not figure prominently in their lives.

Gary Little, former Community Manager at Gloucester Rugby, is a prime example of this : "I'm not sure if Kingsholm is a part of my life or a part of me, if that makes sense. My father would bring me along as a young boy to watch games, he would meet up with his friends in the old clubhouse bar and then gather under the clock for the match. As a child I probably didn't take too much notice about what was going on on the pitch, I would be running around on the 'Tump' playing with other kids, no doubt to the annoyance of those trying to watch the game. As I got older I began to appreciate the game a bit more and would join my own friends to watch games in the Worcester terrace. The clubhouse bar in the old stadium used to open regularly, being a venue for Club members to enjoy a social drink throughout the week and a venue for skittles, darts and shove ha'penny teams. In those days it was a social club, it was much more than just a rugby club. Ah, the good old days. After spending a few years away, whilst studying at university and travelling the world, I was drawn back to the Club and was very fortunate to be offered the job of Community Manager, a role created just after the game had gone professional. The role was specifically geared toward developing grassroots rugby, engaging young people in a variety of community programmes, and hopefully helping to make a difference to the lives of those in our community who are less fortunate than others. It enabled me to work with players, both old and new, and to work with some great people who support the Club in so many ways, the many supporters, business people and local dignitaries, and a fantastic group of volunteers who formed the Gloucester Rugby Heritage group. I love the rugby, I love the old Club, I love the people and the characters that surround the Club. I enjoy the victories and bemoan the losses! So the question of what does Kingsholm mean to me, is not that easy to answer - I suppose it's in my blood and no matter where I am or where I go, it will always be a part of me."

I would add only that, without Gary's initial intervention and continuing commitment, Gloucester Rugby Heritage and this book, would never have happened.

One of the delights of the Heritage Project is that it has given me the opportunity to get to know a lot of people who are devoted to rugby at Kingsholm. Many have enjoyed a longer association with the ground than myself, but I hope that even they will discover amongst these pages some information which is new to them. Indeed my dearest wish is that all my readers will find the content interesting and educational. For me, the writing of this book has been a labour of love, and I dedicate it to those many people, including players, fans and officials, who have helped to make Kingsholm a unique and special place over the past 125 years.

Malc King
Chairman, Gloucester Rugby Heritage

Acknowledgements

The team behind the book – from the left – John Theyers, Dick Williams, Malc King, John Cowen, Chris Collier [Malc King]

Although I have had the pleasure of writing this book, there are many others who have contributed to its production. The whole Gloucester Rugby Heritage Project has succeeded only because of the huge effort put in by a devoted team of volunteers, who have contributed more than 30,000 hours of their time over the past nine years. The Project has also benefited enormously from the professional expertise and assistance of our partners, Gloucester Rugby and Gloucestershire Archives; from the financial backing of our sponsors, the National Heritage Lottery Fund and Ecclesiastical Insurance; and from the enthusiastic encouragement and support of a great many people who cherish Gloucester Rugby and Kingsholm.

The research work behind this book and the many other Gloucester Rugby Heritage outputs has been undertaken by a core team of volunteers, who continue to labour in the Archives and lunch in the Queen's Head at Longford with utter dedication. They are John Theyers (treasurer), John Cowen (cataloguer), Chris Collier (statistician) and Malc King (chairman). Without their efforts the whole Project, including this book, would not have been possible.

Dick Williams, the mastermind behind the Gloucester Rugby Heritage website, also maintains our digital library of photographs, and his monumental efforts have ensured that this book is richly illustrated. He was also kind enough to take on the task of compiling the index. When we have had only poor quality images, Martin Bailey has dazzled us with his expertise in digitising and enhancing documents and photographs, and many of the illustrations in this book are much the better for the application of his skills. Annette Chapman has improved the book by exercising her editorial skills to very good effect, although the author readily confesses responsibility for any remaining errors. We have also been fortunate in contracting John Chandler, famous locally for his work on the Victoria County History, to exercise his design and type-setting skills to produce a polished publication.

I am grateful to Chris Brind for his help in the early days of our research, and to Dave Smith who has become secretary of our Project, is our expert on video material, and who designed the cover of this book. David Halliday has sent us a stream of transcripts of our interviews, many produced whilst touring the outback of Australia in his camper van (the interviews themselves can be heard on our website). Others too numerous to mention have also contributed, but they know who they are and they have my gratitude.

I owe particular thanks to Mike Tindall, Heather Forbes, Martine Walkinshaw and Martin St Quinton for kindly writing forewords to this book.

Gloucester Rugby has been very supportive throughout, particularly with the time and enthusiasm of Gary Little, until recently their Community Manager, who sat on our Project Committee for eight years and who regularly made things possible for us. The Walkinshaw family and Martin St Quinton as owners of the Club; Ken Nottage and Stephen Vaughan, as successive Chief Executive Officers of the Club; and David Foyle, Peter Ford, Allan Townsend, Eric Stephens and Fred Reed, successive Presidents of the Club, have never wavered in their encouragement. Dave Balmer, Stadium Manager, has been ever willing to contribute his long and unique knowledge of the inner workings of Kingsholm. The Club has kindly made space for displays all around Kingsholm, has provided facilities for events, has responded very positively to requests for help, and has put us in touch with many of the contacts who have enriched the Project and this book

Gloucestershire Archives has been equally active in promoting and supporting Gloucester Rugby Heritage. Their professional expertise has been invaluable, and the Archives provide a home for our physical archive in climate controlled conditions. This will ensure that the many photographs, documents and interviews which have been gathered together, will be available in good condition for generations to come. The support and professional guidance of the County Archivist, Heather Forbes, has been much appreciated, as well as the time and skills of many of her staff, but in particular Jill Shonk, Kate Maisey and John Putley, all of whom have served on our Project Committee at various times. In compiling the chapter on Kingsholm before rugby, useful inputs have been made by John Rhodes, Anna Morris and Andrew Armstrong.

Whilst many of the documents and photographs in our archive have come directly from the Gloucester Club, we are also grateful to more than ninety individuals, many of them former players, who have donated memorabilia to our archive. Special mention should be made of a couple of donations which were particularly useful in the production of this book. Pride of place must go to those Club officials who cared sufficiently for the heritage of Gloucester Rugby to take care of the legal documents relating to the purchase of Kingsholm in 1891; these were passed down from one generation to the next and ended up with Harold Symonds, a former player, who has now kindly placed them in the safe hands of the Gloucestershire Archives. John Horner, another former player and chartered surveyor, was responsible for many of the developments to the fabric of Kingsholm in the last fifty years, and he sorted through the archives of his company to extract a selection of his plans, which also now reside in the Gloucestershire Archives. John Hudson has been helpful not only in providing material passed down in his family but also in generously facilitating the sale of our previous books. But I am grateful to all those, too numerous to mention individually, who have donated material - their generosity has greatly enriched our collection and added to our knowledge of the history of the Club.

Many of the details of matches and photographs in this book are drawn from the Gloucester Citizen and sister publications, and I am grateful to Jenny Eastwood, Editor of the Citizen, for allowing us to reproduce both text and images from these sources. I am also grateful to Phil McGowen at the World Rugby Museum at Twickenham for his expert advice and provision of material from his archive; to Pete Wilson for quotes from some of the people he has interviewed on BBC Radio Gloucestershire; to Douglas Gatfield for his collection of photographs recording the construction of the new stadium in 2007; and to Paul James and Adam Balding for contributing to the RWC 2015 chapter. Duncan Wood, Media Manager at Kingsholm; Martin Bennett, the official photographer at Kingsholm; and his predecessor, Tony Hickey; have been generous in providing photographs of Kingsholm in more recent times. And one of my favourites in the book, the wonderful photograph of Harry Dyke and his horse, was donated by Harry Dyke's granddaughter, Olivia Thompson.

Sources

The Gloucester Rugby Archive contains many photographs (mostly of teams), lots of notebooks giving details of matches, annual reports and accounts, ground development plans, heaps of correspondence and many legal documents. It has been the basis for the research on which this book is based, and it has provided many of the images which illuminate these pages. Whilst the hard copy originals are held in the Gloucestershire Archives, where they are publicly accessible, many items have been digitally scanned and can be accessed on the Gloucester Rugby Heritage website - www.gloucesterrugbyheritage.org.uk.

An impressive amount of research on the history of the Gloucester Club is contained in a thesis entitled "The Civilising of Gloucester Rugby Football Club? – A Historical Sociology of the Development and Management of an Elite, English Rugby Union Football Club, 1873-1997". This earned the author, Andy White, his PhD, and is not only a useful source in its own right but has served to point towards other sources. A copy is lodged in the Gloucestershire Archives, and it can also be accessed on-line at https://lra.le.ac.uk/handle/2381/31040.

The Citizen became the daily newspaper of Gloucester in 1876, only three years after the foundation of the Club, and since then has published many column miles of reporting on Gloucester Rugby. The paper has boasted a sequence of distinguished rugby correspondents, who made it their business to get close to the workings of the Gloucester Club. Most issues of the Citizen, 1876-2004, are conveniently available on microfilm at the Gloucestershire Archives, and the book draws heavily from this source. Indeed, the Citizen has been, by some margin, the main published source of material, and, except where another source is specifically identified, all the quotes in this book are taken from the Citizen.

The Journal is also available on microfilm at the Gloucestershire Archives. A weekly publication, which preceded the Citizen by more than a century, it is a unique source on the first three years of the Gloucester Club, 1873-76, and a valuable source of photographs from the 1930s to the 1960s. Copies can be viewed on microfilm at Gloucestershire Archives up to 1992.

Likewise the Gloucestershire Echo, the Citizen's sister newspaper based in Cheltenham, regularly reported on Gloucester Rugby, but in less detail than the Citizen. Copies are available on microfilm at Gloucestershire Archives for 1930-2005, and are most useful when copies of the Citizen are missing.

The Cheltenham Chronicle and Gloucestershire Graphic was published once a week 1901-41. It did not normally cover Gloucester Club games, except for those against Cheltenham, but it did cover most of the big representative matches at Kingsholm, and is notable for being richly illustrated with good quality photographs. Every issue can be seen in bound volumes at the Gloucestershire Archives, and most of the photographs in this book from that period have been copied from this source.

The Magpie was published weekly from May 1891 to December 1893. It is available in four bound volumes at the Gloucestershire Archives, courtesy of Charles Dancey, of whom you will learn more later in this book. Although disappointingly short-lived, this publication reported at length on the Gloucester Club, and regularly illustrated its reports with cartoons. Fortunately it covered the period when the Club moved to Kingsholm.

In a very few cases, despite diligent searches, it has not been possible to establish conclusively whether copyright exists for certain historical images. This limited edition book has not been produced in order to make a profit, and any income resulting from sales will all be used to further the charitable work of Gloucester Rugby Heritage.

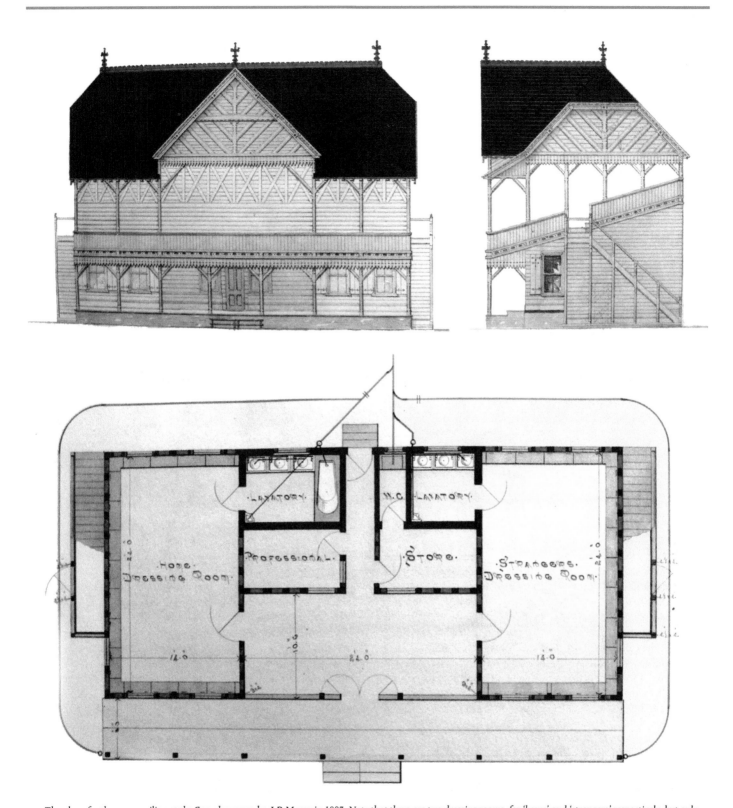

The plans for the new pavilion at the Spa, drawn up by J P Moore in 1883. Note that there are two dressing rooms, for 'home' and 'strangers' respectively, but only the home team players are allocated a bath. This better provision for the home team is a tradition which persists to the present day; as at most grounds, the facilities provided at Kingsholm for the away team are considerably less roomy and well equipped [Gloucestershire Archives]

became the property of the contractor, for which a credit of £27 was allowed for the materials recovered from its demolition.

In the early seasons, there was a lengthy break in fixtures over the Christmas period, but a new tradition was started at the Spa on Boxing Day 1883. A representative London team, the first to visit Gloucester since the Flamingoes, and including the famous England rugby and cricket player, A E Stoddart, proved to be a big draw. Spectators streamed into the 6d and 2d sides of the Spa field and made up the largest crowd ever seen on the ground. £40 was taken on the gate. A London team, normally featuring Stoddart, came to the Spa on Boxing Day for the next five years, but after the Club moved to Kingsholm, Old Merchant Taylors took over the Boxing Day slot.

A photograph taken in 1908 of the pavilion at the Spa, built in 1883, and used by the Rugby Club until 1891 [Gloucestershire Archives]

In 1887, the rent for the Spa field was reduced from £32 to £20, and the Club's share of that as sub-tenant was reduced from £15 to £9. This did not lead to any reduction in admission charges for spectators. Season tickets at the Spa were 5s and 2s 6d; ground entry for individual matches was 6d and 2d; and there was also a charge for transfer to the pavilion. Some insight into the financial position of playing matches at the Spa can be gained from details of the match played against Bath on 29th December 1888. Income from the match was £8 2s 7d (7s 3d from the pavilion, £2 18s 6d from the 6d side, and £4 16s 10d from the 2d side). Expenditure on the match was 14s 6d (6s to gatekeepers, 3s to Baylis, 1s for delivery of bills, 2s for errand boys, 1s to Townsend, 1s to Brent, and 6d on lemons).

The desire to maximise income from gate money caused the Club to fence the ground at the back of the Beaufort goal in December 1887, but this seems not to have deterred non-paying spectators sufficiently. The following year the Committee decided to use seats installed for athletics sports at the Beaufort end, with spectators standing on them to obstruct the view from the Spa walk. A similar arrangement was put in place for 1889-90 with a single row of stands, but this was to form part of the 2d side, and was therefore separated from the 6d side by a fence. The Committee also decided to erect a signboard, 12ft x 2ft 6ins, giving the name of the Club, admission prices, etc. Not more than £3 was to be spent on this, but it was to be erected at the Pump Room corner at the Beaufort end so as to obstruct the free view of the field.

In January 1888, the Club Committee decided that 'two ticket boxes at 10s each and 5,000 tickets at 10d per thousand should be procured for the purpose of checking the gate money'. They soon changed their minds. At the end of the month they voted in favour of a different plan under which 'the tickets for admission to the ground on match days be sold through the railings at a distance of some 10 to 20 yards beyond the gate on the 2d side and at the corner on the 6d side, such tickets to be delivered up to a collector at the gates, by this means avoiding a squash; a table to be provided for each ticket seller; tickets of four colours to be used in rolls as before, numbered and respectively printed; admission 6d, 3d, 2d, 1d; the boxes to be discontinued.'

[NOTE: Throughout this book all financial figures are quoted in the currency in use at the time, which, for the first hundred years of Gloucester Rugby, was £ s d. For the sake of younger readers, familiar only with decimal currency, a pound divided into 20 shillings, and a shilling into 12 pence. So, 10s = 50p, 5s = 25p, 1s = 5p, 6d = 2.5p and 1d = 0.4p. A guinea was £1 1s = £1 5p.]

The Dream of the Club's Own Ground

ALTHOUGH THE HIATUS resulting from the floodlit match had been successfully resolved, this had served to highlight the insecurity of the Club's tenure as sub-tenants of the Cricket Club on a Council-owned park. There was tension every year over matches in March, when the Cricket Club were keen to start their pitch preparation for the coming summer season and nervous of damage from rugby. Another consideration was the growing popularity of rugby in the City, which led to more players joining the Club, and the introduction of regular second team matches. This put additional pressure on the playing surface at the Spa. There was also a financial motivation for change in that the difficulty of screening matches at the Spa was limiting the income derived from charging spectators.

Club officials started to search for a new ground, and to investigate the means to fund its purchase. At the Club AGM in 1888, Jimmy Boughton, as Chairman of the sub-committee appointed to try and procure a new ground, reported that they had done all they could to achieve this. They thought they had succeeded in obtaining Budding's Field, but, after negotiations were opened with the proprietor, the residents in London Road lobbied him, asking him on no account to let the ground to the Football Club, and so negotiations were broken off. Despite this rebuff, Budding's Field was soon being used as a soccer pitch by the Gloucester Association Football Club, and in fact rugby was not totally excluded. In March 1889 the Gloucester 2nd XV played a match there against Stroud, when the Spa had been flooded, and the Club hoped to use it again in 1890, when they tried to organise a fixture with Wigan as an add-on to their Easter tour to South Wales. The Spa was not available, having been given over to cricket for the summer season, so the Club offered £1 to Mr Orchard, the owner of Budding's Field, to rent the pitch for a day, but he would not accept less than £5, and the plan foundered.

The Club then tried to acquire the field at the back of the station belonging to Mr. Vassar-Smith as their permanent new home, but that gentleman informed them that he had promised the friends of the Home of Hope not to let the field to any sporting club. The next option was Beard's Field on the Bristol Road, but it transpired that the Club might have to leave at any time on receipt of 14 days' notice, as the land was up for sale in building lots. A place in Barton Street was also looked at, but that proved far too small, so the sub-committee concluded that no viable option was currently open to the Club. At the AGM, Mr Sloman suggested trying for a piece of land next to Linden Road, but this came to nought, the search came to a halt, and the idea of the Club owning its own ground was shelved for the time being.

With the prospect of continuing their tenancy at the Spa, a General Meeting of the Club at the end of the 1888-89 season took some measures to ease the relationship with the Cricket Club. Because a match had been played on the Spa as late as 31st March, it was resolved that the Cricket Club should be paid an additional £5, and it was agreed that no junior matches should be played on the Spa on Thursdays. A resolution was also passed to the effect that 'it is desirable that the Club should possess an enclosed ground'. It was therefore decided to make another effort to get permission to put canvas round the Spa for all matches, and to consider erecting stands for those who had paid so as to obstruct the view of those outside the ground who had not.

However, the dream of the Club's own ground had not been abandoned. It was noted that £4,000 would be required to purchase and fit up an enclosed ground at Kingsholm which had been thought suitable for the purpose. Whilst little difficulty was anticipated in raising the capital for the formation of a company to acquire and operate such a ground, the problem was perceived to be the inability of the Club committee to take on a long-term lease. The committee was a changeable body, elected every year, and unable to pledge its successors, so thought not to be acceptable as the signatory to a legal contract. No way forward was found, and so the dream that the Club should have its own ground again remained just that for the time being. Meanwhile use of the Spa was expanding and more important matches were being staged there.

New Zealand Maoris

In February 1889, the New Zealand Maoris descended on the Spa to play against Gloucestershire, much to the pleasure of the visitors who believed that the Gloucester Club side would have been more difficult opponents. Qualification for the Maoris depended upon being born in New Zealand rather than being exclusively of Maori ethnicity, and they were the first international touring team to visit the British Isles. They aroused a lot of interest amongst rugby followers and the Citizen reported that

This match, the event par excellence of the football season at Gloucester, came off before an immense concourse of spectators, the weather being bitterly cold. Special permission had been obtained from the Corporation of the City to enclose the ground for the occasion, and accordingly the match was shut off from the view of outsiders by canvas, and the thousands who usually obtain a good view of the Gloucester matches "on the cheap", either had to pay for the entertainment in common with the more practical supporters of the club, or put up with the only alternative of missing one of the most interesting and important matches of the season, as well as the novelty of seeing a team of New Zealanders, who have gained the reputation which has been attained by the Maoris, give an exposition of the game. The mass of people who lined the ropes included a great many who had come in from the country as well as a large number from Cheltenham, Stroud and the neighbouring towns, while the grand stand would not contain all the ladies who graced the ground by their presence. Indeed, such a muster has probably not been seen in the Spa before, and it will probably be some time before such an one is seen again. A trophy on the pavilion, bearing the New Zealand Standard, and a string of flags at the entrance gate, amongst which was the National Flag of New Zealand, were provided by Mr Conway Jones free of charge. The ground was kept by a number of committee men, and a special force of police. The money taken at the gate amounted to £193 odd.

A close match resulted in victory for the Maoris by one goal and one try to one try.

The County Championship

The County Championship was started in 1888-89, but for the first two seasons, counties made their own fixtures, and a winner was declared by the Rugby Union based on the results from a fairly random assortment of matches. Then, in 1890-91, the Rugby Union organised the counties into groups, and the winner of each group went into knockout stages to decide the Champion. Gloucestershire was grouped in the South West with Somerset, Devon and Midland Counties. The first, and as it turned out, the only match played by Gloucestershire under this system at the Spa was on 15th January 1891. It was won 5-0 (three tries and one conversion) against Midland Counties. The County Championship soon became the stepping stone from club to international rugby and county caps came to be treasured by the players. For the best part of the next century, the County game was often the biggest match of the season played in Gloucester.

Easter 1891

In November 1890, the Club received a challenge from the Barbarians for a match in Easter week 1891. This would represent another step up in the status of the Club, so they were keen to accept the fixture. The problem was that by Easter the Spa would be back in the hands of the Cricket Club. They enquired about playing on Budding's Field, but that was not available, and a desperate Club Committee declared that no expense should be spared to find a ground.

This was all to no avail, so in December 1890 they decided to try to persuade their landlords to allow them to play on the Spa by offering to pay a proportion of their gate money to the Cricket Club if they would allow the rugby season to be extended. The Cricket Club replied positively:

The Gloucester Cricket Club do hereby sanction the use of the Spa field by the Gloucester Football Club down to and including Wednesday April 1st 1891, on consideration that 10% of the gross receipts taken at all matches played on the ground after the 7th March shall be paid over to the Treasurer of the Cricket Club, and that such sum shall not in the aggregate amount be less than £20. And further, that the ground shall immediately after April 1st next be put in order by, and at the expense of, the Gloucester Football Club, to the satisfaction of the Cricket Club Committee. And it is to be distinctly understood that this sanction is given in the present instance, and is not in any way to be deemed a precedent for future years.

These conditions were agreed and the Club set about organising fixtures. A match was arranged for 30th March, Easter Monday, against the Royal Naval College (Devonport), who agreed to come for £15 plus tea. Easter Wednesday, 1st April, was offered to the Barbarians along with £10 plus tea, but they held out for more and were made an improved offer of £25 plus tea. Advertisements were placed in the 'Sportsman' and the 'Umpire' offering similar terms for a match with any strong team. With the financial commitments to the opposition teams and to the Cricket Club, it was decided to increase income at the Easter Monday game by doubling the admission charges for this match and by applying to the Council for permission to erect canvas screens. Old Merchant Taylors were invited to play on Easter Saturday, 28th March, and if they declined Clapham Rovers were to be asked. This promised to be the most prestigious sequence of matches ever played by the Club, but these plans were about to be overtaken by events which would change the course of the Club's history.

Leaving the Spa

BY 1891, GLOUCESTER was playing the big four Welsh clubs (Newport, Cardiff, Swansea and Llanelly) on a regular basis. The results did much to define the success or otherwise of Gloucester's season. These matches were always keenly contested, and invariably attracted the biggest crowds of the season. On Monday 5th January the Committee discussed the home fixture against Swansea scheduled for the following Saturday, 10th January. There were concerns about the cold weather, so the minutes record that 'the Hon Treasurer (S Starr) was granted full permission to do all possible to get the ground in playing order'. The Committee met again on the ground at 1pm on the Friday, and all seemed set for the match the following day, but there was a hard frost overnight.

An inspection of the pitch on the morning of the match showed it to be frozen hard. Faced with the prospect of losing such a major and lucrative fixture, officials and members were summoned to try to rescue the situation. They fetched tons of salt in carts and spread it liberally across the pitch. This did the trick - the ground thawed, and indeed was reported by 'Goal Post' in the Western Mail as 'quite soft and playable, thanks to the measures taken by the club committee, although skating on the Severn had been indulged in during the week'. The Citizen reported that 'the ground was in remarkably good condition considering the weather which has prevailed of late, the only fault being that the surface was somewhat slippery'.

So, the match went ahead, and Gloucester rose to the occasion in front of the largest attendance of the season, estimated at 8,000. 'The crowd furnished a scene to be remembered, one mass of people extending all round the ground, and every possible position of vantage being tried to its utmost capacity.' £71 17s 8d was taken on the gate, made up of £36 12s 9d from the sixpenny side, £32 0s 2d from the threepenny side, and £3 4s 9d from the pavilion. This included a great many boys who paid one penny admission.

Gloucester scored a try and converted it early on, and never looked back. They eventually won 4-0 with tries from Walter George and Walter Taylor and a conversion by A F Hughes (the scoring system in use at the time awarded one point for a try and two for a conversion). Although the pitch was playable, it was noted that 'Bancroft was playing with both his arms bleeding badly from falling on the frozen snow behind his own goal'.

The pitch seemed to have survived the salt treatment, and the game itself, in reasonable order. Indeed, during the following week an extra match was organised on the Spa at short notice. The Gloucestershire County team played the Midland Counties on Thursday 15th January 1891. The match was originally scheduled for Coventry, and then switched to Burton-on-Trent, but when both of these grounds were declared unfit, it was decided at the last moment to play the game at Gloucester. Thirteen Gloucester players turned out for the County, and they won by one goal, two tries and four minors to one minor. Minors, scored when the defending side was forced to touched down behind its own goal line, were noted as part of the score, but did not have any bearing on the result of the match.

In the succeeding weeks the true cost of the liberal application of salt gradually became apparent as the grass died. On 17th January, Gloucester played out a 0-0 draw against Penygraig on a deteriorating pitch, and on 24th January, Gloucester had a match against Swindon. The description in the Citizen match report was;

The executive of the Gloucester Club had no difficulty in getting the ground soft enough to play upon this week, but on the contrary, it would have improved matters considerably if the softening process which had been conducted by the weather had not been quite so thorough and effective. Water stood on the ground in many places, and the Spa was literally a sea of mud, in which the players wallowed until they were scarcely distinguishable. Under these circumstances it was only to be expected that the football would be of a mediocre and somewhat uninteresting description, whilst amusement was occasioned by the capers of the players, which were suggestive of mud-larking....The vain attempts of both sides to pick up and hold the ball were most laughable....there being more water at the railway end, towards which Gloucester were now playing, some ludicrous situations quickly ensued....Scarcely a minute passed without someone being collared and thrown in a large pool of water, or a bunch of players measuring their length and almost burying themselves in the mud.

Nevertheless, Gloucester emerged from the quagmire with a victory by 2 tries and 7 minors to nil.

The Gloucester Journal was rather more critical in an editorial the following week:

In order to excel on the football field under such circumstances as those which prevailed at the Spa last Saturday, it would almost be necessary for a player to acquire some amphibious capabilities, and that team which contained the best swimmers or water pilots, rather than that which could acquit itself best at football, might be backed to win. The Spa was in a terrible state – all over it was as soft as could well be imagined, the ground to a considerable depth being nothing more nor less than wet slush, whilst near the 25 line at the railway line end stood a pool of water of abnormal dimensions, which proved, much to the discomfiture of some of the players, to be two or three inches deep at the least, and at the other [Beaufort] end a series of smaller puddles extended across the enclosure.

The Club had tried to improve conditions with straw on the pitch, but by 26th January this was described as 'practically fit only for manure', and it was sold off for 15s. On Monday 9th February, the arrival of the Hull team in Gloucester for the first time attracted a big crowd. This time dry weather enabled the pitch to hold up well enough – 'the weather and the state of the turf favoured an open game.' An excellent hard-fought game ended with a win for Gloucester by one goal, two tries and two minors to two minors.

The lack of grass was not putting a stop to rugby, but was clearly going to be a problem when the cricket season came along. The Gloucester Cricket Club, who held the lease on the ground from the local council, and let the ground in the winter to the Rugby Club as their sub-tenants, was unhappy to say the least. The spirit of cooperation between the clubs was evaporating, and the grandiose plans which the Rugby Club had put in hand for Easter were largely abandoned. In the event the match against the RNC Devonport was the only one played by the 1st XV at the Spa after 7th March, but Gloucester won 7-0 thanks to two tries by Walter Taylor and one try and a conversion from Walter Jackson. It was the 2nd XV which benefited most from the extension to the season – they packed in four additional fixtures, including matches on successive days on 30th and 31st March, and enjoyed four victories against Sharpness, Beaufort,

Cinderford and XV Colts of the City. This proved to be the final fling for the Club at the Spa.

W B of The Citizen later described how the Swansea match had been played at 'the cost of the absolute ruin of the ground, which instead of a piece of pasture land assumed, as soon as the frost gave, the appearance of a newly ploughed piece of arable. For the purposes of Cricket the ground was almost entirely spoilt, and the Cricket Club had 1600 square yards in the centre of the field dug up and planted with grass seed.'

Divorce between rugby and cricket was inevitable, but the number of individuals who were members and officials of both rugby and cricket clubs at least enabled the separation to proceed without acrimony. There were already significant developments in hand behind the scenes. Jimmy Boughton had persuaded A V Hatton to lease the Castle Grim estate at Kingsholm from the Church Commissioners, with eventual purchase by the Rugby Club as the hidden agenda. Within a month, the Citizen published the following exchange of letters between A W Vears and H J Boughton, both ardent supporters and officials of the rugby and cricket clubs:

My Dear Boughton,
Referring again to our several conversations respecting the present condition of the Spa field, I am strongly of an opinion that we should at once call together a representative body of the various clubs connected with the Spa, or say, if you like, the full committees of the various clubs, and discuss the situation.

We have now undoubtedly arrived at a climax. The Cricket Club or the Football Club must go. Personally I much regret this, and very much wish the field was a bit bigger so that we could avoid playing football on the cricket pitch, and that the two clubs might go hand in hand on the same field. But this is impossible, and we must face the inevitable. It would be manifestly unfair, looking at it from a football point of view, if the Cricket Club, who are tenants of the ground, were to give the Football Club notice farther on in the summer, or just before the commencement of the football season. That, I think, is a great reason why action should be taken at once.

It is easy enough to point out many reasons why the Football Club should have a ground of their own. I maintain it is to their direct interest to secure a ground over which they would have entire control; and that they can never have on the Spa. It is quite possible public opinion will be in favour of football being continued on the Spa, because the Gloucester public have been very much spoilt by having such a central ground, and I would probably be a bit horrified at first at having to go, say half a mile to the football ground. But all the real supporters of the game would soon get over this feeling in the knowledge of the fact that a properly enclosed ground is necessary for the future welfare and prospects of the club. Football has become such an institution in Gloucester that I question if it would not be well, after the committees have met, to invite a sort of public meeting to consider the matter. Someone must take the initiative, so I address this letter to you with full permission to make what use of it you like, together with your reply.
Faithfully yours,
A W VEARS
25, Brunswick Square, May 8th, 1891.

My dear Vears,
I am in receipt of your letter of the 8th inst., but absence from home has prevented my replying to it before to-day.
I may begin by expressing my entire accord with its contents, and I do not see any better way of solving the difficulty we are in than by a joint meeting of the two committees. I understand from Mr. Smith that a Cricket Committee has been summoned for to-morrow (Tuesday) night for the purpose of discussing the state of the field, when, I take it, the matter will be thoroughly thrashed out from a cricket point of view, and suggestions made for further consideration by the joint meeting, which might be held in the early part of next week.

I will, for a few moments refer to the ground as a cricketer, and, in doing so, I say unhesitatingly it has been absolutely ruined by football, and can never be of any real use again until it has been re-turfed, whilst it must be plain to everyone that if it were re-turfed now the new turf would be cut up irretrievably the very first time football was played on it. It is useless attempting to disguise the fact that there can be but little probability of the Gloucestershire v Surrey match being played here in August, and if we lose this match Gloucester may as well bid good-bye to county cricket for ever. I am, and have always been, averse to taking a pessimistic view of things, but I really see little prospect of bringing off all our own first and second XI matches this year.

Now, as regards the Football Club, I feel with you that it would be unfair and – having regard to the cordial relations which have hitherto existed between the Cricket and Football Clubs – unsportsmanlike in the extreme to delay giving the club notice to quit a day longer than we can possibly help; and I even go further than this, and say that seeing how popular the winter game is with the citizens, we ought not to give such a notice unless we can find a suitable field elsewhere upon which the Football Club can play. A ground over which the Football Club would have entire control all the year round would be of great advantage to them, and if once procured – as it might be by a very small pecuniary sacrifice on the part of the thousands interested – it would, I am sanguine enough to believe, be a source of profit to those who found the sinews of war.

I gather from the last sentence in your letter that you anticipate my thinking it worth while to publish it, together with my reply, and this I will do in the hope that it may lead to useful suggestions being made by some of the many readers of the Citizen who take an interest in two of the best games ever played by Englishmen.
Yours very truly,
HUBERT J BOUGHTON
Linden Grove, May 11th, 1891.

A W Vears and H J Boughton, who jointly masterminded the acquisition of the Kingsholm ground [Gloucester Rugby]

The publication of these letters generated further correspondence from readers of the Citizen. On 14th May 1891:

Dear Sir, - After reading the correspondence published in your issue of Tuesday evening between Messrs. Vears and Boughton with reference to football on the Spa field, it is quite apparent from a football point of view that a field over which the club could have entire control should be procured, so that it may be fenced in, and thereby greatly increase the gate money.

The question now comes as to where there is a suitable field. It has often occurred to me that the field near the Kingsholm end of Denmark-road, opposite Messrs. Wheeler and Son's entrance gates would be most suitable. There are several advantages: the trams pass within fifty yards of it; the field could be easily fenced; it is well drained, and there is no danger of it being flooded. The field in question, I have been informed, is the property of the Charity Trustees, which body is composed of business men, who would be, I am sure, pleased to accept the club as tenants, as they would be prepared to give a higher rent than could be secured for land used for agricultural purposes only, and at the same time afford enjoyment to the many thousand citizens who flock to witness the favourite winter game. Thanking you in anticipation,

I am, yours faithfully,
A LOVER OF THE GAME.

On 16th May 1891:

Dear Sir, - Your correspondent who signs himself 'A Lover of the Game,' has evidently been misinformed respecting the drainage of his would-be football field in Denmark-road. Had he lived in the neighbourhood as long as I have, not a few times would he have seen the field in question almost entirely under water; and I believe I am right in saying that this was the reason which a few years ago induced the occupier of the land (which till then had been used for agricultural purposes) to lay it down. I might mention other disadvantages which his field possesses, but this alone will suffice to show that it is not at all suitable for the Gloucester Football Club. Thanking you in anticipation,

I am, yours faithfully,
A RESIDENT IN THE NEIGHBOURHOOD

On 18th May 1891:

Dear Sir, - Your correspondent who signs himself 'A Resident in the Neighbourhood,' whose letter you published in your issue of Saturday, is evidently not a lover of football, and does not therefore wish to see the game played near his residence, as his argument with reference to the drainage of the suggested field is scarcely correct. A resident whose house overlooks the field informs me that he has seen the Spa field half under water, and at the same time the field in question was quite dry. The field has a good fall towards a ditch, which skirts the lower end (and is never full of water, as it runs off faster than it accumulates) and is carried into the sewer on the Tewkesbury-road; hence my stating that 'the field is well-drained.' As to your correspondent's remark with reference to the field being laid down some short time ago because of it being frequently flooded, it is strange that for some 35 years, to my knowledge, this land has been in the occupation of the family of the present occupier, and that until recently they planted alternately potatoes, wheat, and other crops (which certainly cannot be grown with advantage in a field subject to flood) seeing that as a market gardener the late Mr. Roberts had few equals. If the other 'disadvantages' which your correspondent says he has in store are as weak as the one he brought forward, I am afraid his opinion is not worth much, and in conclusion I may say that if the Gloucester Football Committee have to procure a ground in or near the city to which there are no resident objectors, football in Gloucester

may be considered a thing of the past.

Apologising for further troubling you,
I am, yours faithfully,
A LOVER OF THE GAME.

On 19th May 1891, the Club Committee met to discuss the future of the Spa ground, with W A Lucy and Rev J H Seabrook in attendance as representatives of the Cricket Club. The minutes record that:

In introducing the deputation, the Chairman remarked that the ground was now in such a bad state that it was plainly evident that both games could not in future be played there. Messrs Lucy and Seabrook addressed the meeting, pointing out that as a cricket ground the Spa would be this season in great part useless, and that the Cricket Club were of the opinion that the Football Club ought to now find a ground elsewhere. A short discussion ensued, and the deputation then withdrew. It was resolved that a sub-committee consisting of Messrs Boughton and Vears be empowered to make enquiries and obtain all possible information of suitable grounds, and at a later date a committee meeting to be called to learn the results of their labours.

The acquisition, and preferably purchase, of its own ground, which had previously been seen as desirable by the Club, had now become a necessity. The Committee met again on 16th June to hear a report from their sub-committee. The minutes record that:

Mr Boughton reviewed the various sites offered to and inspected by the committee, and of these three only appeared worthy of consideration, viz – in Deans Walk, Bristol Road and Sheephouse Road. Considerable time was spent in discussing these, each being fully dealt with, and ultimately A W Vears proposed and E Pickford seconded that the meeting decide in favour of the Sheephouse Road ground. The proposition was however withdrawn, on the understanding that the meeting be adjourned until the following evening when the committee would meet on the ground and fully inspect the same.

Of that meeting at Sheephouse Road, the minutes record that:

On the 17th Messrs Bagwell, Boughton, Vears, Jones, Phelps, Hughes, Bailey, Dere, Coates, Pickford and Smith met on the proposed ground in Sheephouse Road, and made an inspection of the same, when it was considered to be a suitable field, and Mr Boughton was instructed to further interview the proprietor (Mr Cullis) and get the necessary particulars in order that a general meeting might be summoned, and the question placed before them.

The minutes of this committee meeting are reproduced as Appendix A.

A General Meeting of the Gloucester Football Club was held in Goddard's Rooms at the Northgate Assembly Rooms on 1st July 1891, with about 175 members present, to consider the various sites suggested by the Committee for the new ground. The Chairman of the Club, 'Commodore' Vears informed the members that the Committee had instructed Jimmy Boughton and himself to obtain particulars of any grounds that were available for a new Football ground. They had reported to the Committee from time to time on the results of their investigations. They all knew the circumstances under which it had become necessary for them to seek a new ground, and decisions were now required if the Club was to be ready for the next season. The 'Commodore' asked Jimmy Boughton to explain the options which were open to the Club.

Jimmy Boughton, who was received with applause, said that they had during the previous six weeks been over a great many sites, but only three grounds remained which they could place before the meeting. He proceeded to mention several grounds which they had visited, or respecting which they had made enquiries, but which had not been available for various reasons. He mentioned amongst these what was known as Hanmans land in Howard Street, the ground at Alma Place, Bristol Road, Buddings Field, a field belonging to Mr Gould adjoining the latter, and Paradise Field.

One of the sites available was the piece of land in Sheephouse Road, and he proceeded to detail the particulars of that ground first. He had a plan of the site which he exhibited to the meeting, and explained that the space allotted to the actual playing enclosure was 110 yards by 75. It stood some 70 yards back from Sheephouse Road, and a road up to the main entrance would be completed shortly, whilst another entrance would be made, so that in every way the site itself was highly suitable. It would cost £35 or £40 to level it, and though he was requested not to make the price public that night, it would be very much cheaper than any other ground, and about a quarter of the cost of Castle Grim. Mr Cullis, who was the owner of the land, was willing to let the whole of the purchase money stay on the land for two years, at 3¾ per cent. As to distance, it would be two thirds of a mile on foot from the Wagon Works, and it would be rather more than two thirds of a mile to drive from the tram terminus. If they adopted the plan, which they hoped to do, and use the baths as their dressing rooms, teams would be able to be driven there from the station, and the Gloucester team also meeting there, all would be driven together to the ground. There would be ample means for spectators to get out to the

matches at a very small cost, and compared with other places, a number of which he enumerated, the distance would not be great. He read a letter received from Mr Cullis, in which some details were set forth, and stated that they would require to fence the site all round, which for a wooden fence, some seven feet high, would cost £175. They would have to spend £50 in levelling, and £250 in erecting a grandstand etc. (or even £450, or £500), in addition to the price of the ground.

He then dealt with the next scheme, which had only very recently been offered them in its present complete state. It was at Castle Grim, Kingsholm, the owner Mr Hatton having made them an offer of the whole of the land, which was just over 7 acres, and extended from Worcester Street to Deans Walk, and from St. Marks Street to the ditch at the opposite end of the land. They would have to play for the first year on one side of the land, on the piece known as the Old College Ground, which would be large enough to play on (and indeed had staged the very first Gloucester match in 1873). After that they would be able to take down the house in the middle (at present let at £35 a year) and have the whole of the seven acres to themselves. He gave the number of square yards fronting Worcester Street and Deans Walk, which might be sold for building purposes, and would perhaps realise £2,000. The price of the land was £4,400, which amounted to about 2s 6d per square yard, and if they floated a Company to acquire the ground Mr Hatton was prepared to take £100 worth of shares.

The question then arose as to how they were to get the money. Several gentlemen whom he had seen about the matter had promised to subscribe materially in the shares if a Company were floated. They would want about £2,500 subscribed, as they could raise £3,000 at least by mortgage on the land. The Company would do everything connected with

Castle Grim shown on the first Ordnance Survey map of Gloucester, surveyed in 1881-3 and published in 1890, before the development of the site as a rugby ground
[Gloucestershire Archives]

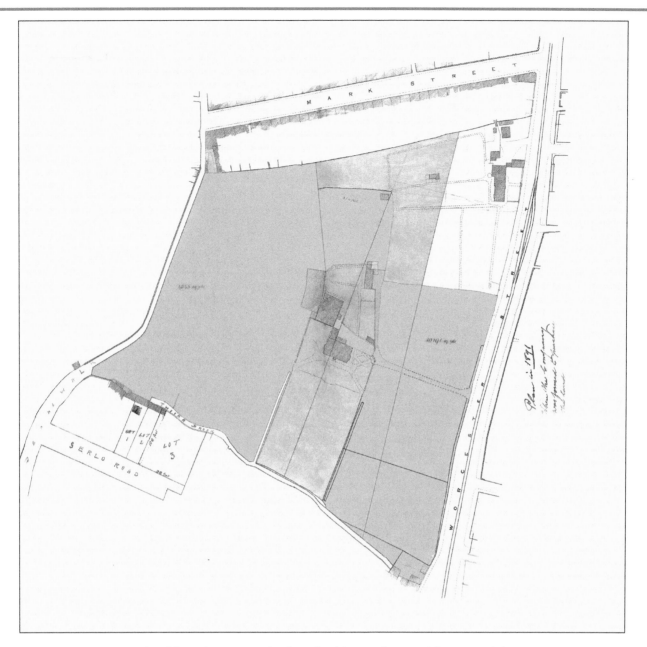

Plan of the Castle Grim estate when the Rugby Club acquired it in 1891 [Gloucester Rugby]

the ground, and for that the Company would require a large slice of the Club's gate money - he estimated at least 40%, and the Club would also have to pay working expenses. If they sold some of the land they would be able to pay off some of the mortgage, and thus reduce their annual interest payments.

He thought this scheme would succeed if all the Football Club's supporters came forward to take up shares, though the Committee had always advocated that the Club should be the owners of whatever ground they got, rather than it being in the hands of a Company, who let it to the Club at a rent. It seemed to him much more satisfactory that the Club should be the owners themselves, because there would otherwise be the potential for conflicting interests between shareholders and Club.

The other option was land in Theresa Street, Bristol Road adjoining Ashbee's Mill, which could be secured to the extent of 140 yards, by 120 yards, for £3,100. Altogether the cost of this ground would be about £3,340, but the frontage land here also might be sold to recoup some of that cost. Like the Castle Grim option, he regarded Theresa Street as too big a scheme for the Club to undertake within its own resources. In

conclusion, Boughton presented the choice as resting between Sheephouse Road, which could be bought and developed by the Club for something like £1,500, and where the Club would own the ground, and Castle Grim or Theresa Street, both of which would involve the Club renting from a Company set up to make the purchase.

Jimmy Boughton's account of the options triggered a long discussion. It was suggested that the Football Club itself should become a Limited Liability Company, but the Chairman expressed his belief that the Rugby Union would regard such an arrangement as a money making venture and therefore contrary to their laws, and would look upon all connected with it as professionals. This would put the whole Club beyond the pale in the strictly amateur Rugby Union game.

It was also suggested that the Club might take on the whole commitment, and raise the money by debentures, which would be paid off at a certain stated premium. Thus the Club would get the benefit of the profits themselves. The Chairman said that might be a better scheme than the one they had thought out, and could be considered when they came to the details, if the Kingsholm ground was selected. Whether it was the Club itself, or a Company outside the Club, that did it, it would be the same gentlemen who would take the shares. Concern was also expressed from the floor that 'the Kingsholm scheme was too gigantic for them as a Club'.

The Theresa Street, Bristol Road, option did not receive any serious consideration, because a more central site was favoured, but there was lively debate on the relative merits of the other two grounds. Mr Pickford thought the Sheephouse Road scheme the best, because it was a question of paying one pound for the Kingsholm site, and five shillings for the other. He believed the other scheme too big for them to undertake. A member, in reply to Mr Pickford, asked whether he would rather pay five shillings a week for a shop in Sheephouse Road, than one pound a week for one in Eastgate Street, or in Worcester Street, which amused the meeting. He thought it purely a business matter, and should be looked at from a business point of view.

Other uses of the ground were queried, and Jimmy Boughton asserted that, if the Castle Grim Estate were procured it would undoubtedly be an athletic ground, and they should utilise it in every possible way to raise money during the summer months. A number of speakers expressed the belief that to go to Sheephouse Road would mean a great falling off in the attendances, and one member anticipated the time, at an early date, if that course were adopted, when there would be no Football Club in existence at Gloucester. The 'Commodore' assured the meeting that it was not true that Association Football would be played on the Spa in future.

The majority of speakers were in favour of the Castle Grim option (although they referred to it at this stage as Deans Walk). Eventually the discussion was brought to a conclusion by Mr Bennett proposing a resolution, which, at the suggestion of Mr Grimes, he amended to read as follows: 'That this meeting is strongly in favour of acquiring the Deans Walk site on the best terms possible'. Mr Phillips seconded, and there being no response to a call for any other proposition the Chairman asked all those in favour of the motion to stand, upon which the whole assembly, with the exception of about half a dozen, stood up, and the resolution was declared carried by an overwhelming majority, amidst loud applause.

Mr Cullis was thanked for his generous offer. Although the Club were no longer pursuing the Sheephouse Road site in 1891, interest in what was probably much the same site was revived some sixty years later when the Club was looking for land on which to build the Memorial Ground for the use of local clubs.

A vote of thanks was accorded to Messrs Vears, Boughton and T G Smith for their efforts in the cause. The Chairman said that several gentlemen had already promised substantial financial support, and he asked those present to give in their names for any number of shares they were prepared to take. He laid stress on the desirability of having as many small shareholders as possible, and before the meeting closed promises had been made by those present of £200, bringing the total committed so far to £750.

Jimmy Boughton recommended that a special committee be set up, to work on what now became known as 'The Castle Grim Scheme' with the Club Committee, and to carry forward the financial arrangements. The following were constituted as this additional Committee: Messrs H W Grimes, C H Dancey, T Gurney, G Cummings, H Mansell, L H Priday, W F Phillips, A J Barnes, H J Berry, T Robinson, L J Simpson, W J Newth, and J Clark. The minutes of this Extraordinary Special General Meeting are reproduced in Appendix A. Given the groundwork already in place through A V Hatton, they were in a position to proceed quickly, and agreement to purchase Castle Grim was reached on 4th July 1891.

There was a hitch before the public were invited to subscribe towards the purchase of the ground. The Ecclesiastical Commissioners refused to convey the property to Mr Hatton, on the grounds that he had offered it for sale to the Football Club before he had himself entered

into a formal contract. This led to some correspondence between the respective lawyers, Messrs Bretherton, Son, & Boughton, acting for the proposed purchasers, and Messrs Whitcombe & Gardom, acting for the Commissioners. A satisfactory resolution was soon reached, aided no doubt by Boughton and Gardom both being founder members of the Football Club. Subject to the purchase money of £4,400 being subscribed by the local lovers of football, a provisional contract to purchase at that sum was entered into with Mr Hatton. The Committee and others interested in the new ground made further promises to buy shares, so that £1,400 had already been pledged before the Company Prospectus was issued in the form of a letter circulated by Boughton and Vears:

GLOUCESTER FOOTBALL CLUB

Bell Lane, Gloucester

PROPOSED NEW GROUND

Dear Sir,

An opportunity has arisen of purchasing the Castle Grim Estate, situate at Kingsholm, Gloucester, comprising 7 acres, 0 roods 21 perches, as a Football and General Athletic Ground for £4,400 (of which sum about £3,000 will be borrowed on Mortgage) and a Limited Liability Company, with a Capital of from £2,500 to £3,000 in Shares of £1 each, is to be formed for the purpose of carrying the scheme into effect.

The property comprises (in addition to the house and buildings in the centre of the ground, which will be pulled down) two houses and a builder's yard fronting Worcester Street, at present bringing in a rental of £39 a year, and which can be sold off without in any way injuring the ground from an Athletic point of view. There will also be a considerable quantity of land, with frontages to Worcester Street and Dean's Walk, which could at any time be sold off for building purposes if thought desirable.

The Ground is in every way adapted for Football, and with a comparatively small outlay can be made ready for play by the beginning of the coming season. It is only eight minutes' walk from the Cross and Railway Stations, and will have two entrances, one from Worcester Street and one from Dean's Walk.

An Agreement has been prepared and is proposed to be entered into between the Company and the Football Club, whereby the former will receive as a rent from the Club one third of the GROSS ANNUAL INCOME of the Club, such aggregate amount, however, not to exceed in any one year £275, and in addition to this source of income the Company will let the ground for Cricket, Cycling, Athletics, and other objects of a similar nature, during the summer months.

The gross income of the Gloucester Football Club last year amounted to £660, and it is estimated that with a ground entirely enclosed, the income will not be less than £1000 during the coming season, especially when taking into consideration the excellent List of Matches which has been arranged; and it is further estimated that with the amount to be received from the Football Club and its income from other sources, the Company will be able to pay to the Shareholders a dividend of certainly not less than £5 per cent per annum.

The Company is not being floated for the purpose of paying large profits, but for securing a permanent and suitable Ground for the use of the Football Club; and it is because of the interest you take in Football, and in the Gloucester Football Club in particular, that we address this circular to you, in the hope that you may be able to assist the undertaking by subscribing for Shares. We may mention that 1400 shares have already been subscribed for in numbers varying from 1 to 100.

If you are desirous of taking shares, will you kindly fill up and return the annexed form to us at the above address on or before Monday, the 27th day of July, instant.

Yours truly,

HUBERT J BOUGHTON

A W VEARS

P.S. - A Draft of the proposed Agreement between the Football Club and the Company, and a plan of the Property, can be seen at the offices of Messrs. Bretherton, Son, and Boughton, Solicitors, Bell Lane, Gloucester.

To MESSRS. BOUGHTON AND VEARS.

I hereby agree to subscribe for .... Shares of £1 each in the Company proposed to be formed for the purpose of purchasing and laying out The Castle Grim Estate as a Football and Athletic Ground.

Name (in full)……………………………………..

Address…………………………………………

Occupation…………………………………….

Date……………………………………………

Later that week, the Citizen published an article, promulgating the details of the above offer, and encouraging supporters to invest –

We understand that shares to the amount of £1,750 are promised to be taken up, but that the responses to the circulars sent out are coming in but slowly. Therefore it is apparent that promises to the extent of at least £700 are required by Monday next to make up the necessary amount. In order to ensure the success of the scheme, for there is no time to be lost if the ground is to be got ready for play during the coming season, intending subscribers (and surely there must be many amongst the thousands of persons who take an enthusiastic interest in football matches) should not further delay to apply for a share or shares.

Club members gathered at the Ram Hotel on the evening of Friday 31st July for a general meeting, presided over by the Club Chairman, 'Commodore' Vears. The meeting was called to consider the report of the special committee appointed to look into the acquisition of the Castle Grim estate. Jimmy Boughton reported that promises of £2,500 had been made to subscribe in shares in the Ground Company, which meant that they had reached the amount asked for. It was sufficient to justify going ahead with the purchase, although he thought it would now be better to increase the share issue to £3,000, as the greater the capital of the Company, the less they would have to raise on mortgage. It was not proposed to call in the amount of shares until the second week of September, which would give the Company time to pay the required amount to Mr Hatton by the 29th September.

Jimmy Boughton also read out the proposed agreement between the Club and the Ground Company, which stipulated that the Club's tenancy should run each year from the first Saturday in September to the fourth Saturday in April, with rent payable on 1st May. The amount of the rent was to be one-third of the gross income of the Club up to a maximum of £275, which was 5 per cent on the capital of the Company. Power was reserved for the Club to acquire the ground at any time at a fair price based on a professional valuation. For the summer months, the intention was to let the ground for cricket, athletics, rounders, etc.

One of the members, Mr Collett, queried whether the Club could afford as much as £275 rent. The Chairman replied that the Club could expect to save at least £100 during the season as a result of having a ground of their own, and that they had every expectation that the Club's income would grow substantially from the £600 which had been taken during the previous season. Mr Boughton reminded the meeting that no matter how low the Club receipts, they would never pay more than one-third of them in rent.

Eventually the main issue came to a vote. Mr J Franklin proposed and Mr D Lane seconded: 'That Messrs Vears and Boughton be authorised to sign a contract with Mr Hatton to purchase the Castle Grim estate'. This resolution was passed unanimously.

The Club was granted the power to appoint a member of the Club Committee as a director on the Board of the Ground Company, and Sidney Starr was unanimously chosen for this role. In thanking the meeting for the confidence placed in him, Sid promised to do his best, and expressed his intention to consult the Committee before taking action on any important matter. Tommy Bagwell intervened, and got a good laugh from the members by saying that he hoped Mr Starr would at least consult the Committee before applying salt to the new ground.

FOOTBALL AT GLOUCESTER

" Now Tommy, give up the key and open the New Grounds !"

A cartoon published in the Magpie on 4th July 1891, which reflects that, despite the attractions of the new ground at Kingsholm, a nostalgic attachment to the Spa ground was felt by many, including Tommy Bagwell, captain of the Gloucester Club at the time [Magpie]

The Acquisition of the Kingsholm Ground

A GENERAL MEETING OF about 75 (prospective) shareholders of the Gloucester Football and Athletic Ground Company Limited was held on 5th August 1891 at the Ram Hotel in Southgate Street, Gloucester. The meeting appointed 'Commodore' Vears to be the Chair of the meeting, and then elected the following as Directors of the Company:

Arthur Williams Vears, age 40, of 25, Brunswick Square, Gloucester, timber merchant

Lewis Henry Priday, age 41, of Longford Road, Longford, Gloucester, auctioneer and land agent

Alfred Woodward, age 44, of Lewishurst, South Hamlet, Gloucester, grain merchant and managing director of a grain warehouse

Samuel Davis, age 35, of 24, Westgate Street, Gloucester, haberdasher

George Cummings, age 56, of Castle Grim, Tewkesbury Road, Gloucester, maltster and saddler

Thomas Gurney, age 43, of 1, Widden Street, Barton St Mary, Gloucester, builder

Charles Henry Dancey, age 52, of 6, Midland Road, Barton St Mary, Gloucester, retired plumber

Arthur Vincent Hatton, age 47, of 1, Kingsholm Road, Gloucester, brewer and maltster

None of these Directors had played rugby for the Club, but they were all committed supporters. 'Commodore' Vears was also Chairman of the Club. The Director nominated by the Gloucester Club was Sidney Stephen Starr, age 30, of 69, London Road, Gloucester, floral contractor, who had played for the Club in the 1880s, mostly for the 2nd XV. He would stand down 18 months later in order to take up the post of Company Secretary from H S Simpson.

Messrs Bretherton, Son and Boughton were appointed as Company Solicitors, which effectively meant that Jimmy Boughton would handle the Company's legal affairs. H S Simpson was appointed as Company Secretary, and B Coombs as Company Auditor. However, Simpson was forced to resign the following year; he worked for a bank, and his employer promoted him and transferred him to the Isle of Wight.

Edwin Knibbs was thanked for hosting this and earlier meetings at the Ram Hotel, but alternative arrangements were put in place for the future. The Registered Offices for the Company were at the Oddfellows Hall, where use of a small room as the Company office, and use of a large room for Company meetings twice a year, was arranged for a rent of £5 per annum. It was agreed that a capital of £4,000 be registered for the Company. At this time, it was still hoped that the new ground would be ready for the first match of the new season on 19th September, but that proved to be over-optimistic.

The Ground Company opened an account with the Capital and Counties Bank. The first entry on 21st August 1891 was for credits into the account from sales of shares in the Company. These amounted to £65 on the first day, had grown to £2,421 by 3rd October, and to £2,822 by 18th December 1891.

On 21st August 1891, a Board meeting was held at the Ram Hotel, at which a sub-committee was formed to procure a Company Seal, and it was agreed that five Directors would make a quorum at Board meetings. The title of the Company was confirmed as 'The Gloucester Football and Athletic Ground Company Limited'. There was a difference of opinion as to the name by which the ground should be known. Vears and Dancey favoured 'the Kingsholm ground', whilst Starr and Hatton preferred 'the

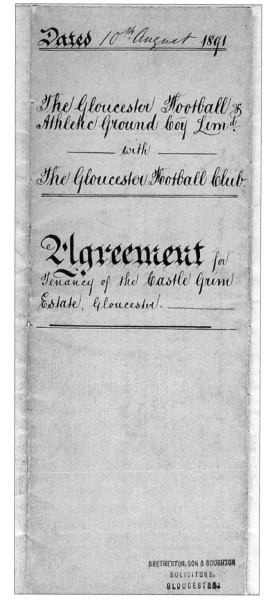

The title page of the Tenancy Agreement, which was signed on 10th August 1891 by Hubert James Boughton and Arthur Williams Vears on behalf of the Ground Company, and Tom Graves Smith and Sidney Stephen Starr on behalf of the Gloucester Football Club, for the tenancy of the Castle Grim ground. The Club would have possession of the ground for the duration of the football season, and the Company would have sole use for the remainder of the year. Annual rent was set at one-third of the gross annual income of the Club for the season prior, but not to exceed £275, the first payment falling due in May 1892. The Company could sell off part of the land, provided enough land was left for the purposes of the Club. The ground was to be levelled and fences erected to shut out the public view, and grandstands, pavilions, and other buildings would be put up by the Company, which would also bear the costs of maintenance and repairs. The Club was not allowed to sub-let, except for International, County or Trial matches, without the permission of the Directors of the Company. The Club were to pay all the costs of matches, and would have the right to purchase the land and buildings from the Company at a fair price fixed by two professional valuers. The full text of this agreement is reproduced in Appendix B at the back of this book.
[Gloucester Rugby]

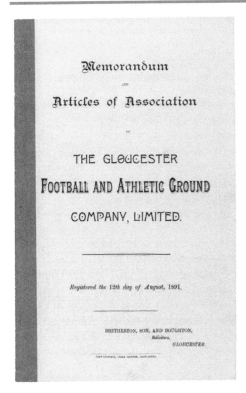

The cover of the Memorandum and Articles of Association of the Gloucester Football and Athletic Ground Company, Limited, which were issued on 12th August 1891 by Bretherton, Son, & Boughton, Solicitors, Gloucester. This document is shown in full at Appendix C. On the same day, the Certificate of Incorporation of the Company was issued by the Registrar of Companies, and this is reproduced at Appendix D. [Gloucester Rugby]

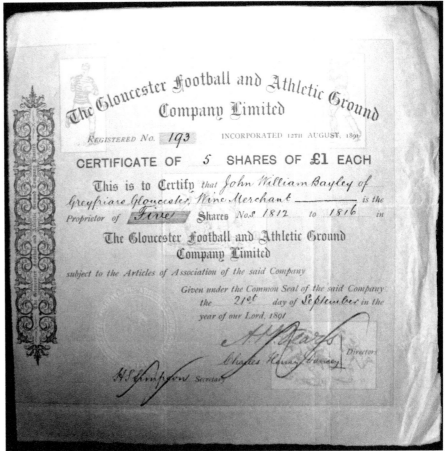

The share certificate in the Ground Company issued to J W Bailey, who played for the Club and was known as 'Down 'Em' Bailey on account of his ferocious tackling; his Club and County caps are on display in the Cathedral View at Kingsholm [Gloucester Rugby]

Castle ground' after the original 'Castle Grim' name of the property. It was put to the vote, 'Kingsholm' prevailed by 5 votes to 2, and 'Kingsholm' it has been ever since.

During September 1891, there was a hitch in the negotiations for the proposed mortgage on the ground. The Trustees of the Conservative Benefit Society would not advance the money without a guarantee that the Company Directors would pay the interest for 5 years. These terms were not acceptable to the Board, because they had to stand for re-election more frequently, and because they hoped for a lower rate of interest. So, they turned to the Company solicitors, Bretherton, Son & Boughton, to seek a lender who would agree to a mortgage of £2,500 carrying interest of 4%. At the end of September, the Seal of the Company was affixed to a mortgage on these terms with Christopher Poytress, Edward Pates and Arthur Vincent Hatton (brewer and Director of the Company), although this was subject to conveyance of Castle Grim being completed. Effectively Hatton was thus using the £800 profit, which he would be making from buying and selling the Kingsholm ground, to then earn interest as a mortgage to the Ground Company.

Although promises to invest in the Ground Company had been registered earlier and some money had been banked, the £1 share certificates did not actually go on sale until 15th September 1891. The first shareholding of 50 shares was purchased by Charles George Clark, a wine merchant of Blackfriars, Gloucester. Next in line were Ernest Wright, a tobacconist, of Southgate Street, and Walter Thomas Herring, a clerk, of Oxford Road. By the end of the day, 703 shares had been sold. There were several share certificate books, and when a certificate was torn out to be issued to the purchaser of a shareholding, a stub was left recording the shareholder's details. These share certificate books have survived and

are now held in the Gloucestershire Archives, so a complete listing of the shareholders in the Ground Company is available.

Supporters of the Club were keen to purchase shares, but the Ground Company was also seen as a good investment, and people from all walks of life in Gloucester subscribed to the share offer:

24 merchants (china dealer, haulier/carrier, miller, ship owner, seedsman, warehouseman, manufacturer, contractor) purchased 406 shares

15 professionals (solicitor, accountant, stock-broker, banker, etc) purchased 350 shares

20 in the drinks trade (including hotel keeper, maltster, brewer, wine merchant and caterer) purchased 311 shares

45 shopkeepers (in trades including draper, grocer, chemists, jeweller, baker, hairdresser, haberdasher, hatter, confectioner and gunsmith) purchased 266 shares

18 gentlemen (addressed as Esquire) purchased 259 shares

28 in the building trade (including bricklayer, builder, decorator, plumber and shipwright) purchased 205 shares

3 Members of Parliament purchased 170 shares

6 house and land agents purchased 168 shares

27 clerks purchased 121 shares

14 journalists (including printer and telegraphist) purchased 111 shares

7 women purchased 95 shares

12 travellers purchased 90 shares

3 architects purchased 35 shares

People declaring no occupation purchased 34 shares

Registered No. *38*

Certificate of *1* Share

No. *324*

Issued to *George Walter Coates*

of *34 Wellesley Street Gloucester*

Boiler Maker

Dated *15th Septr*

1891

6 labourers purchased 27 shares
1 Sergeant Major purchased 20 shares
5 surgeons (including a dentist) purchased 18 shares
1 schoolmaster purchased 10 shares
small numbers of shares were also purchased by people declaring their occupation as coachman, manager, farmer, foreman, elocutionist, boilermaker, salesman, engineer, wagon-fitter, curator, postman, collector, engine driver, and Inspector of Police

This level of interest ensured that the Company was successfully launched. By 21st September 1891, 1,965 shares had been sold; by 24th September, 2,300 shares; by 2nd November, 2,581 shares; by 13 April 1892, 2,878 shares; and by 17th June 1892, all 3,000 shares had been sold. All of the original shareholders in the Company are listed in Appendix E.

The Board decided that the share capital of the Company would not be raised above 3,000. Consequently, the only subsequent share dealings in the Company were in reissued shares following a change of ownership. One shilling was charged for each transfer of shares registered

AN OLD FOOTBALL PHOTOGRAPH.

The Gloucester Rugby team of 1891-2, interesting from the fact that the central figure in the back row is the late Mr. George Witcomb, whose death took place last week. Also to the fact that another of the players (Mr. S. A. Ball, the once-famous half-back) is now seriously ill, and his friends are subscribing to a fund to help him in his distress.

The names are.—Back row: T. G. Smith (hon. sec.), Walter Taylor, H. G. Brown, D. Price, F. W. Mugliston, G. J. Witcomb, C. J. Click, J. Mayo, A. Collins, H. W. Bennett (secretary). Sitting: S. S. Starr (treasurer), D. Phelps, G. Jones, S. A. Ball, Tom Bagwell (capt.), W. George, W. Jackson, C. Jenkins. On ground: C. James, T. Huggins, A. F. Hughes. Matches played 34, won 24, lost 6, drawn 4.

in the Company's books. This facility was soon being used – for example, in 1893, A W Vears, who had initially purchased 100 shares, bought four further small blocks of shares which had become available, to bring his holding up to 165.

Work was required at Kingsholm to prepare the new ground, and it could not be made ready for the first few games of the 1891-92 season, so they were played at the Gordon League ground on Denmark Road (with a flat rate entry charge of 3d).

A conveyance (indenture) dated 11th November 1891 was made between the Dean and Chapter of the Cathedral Church of the Holy and Indivisible Trinity in Gloucester, the Ecclesiastical Commissioners for England, Arthur Vincent Hatton, and the Gloucester Football and Athletic Ground Company. This records that the Dean and Chapter (with the approval of the Commissioners) had contracted to sell Castle Grim to A V Hatton for £3,600, and A V Hatton had agreed to resell to the Gloucester Football and Athletic Ground Company for £4,400. The Ground Company had paid £3,600 to the Commissioners, and £800 to Hatton to purchase the ground. In this document, Castle Grim is described as consisting of 2 cottages, a builders yard, pasture and gardens, altogether comprising 7 acres, 0 roods, 4 perches, and including half the bed of the River Twyver. On 20th November 1891, the newly acquired Company Seal was affixed to this Conveyance Deed.

With the conveyance in place, the mortgage which had previously been arranged with Messrs Poytress, Pates and Hatton could proceed. It was signed the following day, and Poytress, Pates and Hatton were given the deeds to the ground.

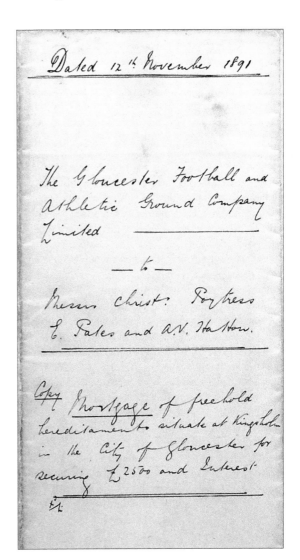

The title page of the conveyance, which is reproduced in full at Appendix F
[Gloucester Rugby]

The title page of the mortgage, which is reproduced in full at Appendix G
[Gloucester Rugby]

Jimmy Boughton

HUBERT JAMES BOUGHTON, commonly known as 'Jimmy' in Gloucester sporting circles, was born in 1859 at Westbury-on-Severn, the son of John Boughton, a farmer and landed proprietor of Adsett Court, Westbury-on-Severn. His elder brothers, John and William A Boughton, were founder members of the Gloucester Football Club, and played in the Club's first matches in 1873. The first 2 matches were against the King's School, Gloucester, where Jimmy, aged 14, was then a pupil. Unfortunately there is no record of the players in the school team, so we do not know if Jimmy played in those matches against his brothers. However, on leaving school he was soon playing for the Club, and was articled to the law firm of Messrs Bretherton and Sons, where he qualified as a solicitor and became managing clerk to the firm.

He was a gifted sportsman, who became involved as player and administrator for many sports clubs in the City. However, his principle loves were rugby and cricket, and he captained the City teams in both sports. He encouraged the expansion of local rugby clubs in Gloucester, and likewise in cricket, was involved in the formation of the Gloucester Cricket League.

Whilst still playing, he became Treasurer of the Rugby Club in 1879. In this capacity, he led the defence of the Club against criticism following the damage done to the Spa by spectators attending the floodlit match against Rockleaze. He had firm views on rugby being played in the right spirit, and went on record as believing that 'to play for the love of the game should be the desire of every footballer'. He stood against rough play, ill temper and partisanship, and therefore opposed the creation of a Cup Competition believing that it would encourage these undesirable traits.

Jimmy was instrumental in the Gloucester Club acquiring its own ground at Kingsholm. He led the abortive search for a ground in 1889, and reacted quickly when the opportunity reappeared in 1891. In January of that year, following the death of Mr Bretherton senior, Jimmy became a partner in the firm of solicitors, which henceforward carried on business as Bretherton and Boughton. In March 1891, it seems quite likely that he may have had a hand in Arthur Hatton, a local brewer and fellow Freemason, buying the Castle Grim estate. In May 1891, he engaged in a public exchange of letters with A W Vears about the need to find the rugby club its own ground in order to get away from the Spa, although they did not advertise that this was already well in hand. His legal expertise was again useful in setting up the Gloucester Football and Athletic Ground Co Ltd, which then purchased the Kingsholm ground from Hatton. Jimmy bought 100 shares in the Company - this stake facilitated his appointment as one of the first Directors, and he also acted as solicitor for the Company.

MR. H. J. BOUGHTON,
From a photograph taken some years ago.

A cartoon of Jimmy Boughton published in 1891 [Magpie]

In 1891, Rowland Hill, Secretary of the RFU, commented on 'the upward-looking and supportive relationship that officials of the club, notably H J Boughton, had with the RFU'. Jimmy became the first President of the Gloucester Club in 1892, resigned in 1896 in order to avoid a conflict of interest with his duties at county level, but then resumed the role in 1900.

Jimmy was very keen to promote rugby at county level, was prominent in the formation of the Gloucester County Football Club in 1878, and served as Secretary and Treasurer. When this was superceded by the County Union in 1891, Jimmy was unanimously elected as the first Chairman and President, and was re-elected every year until he stood down in 1900. He was also instrumental in setting up the Gloucestershire Referees Association in 1892, and was one of the twelve referees appointed, eight of them from Gloucester. In 1897, Jimmy became the first Gloucestershire county representative on the RFU committee, a position he retained up to the time of his death in 1902.

A photograph of Jimmy Boughton published following his death in 1902
[CC&GG]

Jimmy was a talented cricketer, both as batsman and as lob bowler. He was just as influential as captain and administrator for the Gloucester and County Cricket Clubs as he was for their rugby equivalents. He played for Gloucestershire alongside W G Grace, and scored 48 in his last match for the county second team in 1898. He served on the county committee, and was instrumental in establishing the annual county match at the Spa, and in 1902, the year of his death, in expanding this to a full week with 2 county matches played in Gloucester, a legacy which was to last for well over a century. When he ceased playing, he took up golf, again with notable success.

Jimmy died suddenly in 1902 at age 43. His obituary records that:

He was recognised by his contemporaries as a wonderful organiser, and a man tremendously keen on the advancement of the game. What he did for Rugby Football in the West cannot be measured in mere words, but it would not be too much to say that this Gloucester sportsman, more than anyone else, 'made' the game in a centre that was honoured by his activities.

For good reason he was described as 'the father of sport in the City'.

H J Boughton (Gloucester and Gloucestershire) on the opening of Kingsholm in 1891: 'I hope that the new ground will be the headquarters of Gloucester Football for very many years to come.'

Arthur Hatton

ARTHUR VINCENT HATTON, the son of a farmer, was born in Eldersfield, Worcestershire, in 1843. He and his twin sister, Matilda, were the youngest of seven children, and grew up at Chaceley Court, near Tewkesbury, where their father was farming 300 acres and employing six men. Arthur went into business as a brewer, and by 1870 he had set up the Northgate Brewery in George Street, Gloucester, and was employing eight men. This grew into a substantial business with a number of tied houses including the Horse and Groom in London Road, Gloucester, the Anchor Inn at Epney, the Plough Inn at Newent and the Royal Exchange Inn at Hartpury.

By 1891, Arthur, then 47, and his wife and two daughters, had moved to 1, Kingsholm Road, Gloucester, just along the road from the Castle Grim estate. It is not clear whether Arthur himself spotted an opportunity to acquire this neighbouring property, or whether he was put up to it by Jimmy Boughton and/or A W Vears, but Arthur agreed to pay £3,600 to the Church Commissioners for Castle Grim. What is known is that even before the sale was completed, Arthur had already agreed with Boughton and Vears that he would sell the estate on to the newly formed Gloucester Football and Athletic Ground Company for £4,400. When the Church Commissioners heard of this, there was a hitch whilst they queried his right to sell the property before he actually owned it. However, this was ironed out, and indeed Arthur never even had to pay the £3,600 himself. The Ground Company paid this amount directly to the Church Commissioners and £800 to Arthur, who became one of the founding Directors of the Ground Company. This seems a very handsome profit for Arthur as the middle man in the deal, and no explanation for it appears in any of the available paperwork. However, he presumably accepted the risk for several months that the Ground Company would not succeed in raising the necessary funds to purchase the ground from him.

Meanwhile, the Ground Company needed more money than their share issue would raise, in order to complete the purchase and develop the ground, but were unhappy with the terms offered by the banks. Arthur, flush with the knowledge that he would be receiving £800 from the sale of Castle Grim, came to their rescue. He got together with Christopher Poytress, a grocer in Worcester, and Edward Pates, a florist in Cheltenham, and they jointly agreed a mortgage of £2,500 with the Ground Company, earning 4% interest per annum, with Castle Grim as surety. This mortgage was put in place at the end of September 1891, with the conveyance of the ground not completed until November.

That same month the Ground Company entered into negotiations to sell a strip of the ground to a neighbour, John Stephens & Co, but this

COUNCILLOR A. V. HATTON,
Kingsholm Ward, Gloucester.

[CC&GG]

fell through when an acceptable price could not be agreed. Arthur stepped in and agreed a price, but he then tried to alter the conditions of the sale, wanting to secure more frontage onto Worcester Street. His fellow Board members recorded in their minutes that they did not think Arthur had treated them properly and the sale fell through. The minutes of the next meeting record Arthur's objection to this version of events.

In 1896, Arthur successfully negotiated with the Ground Company and his co-Trustees to effect an addition to the mortgage, which was increased by £500. He sold his brewery and business to Ind Coope & Co of Burton, and retired as a Director of the Ground Company in 1897. In 1899 he decided to withdraw from the mortgage, and transferred his interest to his co-Trustees. By 1901, Arthur was living on Cheltenham Road, and working as a maltster. He died in Gloucester in 1911.

Getting Kingsholm Ready for Rugby

As soon as the General Meeting of the Ground Company was concluded on 5th August 1891, a meeting of the Directors was convened, and 'Commodore' Vears was elected as Chairman of the Board. The Board's first decision was to seek tenders to remove 4 walnut trees, so that the ground could be levelled and made ready for play.

Things then moved quickly in order to try to get the ground in a fit condition for matches in the forthcoming season. Three days later, on 8th August, the Board met at Castle Grim early in the morning to decide the layout of the ground, how much levelling was required, and what buildings and walls needed to be pulled down. In order to get the field into use quickly, the pitch alignment chosen for the first season was north-south (at right angles to the layout in every season since) at the western end of the ground. This allowed matches to be played before the buildings in the centre of the ground were knocked down. Later the same day the Board had an evening meeting with J P Moore, architect, to brief him on the work required.

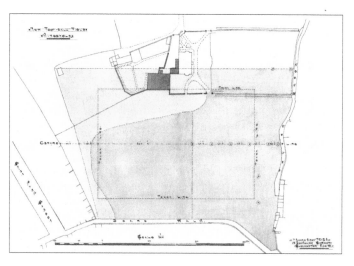

The more precise plan of the new ground drawn up by the Club architect later in August 1891 [Gloucester Rugby]

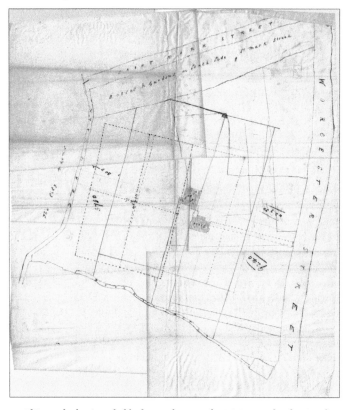

This rough plan is probably the one drawn up by J P Moore when he visited Kingsholm with the Board of the Ground Company on 8th August 1891. It shows in dotted black lines the initial layout of the pitch, 110 yards by 75 yards, squeezed between Deans Walk and the buildings which still remained in the centre of the site. The red lines may show the layout of the pitch and enclosure which the Board intended to implement when the buildings were knocked down, but this never came to fruition, with the pitch alignment being changed by 90 degrees when the pitch was relaid for the 1892-93 season
[Gloucester Rugby]

The September 1891 entries in the Capital Account in the General Ledger of the Ground Company reveals how much work was put in hand during that month to prepare for the opening match in October. The expenditures recorded, in addition to the £4,400 paid for the ground, are:

		£	s	d
J Gurney	Levelling	117	15	0
H S Crump	Deans Walk fence	94	6	6
E Clutterbuck	Kingsholm Road fence	102	3	0
Vears & Baylis	Footboards	10	4	8
H S Crump	Turnstiles	74	18	0
W H Phillips	Painting	7	17	0
A Bendall	Levelling	266	16	1
Bretherton Son & Boughton	Legal costs	155	18	4
J Bellows	Printing	18	14	8
J P Moore	Architect		6	10
A V Hatton	Fruit		4	0
E Clutterbuck	Extra fencing	21	0	0
Brooks Bros	St Marks Street fence	62	10	0
J Griffett	Levelling etc	217	0	0
J M Butt & Co	Iron roller	24	15	0
D Lane	Fence, wall & doors	28	5	0
H S Crump	Sundries	11	10	6
Chance & Bland	Advertisements	5	17	6
W J Jenkins	Turf	66	13	0
Secretary	Extra work	20	0	0
Roberts & Starr	Grass seed	7	6	0
Sundries in petty cash account		57	18	9
Sundry labour reclaiming land by ditch		20	3	0

The initial levelling of the ground was undertaken by Joseph Gurney (brother of Thomas Gurney, a Director of the Company, and also a builder), for which he was paid both in cash and in kind by taking possession of the bricks and timber which required removal. By the middle of September, it was apparent that more earth was required to fill in the lower, western, end of the field, so agreement was obtained from the tenant to take more from the higher part of the field, and in December, Joseph Gurney was paid an additional £77 15s 0d for this work.

The Young Men's Christian Association had a small shed on the ground, which interfered with the Ground Company plans. Agreement was reached with them that the Company would buy the shed for 10s, so that it could be removed, although half this amount was then raised from the sale of the recovered materials.

During September 1891, there were meetings with representatives of the Gloucester Wagon Works to discuss the erection of a grandstand. Originally the Company decided that they would not be willing to pay more than £30 for this. After negotiation a deal was done for the hire of a grandstand 50 yards long and a dressing room 20 feet by 8 feet for 6 months for £50, although the Wagon Works was required to accept liability in the event of accident resulting from faults in the building. This was duly erected, and a portion was railed off for the press. Before the end of the year a further £2 was allocated for improved accommodation for the press. The grandstand appears to have been placed in what is now the centre of the ground, facing west. However, this was only ever seen as part of the temporary arrangements necessary for matches to be played during the 1891-92 season, and did not form part of the longer term plans for the ground.

The longer term plans were laid out in an exhibit designed to show people how the ground would be developed, and on 26th September 1891, the Gloucester Magpie reported that:

> The new ground at Kingsholm is assuming a playable form, and will, it is anticipated, be in readiness for the first important home match, that with Burton-on-Trent, on the 10th, which, weather permitting, ought to prove a big draw. The plans, which are now on view, show that, when completed, the ground will be one of the best in the West. There will be a cycling and running track a quarter of a mile in circumference, and refreshment stands and pavilions at convenient distances, a large pavilion occupying the centre of the sixpenny part. These works cannot, of course, be all carried out until after this season, meanwhile a contract has been entered into with the Gloucester Wagon Company for the erection of a temporary grand stand.

These plans were not finally approved by the Board of the Company until January 1892. Even then the decision on the purchase of a grandstand was deferred to the end of the season. Although a cinder track was originally intended, the grass surface was all that was ever available for running and cycling, and some of the facilities displayed in the plans never came to fruition at all.

The Club had suffered problems for many years at the Spa in terms of preventing spectators watching matches for free. In order to maximise the income to the Club from gate money, it was an imperative at Kingsholm to secure the ground. Fencing on all sides of the ground was therefore given a high priority. Company architect, J P Moore, was given the job of requesting tenders for corrugated iron fencing for both the Dean's Walk and Worcester Street ends of the ground. [In the Club and Company records, the eastern side of the ground is sometimes referred to as the Worcester Street end, and sometimes as the Kingsholm Road end. This is understandable since the Kingsholm Road becomes Worcester Street when it reaches the ground. For the sake of clarity, only the Worcester Street designation is used in this book.] A tender from George Cummings (a Ground Company Director), which quoted £87 10s 0d for this fencing work, was initially accepted.

However, concern was soon expressed about children getting under the Deans Walk fence, holes there had to be blocked, and it was decided to erect more substantial solid wooden fences round at least three sides of the ground, the south side being protected by the River Twyver and neighbouring buildings. The work was spread around various bidders. Brooks Bros looked after the northern, St Marks Street, side at a cost of £62 10s 0d.

On the east side, the old Worcester Street fence was sold off to Thomas Toomey for £16 10s 0d, and Enoch Clutterbuck erected new fencing at a cost of 8s 9 ½ d per yard. Enoch had completed the work to the satisfaction of the Company by the end of the year, and he was paid £102 3s 0d. Enoch's son, George, age 15 in 1891, who may well have helped his father in this work, would later become a leading light on the Kingsholm ground, as a powerful wing three-quarter, who made 131 appearances and scored 58 tries, including 6 in one match against Clifton. Barbed wire was later put along the top of the Worcester Street fence as a further deterrent to unauthorised entry.

H S Crump was paid £94 6s 6d for installing a more secure fence on the western side of the ground alongside Deans Walk. Even after this more substantial fence was built, boys still managed to climb over a wall beside the Deans Walk entrance. Indeed, records show that over the next several generations, the ingenuity of boys to get into the ground on match days without paying continued to outwit a whole succession of measures which were designed to thwart them.

The need to secure income from spectators also resulted in tenders being sought for turnstiles, which were procured at a cost of £66 for both the Deans Walk and Worcester Street entrances from H S Crump. Including installation and huts for the attendants, the turnstiles ended up costing £74 18s 0d.

Season tickets were put on sale, with ladies and juniors at half price. One consequence was that revenue was lost because some men were gaining entry to the ground using boys' tickets. This even led to a suggestion that boys should be banned from the ground altogether, but this draconian solution was dropped in favour of issuing tickets of different colours for adults and juveniles.

A sub-committee was formed to negotiate terms with the various tenants of the Castle Grim property, and by the end of the month arrangements with all the tenants had been agreed. Mrs Bick was to leave on 29th September; Mr King would pay £4 for his tenancy up to Christmas, and Mr Lane would become a quarterly tenant at £4 pa for the 'Vinegar Works' Corner', but he vacated his tenancy a year later. The 'Vinegar Works' Corner' was in the south-east part of the ground, and gained its name from the vinegar and pickle factory which John Stephens had set up next door on Skinner Street in 1870. By 1897, the company had become J Stephens & Son Ltd, the factory had extended its production to jam, and employed about 400 people. It was a major landmark in the Kingsholm area of the City and can be seen in the background of many photographs of the rugby ground, especially the tall chimney which towered above the works. It closed down around 1967 and the buildings were pulled down.

Advertising the sale of season tickets for the first season at Kingsholm [Citizen]

The Opening of Kingsholm

WITH THE GROUND now ready for matches, considerable effort was taken to ensure that the opening of the new ground on 10th October 1891 would be a grand and memorable event. The Engineers' Band was engaged to entertain the crowd before kick-off, and the local Member of Parliament, Mr T Robinson, was invited to declare the ground open and to start the match with a ceremonial kick-off. The opponents were Burton-on-Trent, a club which had been founded in 1870, making it the oldest in the Midlands. Burton looked resplendent in white jerseys with black sashes, whilst Gloucester lined up in the colourful jerseys in which they played at the time - red, yellow and black. The Directors of the Ground Company arranged to entertain the two teams and the Football Club committee to dinner after the match, Messrs Boughton and Simpson offering to contribute to the cost of the banquet.

FOOTBALL.

GRAND OPENING

OF THE

NEW GROUND AT KINGSHOLM,

SATURDAY, October 10th.

GLOUCESTER V. BURTON.

T. ROBINSON, Esq., M.P., will kick off at 3.30 p.m.

ADMISSION—

Worcester Street Side, 6d. Dean's Walk Side, 3d.
Grand Stand 6d. extra.
NO HALF-PRICE.
Members' Entrance - Worcester Street.

SPECIAL NOTICE.

Members' Cards will NOT BE issued on SATURDAY, therefore those intending to become Subscribers must apply before 8 p.m. on FRIDAY, to SIDNEY & STARR (ROBERTS and STARR), 92, NORTHGATE.

MEMBERS 5s., LADIES AND JUNIORS 3s. 6d.

FOOTBALL.

OPENING OF THE KINGSHOLM GROUND.

THE DIRECTORS entertain the Players of both Teams at PUBLIC DINNER, to be held at the SPREAD EAGLE HOTEL at 6.30 p.m.

Tickets, 3s. 6d. each, to be had at the Hotel on or before FRIDAY NEXT. Early application requested.

WANTED, strong, useful Stable Boy, one accustomed to horses. — Apply Weighill, Veterinary Surgeon, Southgate Street.

WANTED, at once, a good General Servant; from the country preferred; age 18 or 19.—Apply 1" Royal Crescent, Cheltenham.

The advertisements in the Citizen for the opening match at Kingsholm and the dinner in the evening [Citizen]

The Citizen reported that:

The new ground at Kingsholm, known as Castle Grim, which has been acquired and laid out by the Gloucester Athletic Ground Company, at a cost of about £5000, was formally opened on Saturday. It will be remembered that, owing to the damage football caused to the cricket pitches at the Spa, the Football Club received notice to quit from the Cricket Club, who rent the field from the Corporation, and who, in their turn, were in danger of being dismissed by that body, who thought of adding the field to the public park; but that idea has apparently for the present been abandoned, and the notice to terminate the tenancy has been withdrawn. The Football Club being thus without a ground, it was decided to float a company for the purchase of the Castle Grim site, and this, though fraught with many difficulties, was successfully accomplished. Though the footballers will be the company's best customers, the ground will also be used for athletics generally, and it is unanimously conceded that, when laid out as contemplated, with pavilions, stands, cycling track, etc., it will be one of the most complete in the kingdom. It is over seven acres in extent, and centrally situated, being on the tramway system, and within five or six minutes' walk of the railway stations and the Cross.

Unfortunately the weather was not kind for the opening, but perhaps Castle Grim was just living up to its name. The Gloucestershire Magpie reported that:

With rain falling in a perfect deluge, and the sky dark with heavily charged clouds, the prospects for the opening of the new ground on Saturday were certainly not cheerful, and it appeared that the event would have to come off under conditions the reverse of favourable to players and spectators. The gentle shower, which ushered in the morning gradually increased as the time wore on and at midday the floodgates seemed to be opened to their widest extent, the rain falling in a perfect torrent. But this notwithstanding, no one thought of the postponement; who has ever heard of a match being stopped by unfavourable weather? The only drawback was that it would be likely to reduce the attendance – to injure the 'gate' as it is now fashionable to express it.

And that it did, although the attendance was still judged to be remarkably good.

Before the kick-off there was a ceremony to mark the official opening of the ground. The Gloucester team lined up in front of the grandstand. They were joined by Club officials, T G Smith and H W Bennett (Secretaries), S S Starr (Treasurer), H J Boughton, A W Vears, H S Simpson, C E Brown, G Coates, W C Bailey, G F Dere, F E Jones, N Phelps, J W Goddard, and E Pickford (Committee); and A Woodward, A V Hatton, G Cummings, C H Dancey, S Davis, T Gurney, L H Priday, and F H Bretherton. A W Vears addressed the assembled company, saying: 'In the name and on behalf of the directors, I now hand over to you this football field, for your use during the season. May your efforts stimulate and safeguard the game of football, and thereby add to prosperity of athletics in the county, and conduce to your future success.' He then asked Mr. Robinson to open the ground.

T. ROBINSON Esq., M.P., SETS THE BALL IN MOTION ON THE NEW GROUND.
Drawn in anticipation by *our artist, who is slightly out of form*

A cartoon published in the Gloucestershire Magpie shows Mr Robinson, the local Member of Parliament, doffing his top hat to kick off the match, watched by Rowland Hill, Secretary of the RFU, who refereed the match, and Tommy Bagwell, captain of Gloucester [Magpie]

Mr. Robinson, who met with a splendid reception, said he knew it was no time for making a speech, as they were all wanting to commence business. He was sure great thanks were due to the directors of the new ground for the public spirit they had shown in connection with the matter, and he felt quite sure that they had worked very hard to get the ground into its present state, for he remembered that only a short time ago the place was in a deplorable condition. Although much had been done, he believed there was still a great deal more to be done. He was sure that the directors would use their very best endeavours to make the ground one of the finest football grounds in the country. He welcomed the Burton team to Gloucester. He was sure his Gloucester friends would find in them honourable opponents. He trusted that the Gloucester team would have a successful season, and he also wished that the best side that day might win the match. He should not detain them any longer, but proceed to kick off.

He was given the honour of kicking off, which he did poorly – 'the kick-off was not a powerful one, and the leather was only sent a few yards into the visitors' half, which was on the city side' - but he was given credit for trying.

Gloucester went into the match with four three-quarters and eight forwards, whereas Burton selected three three-quarters and nine forwards; both teams played one back and two half-backs.

Gloucester: A F Hughes; T B Powell, T Bagwell (Captain), W Jackson, W H Taylor; W George, S A Ball; A Cromwell, A E Healing, A Henshaw, J Williams, H V Page, C Williams, T Collins, A Collins

Burton: J P Ward; G A Marsden, W S Lowe, F M Sadler; W Smith, J C Gorton; H Mayger, E Evershed, J Clitheroe, W N Greenwell, A Gorton, H C Gorton, F Browne, F L Lloyd, F Evershed

Within five to eight minutes from the start (depending on which reporter you believe), Gloucester had scored their first try at Kingsholm, when A E Henshaw kicked the ball over the Burton line, and S A Ball following up touched it down. Walter Jackson duly kicked the first conversion, sending the ball over the hedge, so that a new one had to be brought on. A few minutes later, they had their second try – 'Trevor Powell getting it out of the squash, made a good effort to get away, but finding this would be impossible neatly passed to Bagwell, who by a sharp dodgy run, got in near the corner.' Shortly afterwards George took the ball from a scrum close to the goal-line, and ran round to score under the posts; Jackson again converting. Powell scored his second try in the corner, and Hughes narrowly missed with a dropped goal, which just slipped under the bar. Half-time arrived with Gloucester enjoying a healthy 14-0 lead.

A Scrum in the centre.

This is the first known image of a match at Kingsholm. It was published in the Gloucestershire Magpie, a weekly magazine, on Saturday 17th October, so must have been drawn at the first match against Burton a week earlier. The artist was probably seated in the temporary stand on the east side of the pitch at the northern end. It could not be centrally placed because of the buildings in the middle of the ground which had yet to be demolished. The view seems to be towards the south-west and shows the trees alongside Deans Walk, although the detail of the drawing suggests that a good deal of artistic licence was applied. [Magpie]

It is perhaps no surprise that on such a wet day the players experienced some problems with their woollen jerseys, and in the second half, 'Jackson lost his second jersey, and had some difficulty to struggle into a new one, his efforts to find the opening for his head, causing no little amusement, and a slight delay'. A dribble by H V Page led to a try by Jack Williams in the corner, and on the stroke of time 'by some capital play on the part of S Ball, A Collins and Powell, the last named got in on the corner of the goal' to complete his hat trick. Gloucester thus started their record at Kingsholm with a resounding win by 2 goals, 4 tries and several minors (18 points) to 2 minors (nil). The scoring system at this time awarded two points for a try and three for a conversion; minors (when the defending side touched down behind their own line) were still being noted, but earned no points. The referee, Rowland Hill, was assisted by T G Smith and T E Lovel as touch judges. Many years later, in 1930, the Club was to receive a framed photograph of the then late Sir Rowland Hill from the RFU, which was hung in the gymnasium.

Season tickets for Kingsholm had been sold for 5s and 3s 6d, and 717 members had subscribed by the time of the first match. Takings on the gate were £46 7s 3d made up of £19 9s 6d on the 6d side, £22 7s 3d on the 3d side, and £4 10s 6d for transfers to the pavilion. This suggests that more than 3,000 attended the match. The Club accounts show that expenditure on the match included one shilling on lemons for the teams to suck at half-time, two shillings each on the nine gatemen, one shilling on the delivery of bills to advertise the match, one guinea on ten policemen

from the Gloucestershire Constabulary, £1 13s 6d on the expenses of the referee, £2 3s 1d towards the cost of entertaining the Burton team to dinner after the game, 2s 4d on telegrams, 12s 6d on five men rolling the pitch, and 15s to others involved in preparing the ground. Total expenditure amounted to £8 0s 5d, which left a profit of £38 6s 10d on the match. This was regarded as a very satisfactory outcome.

A dinner was held that evening at the Spread Eagle to celebrate the opening of the ground. There was a profusion of speeches followed by copious toasts. A full account of the dinner is reproduced at Appendix H, but the Citizen summarised the whole splendid day as follows:

NOTES ON THE OCCASION

Owing to the length at which the opening ceremony, the match itself, and the proceedings at the dinner are reported in our columns, our notes on this auspicious occasion must be extremely brief. Those who had been looking forward to the match with so much interest must have hailed last Tuesday's deluge as a great blessing, for it was surely to be expected after such a grand display of their forces, the watery elements would have left us completely alone for a season. But it was not to be so. Following up the stormy days which had succeeded the great deluge of Tuesday, Saturday bid fair to rival even that well-nigh unprecedentedly wet day, and gloomy indeed was the outlook for the day's proceedings. There had been considerable doubt as to the effect of playing on the turf so recently laid, but it was confidently said that if it was only fine no damage could possibly be done, the turf being on a sandy, quickly-drying soil. The hopes of the greatest optimist must, however, have gone down to zero when he awoke and saw the pitiless downpour of the morning. Doubts were generally entertained both in Gloucester and in Cheltenham as to whether the match would be played. But, of course, such a thought could not be entertained by the management. The match was played rather as a matter of necessity than of choice, but the result, so far as the ground itself was concerned, was such as to scatter the fears of the most extreme pessimist, and to justify more faith in its properties than was entertained by the most hopeful. We never saw such an open and a fast match played under such meteorological conditions, and the turf did not appear to be damaged in the slightest. Let it be thoroughly rolled this week, and the ground will be quite equal to the heavy strain which will be put upon it in the coming six months. Had the match been played on the Spa on Saturday the turf would have been spoiled for the season.

As for the match itself, while it may be said that Gloucester outplayed their opponents at all points, yet it cannot be said that the home team made any rings round the Burton men. Each point had to be fought for, whilst the city men had themselves to act on the defensive on more than one occasion. Gloucester began to press from the start, and the Burton men were on the defensive for almost the whole of the first half, and any hope which might have been entertained by the Burton men prior to the match must have been relinquished entirely after the first quarter of an hour's play. The visitors, however, played very pluckily during the second half, and though they did not succeed in making any points they prevented what at one time seemed possible — the adverse score reaching outrageously heavy proportions. The feature of the Gloucester forward play was the grand dribbling. Page and Healing were far ahead of their confreres in this department, the judgement shown (especially by Page) being exceptionally good. It would be well if the other Gloucester forwards would take a lesson from these two in this respect. They all have an idea of propelling the ball with their feet but very little notion of guiding it to their fellow forwards, and away from their opponents. Once or twice, too, the effect of beautiful passes by Page was quite lost on account of his fellows not quite knowing where to place themselves when he was on the dribble. Ball played a very fair game on his re-appearance on Saturday. He and George played well together, but the heeling out of the forwards and the extraction of the ball from the scrums by the halves was not so conspicuous as usual. Bagwell and Powell played very well together, but Jackson and Taylor have yet to adapt themselves to one another. But very few opportunities presented themselves to the flyer, and those that did were lost through the passing going wrong, greater judgement in the use of Taylor's great speed being necessary. Hughes hardly ever played a better game, his saving on more than one occasion being A 1. The two Eversheds and A Gorton were most prominent in the opposing pack, Marsden was the pick of the three-quarters, whilst Ward, who showed sterling qualities as a full-back, somewhat nullified the good impression which he created at times, by a number of mistakes.

The feature at the dinner in the evening was the admirable speech of Mr Rowland Hill. A great authority on Rugby football, the Union has in him the ablest defender of the game. A little soreness has at times been felt in these quarters at the apparent oversight of this district by the Union in the selection of representative teams. It was well that this should be ventilated in Mr Rowland Hill's presence. His answer shows completely that, if there is anyone who should be played in international matches, who is left out, the Union cannot be blamed. In less than three weeks' time a match is to be played in Gloucester under the auspices of the Union with a special view to finding international merit, and the authorities cannot do more than this. Mr Starr was able to report a very good attendance at the match, taking the unfavourable conditions into consideration. More remarkable is the growth of membership which has taken place this year. On Friday Mr Starr disposed of no less than 177 tickets, over 100 being got out in 75 minutes, and there were a large number of applications on Saturday. The number purchased up to Friday night was 665, or 113 more than were sold in any previous season. The extent to which Mr Starr has pushed the interests of the club is evident in the following figures, it being borne in mind that Mr Starr's first season was 1889-90. In 1885-6 there were 273 members; in 1886-7, 276; in 1887-8, 320; in 1888-9, 318; in 1889-90, 428; in 1990-1, 570; in the present season, 685.

An incident, which was more than regrettable occurred at the end of the evening's proceedings. Two individuals, well-known on the football ground, came to strong words over an incident of the past, in which the personal honour of one of the disputants was involved. Epithets of a far from complimentary character were bandied about, and an invitation to 'come outside' was acted upon. Here reputations and persons were alike treated to indignity, and it is rumoured that legal proceedings are to follow. A further rumour, however, states that mutual sorrow at the occurrence prevails.

Tom Voyce, perhaps Gloucester's finest player and Club Chairman and President, looked back many years later and said:

One must always value the good fortune that we had such great sportsmen in the past who, with their added business acumen, chose Kingsholm as the home of rugger for this whole area; indeed, the West Country, one might say!

The First Season at Kingsholm

PRINCIPALLY IN ORDER to increase revenue, although also to meet rising ambitions, the Club extended their fixture list on the move from the Spa to Kingsholm, from 25 matches in 1890-1 to 34 in 1891-2. In this first season at Kingsholm, entry charges for 1st XV matches were 1s and 6d according to the part of the ground, with an extra charge to sit with the members in the pavilion.

The matches against the Welsh clubs were the most popular, and the first of these at Kingsholm was the visit of Newport on 28th November 1891. It proved a big attraction, and 2061 spectators paid £64 11s od at the turnstiles; this was in addition to the members, to whom 1114 season tickets had been sold by this time. Expenditure for the match amounted to £2 6s od (1s on lemons, 18s on gatemen, 13s on policemen, 2s on sorting tickets, 1s on delivery of bills, 2s on Romans, 3s on Dyke, 5s on Haines, and 1s on a boy), leaving a handsome profit of £62 5s od.

On 27th February 1892, the visit of Cardiff generated £60 1s od, and the London Scottish match on 26th March attracted the largest crowd of the season at Kingsholm, with £80 3s od taken in gate money. The novelty of persuading a London team to come to play in Gloucester would have added to the draw of this fixture. Doubtless by way of encouragement for the future, the visitors were well entertained at the Spread Eagle Hotel after the match at a cost of £11 14s 11d plus 5s for a pianist, W H Morgan. These big crowds allowed the Treasurer to announce that the Club had a healthy balance of £75 10s 9 ½ d at the end of the season, by which time membership had risen to 1127.

The County Comes to Kingsholm

Jimmy Boughton of Gloucester was determined to put the game in the County on a wider and more substantial footing, and he organised a meeting on 11th November 1891 at the Spread Eagle, Gloucester, to achieve this. The Gloucester County Football Club reconstituted itself as the Gloucester County Football Union (the later nomenclature of Gloucestershire Rugby Football Union was not adopted until 1908). All the major posts in the new GCFU were filled by Gloucester men – Boughton was elected President, H V Page as Captain, Tom Graves Smith as Secretary and H S Simpson as Treasurer. Boughton also became the first Gloucestershire representative on the Committee of the Rugby Union.

The meeting was arranged for the same day as the County's first use of Kingsholm, a County trial match. H V Page's XV beat Tommy Bagwell's XV by six points (three tries) to nil, although the match was reported to be a farce, with only 25 players taking part. However, the annual County trial match soon came to have more substance, and was played at Kingsholm in each of the next four seasons, although the names of the sides changed to Probables v Possibles and then to Reds v Stripes.

The first match against another county in 1891-92 was lost 4-5 to Somerset at Bath, but because of the bad state of the ground the teams agreed to play an exhibition match of only 20 minutes each way. The second was lost 0-9 to Midland Counties at Coventry, but the third, against Devon, was Gloucestershire's only home match of the season and it was played at Kingsholm. This fixture was originally arranged for 25th November 1891, but was postponed because of the death of the secretary of the Devonshire County Club. It was rearranged for Thursday 17th December 1891. Unfortunately this turned out to be a cold and foggy day and despite it being early closing day in Gloucester, few spectators turned out to watch. Nevertheless they were able to enjoy a Gloucestershire win by one goal, two tries and one minor (9 points) to one minor (nil).

Sid Starr is clutching the gate money from the Newport match in November 1891, although complaining like any good club treasurer that it might have been more; George Symonds taxi service was regularly used by the Club [Magpie]

The County Union declared themselves delighted with the new ground, and were keen to bring more matches to Kingsholm. The following season, they paid a hire charge of £1 15s 0d to the Ground Company in order to stage a county trial match at Kingsholm on 15th October 1892. They came to a different financial arrangement for the subsequent county match against Somerset on 29th October 1892, the County Union paying 25% of the net gate to the Ground Company, which amounted to £15 10s 0d. This match attracted the largest crowd yet seen in Gloucester for a County game, but it was a dour affair, which ended in a 0-0 stalemate. The report in The Magpie dismissed it with a witheringly short report: 'the game would have been more interesting if more open, but it wasn't, and there's an end on't'.

In 1892-93, Cornwall replaced Midland Counties in the South West Group, and from then on Kingsholm periodically staged one of the group games, but Gloucestershire were not a power in the rugby land during the 1890s and never won the group.

International Trial

The Rugby Union was just as impressed as the County with the initiative taken by the Gloucester Club in acquiring the Kingsholm ground, and they were quick to take advantage of this new rugby centre. Less than three weeks after the opening of the ground, an England trial game was staged on Thursday 29th October 1891 between Western Counties and Midland Counties. The six Gloucester players selected for the Western Counties ensured plenty of local interest and five of them were easily identifiable because they wore their club jerseys. The referee was saved from confusion by the all-white attire of the Midland Counties, who ran out winners by one dropped goal, two tries and ten minors (8 points) to three minors (0 points).

The Citizen reported that:

The Rugby Union Committee are, we understand, very well satisfied with their first official visit to Gloucester, and it is more than likely that yesterday's trial will not be the last played in this city. The crowd was quite a Saturday one as regards its proportions, and though the money taken (£31 12s) will barely cover the expenses, if that, yet is probably more than would have been found anywhere else, whether the match had been played in London, the Midlands, or any other place in the Western Counties. There were over 3,000 present, but among these were included the majority of the 852 members now numbered in the city club, and a few dogs. When shall we see the notice 'Dogs not admitted' displayed, and enforced against the whole canine race? The committee ought to find time on Monday next to decide on action in reference to this matter. The officials of the [Rugby Football] Union present were Mr E T Gurdon (president), Mr Rowland Hill (secretary), Mr H Vassall (treasurer), and Messrs C J Currey, A Budd, R S Whalley, F H Fox, and C Stuart (members of the committee). Mr Vassall officiated as referee. Rowland Hill acted as one of the touch judges.

The Barbarians

Another early feather in the cap of Kingsholm was the visit of the Barbarians at the end of the first season on 28th March 1892. They were advertised as '15 members of a crack combination of the country'. The points system at the time, with two points for a try and three for a conversion, secured a narrow 10-9 victory for Gloucester. Although outscored by three tries to two, the home side kicked both conversions whilst the visitors managed only one. Money taken on the gates totalled £31 14s 0d; but half of this sum, £15 17s 0d, was paid to the Barbarians. Expenses amounted to £4 11s 6d, leaving the Club with a profit of £11 5s 6d.

The Gloucester Thursday Club

A separate club was set up in November 1891 by Sid Starr and others to play matches on Thursday afternoons. It grew out of the Gloucester Early Closing Association, an organisation which represented local tradesmen, and which campaigned successfully for half-day closing on a Thursday. In the first season they must have used the only available pitch at Kingsholm, but thereafter they played on their own pitch in the part of Kingsholm now occupied by the car park. Many of the Gloucester players, including Jimmy Boughton, also turned out for the Thursday Club, but none of its dealings appear in the Gloucester Club accounts, and the two clubs seem to have remained quite separate organisationally. Opponents for the Thursday Club were generally local, including Gymnasium, Liberal Club, Harlequins, Newnham, Gordon Wanderers, Post Office, St Lukes, Gordon League and Sandhurst. The club prospered with both players and spectators, and it quickly expanded to run a Thursday reserve XV.

The Thursday XV played a match against Newnham on 21st January 1892. Income was generated from an entry charge of 3d for access to any part of the ground, which produced £1 12s 3d from 129 spectators. Expenses amounted to 11s, which left a profit of £1 1s 3d. A week later on 28th January, the Thursday Reserves played Harlequins, which raised 10s 9d from 43 spectators, whilst expenses came to 8s, leaving a profit of 2s 9d.

By comparison, the Gloucester 2nd XV played against Lydney on 30th January 1892, 199 spectators paid £4 2s 9d at the entrance gates, but the crowd would also have included many members holding season tickets. Expenses added up to £1 14s, leaving a profit of £2 8s 9d.

In some respects the Thursday Club were second class citizens at Kingsholm – the Gloucester Club were asked by the Ground Company to practise on the Thursday pitch in order to keep their own playing surface in good condition for the Saturday matches. The Thursday Club argued that they should only be employing Harry Dyke, the groundsman, for half a day on their match days, but the Company Board insisted that they pay for a whole day.

Development of Kingsholm during the First Season

WITH MATCHES NOW underway at Kingsholm, the Company pressed ahead with the work necessary to make better use of the ground. The Company wanted the quick removal of at least some of the buildings in the centre of the ground, and believed that they could turn a profit by selling them for their salvage value. By the end of October 1891, they had received four offers, varying between £27-10-0 and £35, for the demolition and removal of the house, garden walls, and 'pigscots'. However none of these was regarded as acceptable. Renewed advertising of the work attracted four further tenders on 5th/6th November 1891 for amounts varying between £26-10-0 and £35. The tender from Freeman & Jones of St Marks Street (next door to the ground) for £35 for purchase and removal was accepted. It was decided that the foundation of the house should be taken up at least 18 inches (45cms) below the cellar floor. However, to this day the groundsman at Kingsholm is able to identify where the remaining foundations were left in place (roughly in the middle of the present pitch).

The Company also looked to raise revenue by selling advertising space at the ground, and a tender was accepted from Alexander Storey offering £50 for the advertising rights on the Kingsholm Road fence. However, this arrangement did not work out too well. Storey collected money from advertisers and kept his 50% commission, but proved reluctant to pass on the other 50% to the Ground Company. The Company's solicitors had to chase him for it. Although he was eventually forced to pay up, his contract was terminated.

For the first season, a contract was signed with Mr Wright, who agreed to pay 50 shillings for space on the ground up to the end of the season for a kiosk in which to sell cigars. The Company also came to an agreement with Mr Moffatt, a butcher, who paid £2 for sheep grazing rights on the ground from October to the end of March. Only the western end of the ground was being used for rugby, but development work and other uses of the ground inhibited his access to the grazing. In May 1892 he offered £3 for the grazing rights over the summer, but was still concerned about security and water supply at the ground. In September 1892, he was offered the grazing rights for the next twelve months for £5.

In January 1892, it was decided to advertise for tenders for the purchase and removal of two cottages and stables, for the purchase and removal of sundry trees, and for the rights to supply non-alcoholic refreshments. The following advertisement was placed in the Citizen:

The Gloucester Football and Athletic Ground Company Limited
Tenders wanted as follows:
1. To purchase, grub up, and clear off the ground at once 63 Apple, Pear and Fruit Trees, 2 Poplars, 3 Holly Trees, and about six dozen Gooseberry and Currant Bushes. Work to be completed by February 11th.
2. To purchase, take down, and clear away two Cottages, Stable and Front Wall, now situated on the Company's ground facing the Kingsholm Road. Work to be completed by March 1st.
3. Tenders for the sole right of providing Tea, Coffee, and other Non-intoxicants on days when there are Football Matches up to the 1st May 1892.
Tenders to be marked 1, 2, or 3, as the case may be, and sent to the Secretary, 81, Barton Street, Gloucester, by 6:30 on Wednesday January 13th.

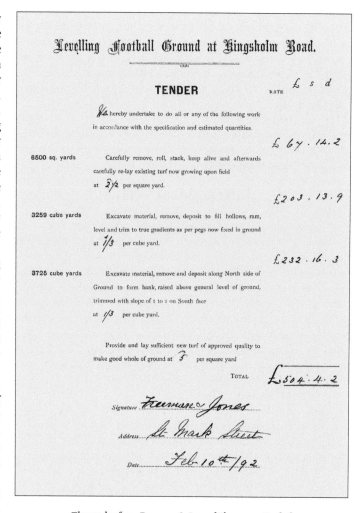

The tender from Freeman & Jones [Gloucester Rugby]

Moffatt's letter about grazing rights for the summer of 1892 [Gloucester Rugby]

An early image of the Kingsholm ground shows Tommy Bagwell scoring against Old Edwardians in a game which Gloucester won by 4 goals and 5 tries to nil on 7th November 1891. The spectators behind the goal are standing on a bank in front of houses in St Marks Street [Magpie]

In April 1892, Albert Bendall of Bowbridge, Stroud was interviewed with a view to giving him the contract to level the ground for £176 6s 1d, which was only part of his tender. He was required to dig out to a depth of 18 inches, and at least nine inches of best soil was to be kept under the turf. There were to be staged payments; and the work was to be completed in 10 weeks. He was given the contract, but only after he had been beaten down from 6d to 4d per square yard for supplying 2,000-3,000 square yards of turf. By the end of May 1892, Bendall had been paid £266 16s 1d for this work.

The Company accounts show that income received was £35 for the sale of the Castle Grim house, £22 15s od from Enoch Clutterbuck for the cottages (believed to have been in the north-east corner of the ground), £16 10s od for iron railings, 5s for a holly tree and 17s for iron hurdles.

W Buckley's tender of £2 for the right to supply refreshments was accepted, although by the end of the month he was asking that this contract be cancelled because he was making a loss – he was persuaded to continue with the experiment for a while longer. The Company perceived a need to safeguard these revenue streams from competition on the ground and wrote to the Rugby Club, reminding them that the Company had the sole right to supply refreshments on the ground, and insisting that the hawking of cakes, oranges, etc must be stopped.

No tender had been received for removing most of the trees, so that was included in a further levelling contract, for which tenders were sought via another advertisement in the Citizen:

Gloucester Football and Athletic Ground Company Limited
Tenders are Required for Excavating, Filling, Levelling and Turfing the remaining portion of ground at Kingsholm. Specifications and Bills of Quantities to be had, and Plan to be seen, on application to the Custodian at the Registered Office, Oddfellows' Hall, Barton Street. The whole of the work to be completed within three months from signing the contract. Tenders to be sent in by noon on Wednesday 10th February.

The specification was for removing, storing and relaying 6,500 square yards of turf, to level the ground, and to deposit 3,259 cubic yards of earth on the northern side of the ground (which would form the bank on which the Shed was built many years later).

Dated 15th February 1892.

The Gloucester Football & Athletic Ground Coy Ld.

with

Messrs Albert Bendall and Albert Jos. Bendall.

Agreement for Levelling Land at Kingsholm.

BRETHERTON, SON & BOUGHTON
SOLICITORS,
GLOUCESTER.

The cover of the contract for levelling the ground. The documents detailing the specification, tender and contract for this work, which effectively laid out Kingsholm in the way which has persisted to the present day, are reproduced in full at Appendix I [Gloucester Rugby]

Work on the Ground during the Summer of 1892

HAVING PUT ALL the necessary legalities in place for successful operation of the Company, and having done what was immediately necessary to play matches at Kingsholm during the 1891-92 season, the Board concentrated in 1892 on the further development of the ground. By March 1892, the Company's architect, J P Moore, was being paid for planning work, and the Company's solicitors, Bretherton Sons and Boughton for further legal work. It was recognised that further development required more capital, over and above that raised from the sale of shares in the Company. In April 1892 a portion of the ground was pegged out for sale, and Messrs Stephens and Hatton were both seen as potential buyers, but this seems to have fallen through.

As soon as the 1891-92 season was over, the Wagon Works removed the temporary grandstand. In early May tenders were sought for the supply of a roller, which was to be over one ton in weight and drawn by a horse. At the end of the month, seven tenders were received for removing earth to form a bank at the western Deans Walk side of the ground, which would be 12 yards wide, 3 feet 6 inches high at the crest, tapering down to nothing. This would later be built up further to become the Tump. A similar bank was to be built up on the eastern Worcester Street side of the ground, taking earth from a bank in the centre of the ground. This would initially be an open terrace before forming the base for the Worcester Street stand many years later. Sand and gravel recovered during this work was to be moved to the Vinegar Works (south-east) Corner of the ground.

'Commodore' Vears, the Chairman of the Ground Company, made arrangements with Bendall for the completion of the excavating, filling, levelling and turfing of the ground, the turfing to include areas in the centre of the ground which had been occupied by the stable and the temporary grandstand. Harry Dyke, who had been taken on as the first groundsman at Kingsholm, also acted as Clerk of Works on Bendall's contract. The contract did not go entirely smoothly. It was soon apparent that the turf laid by Bendall was dead, and he was instructed to make good or be charged for it to be done. Arrangements for turf to be purchased and laid by Dyke and Lauder were made in case Bendall did not replace the turf. Instead he offered to reseed, but this proposal was rejected. J Griffett was hired to do more levelling, for which he was paid £167 in instalments in July and August 1892; and turf was purchased from Jenkins at 4d (1.7p) per yard at a total cost of £66 13s od. The argument with Bendall was still rumbling along into the next season. In September 1892, he invoiced the Ground Company for 15 guineas as the balance of his various contracts, but the Company maintained that he actually owed them money and counter-claimed £16 15s od from him for the cost of having to do the returfing.

Although the ground was let to the Rugby Club for the rugby season, the Company looked to generate more income from lettings during the summer of 1892, and it was agreed that cricket should be played at Kingsholm. The Young Men's Christian Association Cricket Club agreed to rent a pitch from 1st May to 31st August for £7 10s od, which still allowed Rugby Club use on specified days. Cricket pitches were also let to the Police Cricket Club for 2 guineas, and to the Grocers' Assistants' Cricket Club for £5. Other summer hirings in 1892 were to Sanger's Circus on 2nd May for £10; to the Oddfellows & Forresters for a Whit Monday fete for £25; and £5 was charged for extending Mr Moffatt's contract for grazing rights up to 31st August. Volunteers under Capt Thorpe were allowed to drill on the ground, for which they were charged 10s each time the full force drilled, and 5s for a single company. Members of Gloucester Athletic Club were permitted to train on the ground, but only for foot racing. The ground was also let out for various school treats, for which a minimum of 2 guineas was charged, and to Gloucester Trades and Labour Council for £25 for a demonstration on 1st August.

Summer lettings were only entered into if they could be accommodated without interfering with the development of the ground. Attention next turned to the northern, St Marks, side of the ground, and tenders were sought in May 1892 for removing earth, levelling, forming a bank, etc, and for erecting a fence on that side of ground. On 1st June, the tender of J & W Brookes of Bristol Road, Gloucester, was accepted to erect the fence for 5s 5d a yard (although an increase to 6s per yard was later agreed), on condition that the work was completed by 7th July. The tender of J Griffett to carry out the earthworks for £110 was accepted with a completion deadline of 21st July

The minutes of a Board meeting on 1st June 1892, record that the Chairman had calculated that further capital of £700-£800 would be needed for future requirements. The manager of the Capital & Counties Bank was prepared to recommend to his Directors that a credit of £800 be granted on the joint guarantee of the Company Directors. Interest on the overdraft would be 4.5% when the bank rate was at or under 4%, and 5% when above 4%, the commission to be 0.125% to be charged only when the Company's account was overdrawn. The Board agreed to this arrangement. These additional funds were earmarked to build a pavilion on the ground.

The first issue of 3,000 shares had now been fully subscribed, and the Board decided that no more shares would be issued. However, payments were going out on the mortgage - on 20th July 1892, the Board approved a payment to be made to A V Hatton of £48 15s od, representing a half year's interest on the mortgage.

At the Club AGM in 1892, it was agreed, despite some opposition, to increase the annual subscription from 5s to 10s for members to sit in the new pavilion or to stand in the enclosure. The subscription for any other part of the ground was 5s, cheaper rates were available for women and children, and subscriptions for playing members were waived altogether. One membership problem had to be resolved – some members were reported to have obtained their membership cards which folded into three parts and then 'resorted to the mean and miserable subterfuge of tearing them in three, and thereby securing the entrance of three persons for one.' This led to the introduction of single fold membership cards.

In July 1892, a fresh attempt was made to let a contract to make money from advertising spaces around the ground. An advertisement was placed in local newspapers: 'Mr Storey having assigned his lease of the advertising station in the Kingsholm Road to the Gloucester Football and Athletic Ground Company, the Directors are open to receive tenders for canvassing on commission for letting spaces for advertisements and collecting the rents.' Billposters were also canvassed for offers to advertise on the Deans Walk fence. The tender from William Dancey, an auctioneer and house agent, was accepted, and the Ground Company signed a contract with him on 19th August 1892. This allowed him commission of 20% in the first year that an advertising space was let, and 5% for repeat lettings in subsequent years.

On 17th September 1892, the Gloucestershire Magpie reported on the changes made at Kingsholm:

> A great improvement has been effected at the ground. The goal posts occupy opposite lines to those in which they were placed last season; at each end sloping banks have been made, and will prove

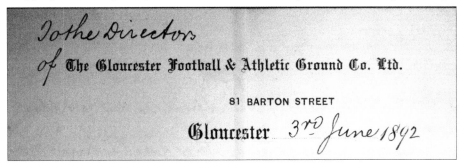

The letter at top shows:

> WILLIS BROTHERS
> Auctioneers,
> Valuers, Property & Estate Agents.
>
> W. H. WILLIS.
> E. J. WILLIS.
>
> BARTON CHAMBERS,
> EASTGATE,
> GLOUCESTER
>
> Gentlemen,   August 4th 1892.
> We shall be glad to canvass & collect the Rents of your Advertising spaces, for 25% & pay you cash in advance.
> We can assure you we shall give a lot of time to the work and have no doubt but that amongst our numerous friends and customers we shall soon fill the spaces. We presume you will appoint us Agents for five or more years.
> We are, Gentlemen
> Yours faithfully
> Willis Bros.

Listed percentages:

Willis	25%
Dancey	5%
Watkins	5%
L.P.S.	2½%
R. Son	15%
Brown	15%
Workman	25%

The tender from Willis Bros for the agency for advertising at Kingsholm; also listed are the percentages to be taken by each agent from all the tenders submitted
[Gloucester Rugby]

an advantage spectators will not be slow to appreciate. A capital exit has also been made into Worcester Street, whereby the crush which invariably followed every match last season, frequently causing much ruffling of temper, will be entirely avoided. The committee are, in fact, carrying out the work they have undertaken thoroughly and well, and when the pavilion is complete the Kingsholm ground promises to be what Mr Vears said at the annual dinner it would be, 'one o' the prettiest in the West of England'.

It was recognised that the Company Secretary, H S Simpson had been faced with a heavy workload in the first year at Kingsholm, and so the Board decided that he should be paid £40 (£20 salary and £20 for extra work); he was also given £25 petty cash and £5 for a year's rent of the company office. Unfortunately Simpson was unable to stay in the job for much longer – in February 1893, he resigned as Secretary of the Company, because his bank employer had transferred him away from Gloucester. There were five applicants to replace him, and the Board selected Sid Starr; he in turn was replaced as the Football Club representative on the Board by Tom Graves Smith.

The Ground Company accounts for the first year of trading showed income of £388 0s 3d, and expenditure of £234 7s 10d, leaving a balance in credit of £153 12s 5d, on the basis of which the Directors decided to return £150 to their shareholders by way of a 5% dividend. These accounts were presented at the first Annual General Meeting of the Ground Company and are shown at Appendix J. Both Company and Club had made a good start in the first year at Kingsholm.

> To the Directors
> of The Gloucester Football & Athletic Ground Co. Ltd.
>
> 81 BARTON STREET
>
> Gloucester 3rd June 1892

The letterhead used for early Ground Company correspondence

The Pavilion

Having secured the necessary funding for the new pavilion by way of an agreed overdraft with their bank, the Ground Company tasked their architect, J P Moore, with preparing plans. These were put out to tender, but the lowest tender was £500, so Moore was instructed to strike out any work not absolutely necessary in the hope of bringing the cost down to £375-£400. The next round of tenders brought one from J C Leat for £405, and from William Williams for £417 5s 0d, but the Board still felt that they were excessive, and demanded further reductions and more tenders. The third round of tenders produced offers of £370 10s 0d from Enoch Clutterbuck and £385 from Alfred Gyde, and the Clutterbuck bid was duly accepted.

J C Leat tried to claim £5 10s 0d for the time and trouble he had expended in compiling his unsuccessful tender for the new pavilion. The Company felt no obligation to pay him, and the dispute rumbled on until September 1892, when the Company eventually offered him £2 to put an end to the matter.

In July 1892, Moore drew up a plan showing the proposed siting of the new pavilion alongside the planned running track. In fact the pavilion was built slightly further to the east and at an angle. The athletics track seems never to have been built as shown on this plan. Although athletics took place on the ground, the track was marked out on the grass during the summer and had to fit into the shape of the rugby pitch.

The new pavilion was not ready for the first pre-season match of 1892-93, which was played at Kingsholm on 10th September, when the Gloucester 1st XV beat the Gloucester Colts XX 26-0. WB (or Bill Bailey, of whom much more later in this book) approved of the changes to the ground, writing in the Citizen that 'the ground at Kingsholm has been laid out splendidly. The field of play this season is just the opposite to last, being from the Deans Walk to Worcester Street, instead of St Marks Street to the City, which is a decided improvement for the spectators, a splendid view being now obtainable from any portion of the field.' The pavilion was first occupied a week later for the second pre-season game between the

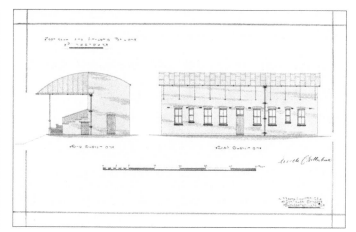

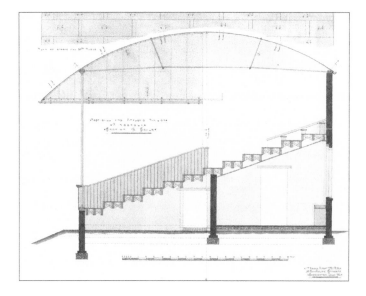

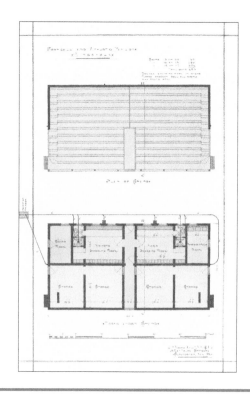

The plans which the Club's architect drew up in May 1892 for the new pavilion.
He was paid £13 1s for this work [Gloucestershire Archives]

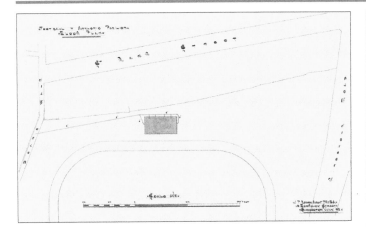

Moore's original plan for the siting of the pavilion [Gloucestershire Archives]

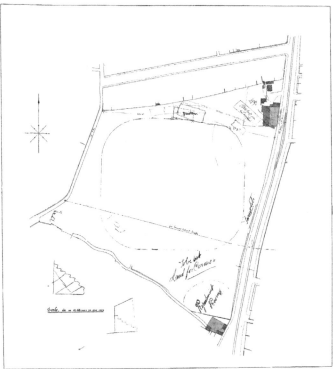

A rough plan showing the amended siting of the pavilion [Gloucestershire Archives]

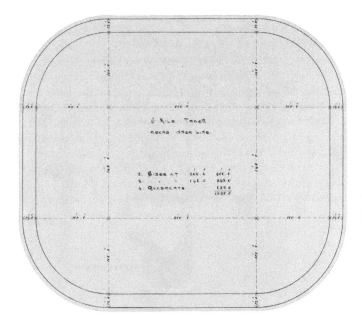

The plan for the athletics track at Kingsholm [Gloucestershire Archives]

1st XV and the Next XX, which resulted in a 2-2 draw, a try apiece. This enabled the members to try out the new seating before they packed it out for the first competitive game of the season on 24th September, when Gloucester beat Bristol 15-0, scoring a goal, a dropped goal and three tries. By then 1085 members had paid their subscriptions for the season. With 132 spectators paying £6 12s 0d to watch from the 1s side, 619 spectators paying £15 9s 6d to watch from the 6d side of the ground, and other spectators paying 16s 6d to transfer to the pavilion, total gate takings amounted to £22 18s 0d.

Enoch Clutterbuck was paid in instalments for his work in constructing the pavilion. The general ledger of the Company shows that he was paid £100 on 27th August 1892, £150 on 24th September, £150 on 29th October, and a final instalment of £28-2-6 on 22nd February 1893, making the total cost of the pavilion £428-2-6. This caused the Company's overdraft with the Capital and Counties Bank to rise to £584. Rather than issue more shares to raise additional capital, the Directors of the Ground Company made themselves personally responsible to the bank for this debt.

A club game being played in front of the pavilion – although the exact date is not known, it is before the gymnasium was built in 1905 [Gloucester City Museum]

Sid Starr

SIDNEY STEPHEN STARR was born in Gloucester in 1860, the son of a sack contractor. Records in the early years of the Club are incomplete, but the first time that Sid appears on a Gloucester team sheet is during the 1880-81 season, when he played at least two games for the Gloucester Second XV. The following season, 1881-82, he appeared for the First XV in the opening two games of the season. The first against a Colts XXII, was won by three goals to one, and was notable for the first appearance of Tommy Bagwell, who scored the Colts' try. Sid stayed in the First XV for the next fixture away against Swindon Rangers, but thereafter reverted to the Seconds, for whom he continued to play until the 1887-88 season.

Sid may not have been a star player, but he became truly devoted to the Club, and his major contribution was to be as an administrator and as the ultimate Club man. He served on the Committee in various roles, including Secretary and Treasurer. In 1890 Sid married Laura Glover Roberts, and the couple lived with Laura's parents at Paradise Nurseries, 69, London Road, Gloucester, where Sid had moved into the family business as a floral contractor. In 1892, the Gloucestershire Referees Association was founded, and Sid was one of the first referees to be appointed by them.

HON. TREASURER GLOUCESTER FOOTBALL CLUB

A cartoon of Sid Starr published in 1891 [Magpie]

It appears that Sid was the Committee man most heavily involved in the laying of salt on the Spa, and for a long time after the event, the members of the Club continued to tease him about his role in this incident. The record of the Club AGM in September 1891 relates that:

In moving the re-election of Mr S S Starr as treasurer, Mr H J Bennett, who with Mr T G Smith is joint secretary, pointed out that Mr Starr had done everything he possibly could in the interests of the club, even to the use of salt on the ground, which drew from Mr Starr the explanation that although he had the credit, he was not altogether responsible in that matter. The subject had been discussed many times and one member was so anxious that the ground should be in a playable condition for the Swansea match, that he suggested the use of a whole warehouse of salt rather than have the match called off. The explanation was justifiable but unnecessary; the pickling of the Spa was an evidence of the energy and forethought of the committee.

In the subsequent endeavours to obtain a separate ground, Sid was doubtful as to whether it could be afforded, but was an enthusiastic proponent of the scheme to purchase Castle Grim, and delighted when it happened. When the Gloucester Football and Athletic Ground Co Ltd had been set up, it was decided that the Gloucester Football Club should be represented on the Board of the Company, and Sid was selected as the first such Board member.

At the first meeting of the Board in 1891, Sid proposed H S Simpson, a banker, for the post of Company Secretary, and he was duly appointed. However, some 18 months later, in February 1893, Simpson was forced to resign because his job took him away from Gloucester. The Company invited applications to replace him, and received five responses. They duly offered the post to Sid for a salary of £20 per annum. He was to serve as Company Secretary for more than 50 years.

Much of the day-to-day running of the Company was left to Sid as Secretary, and in July 1895, he hired the ground for £5 to Mr McCrea for pony races. However, when the Board met later in the month, some Directors thought that the rent of £5 was too low, although they accepted that it could not now be increased. Sid was mortified by the implied criticism of his judgement, and believed that he had lost the confidence of those Directors. He tendered his resignation to take effect at the end of that financial year. Now it was the turn of the Directors to eat some humble pie, and a week later Sid was informed by the Board that he had not lost their confidence, and he was persuaded to withdraw his resignation.

At the Company AGM in 1899, Sid's minutes record the Chairman saying that 'Mr Starr was a most invaluable servant, and saved the board of directors a good many hours' work by the business-like manner in which he fulfilled his duties.' In 1903, they awarded him an honorarium of

Sid Starr and his son attending the match against the Australians at Kingsholm in 1908 [CC&GG]

£10 for persuading Buffalo Bill to pitch his tent at Kingsholm.

Sid was also singled out for praise during the AGM in 1913 – 'Mr C E Brown thought they might congratulate themselves on the excellent way in which Mr Sidney Starr had looked after the affairs of the company. Ignoring the special costs in connection with the sale of a portion of the land, the total expenses were £21 less than in the previous year.'

Sid's wife, Laura, died in 1943. Sid outlived her by four years, but resigned as Secretary of the Ground Company in 1944, and died in 1947, aged 87.

Tom Graves Smith

Tom was born in 1859, the son of a Cambridgeshire farmer. His second name, Graves, was the maiden name of his mother, who died when he was only four. He came to Gloucester as a young man of 16, in 1877, and lodged at 8, Arthur Street. He found employment at the Atlas Works of Fielding and Platt as a mechanical engineer's pupil. He took up rugby and enjoyed a distinguished career as a forward in the early days of both Club and County teams. He made 118 appearances for the Gloucester Club, 1881-89, and was a member of the Invincibles team of 1882-83, which went through the season unbeaten. Tom was captain for four seasons, 1885-89, during which the Club won 48 and lost only 19 of its 78 games. At this time the Captain also acted as Chairman of the Committee, so Tom was the leader of the Club off the field as well as on it. He started to play for the County side in 1884-85 and became captain in 1887.

When he stopped playing he continued to serve Club and County as referee and administrator. He was one of the original referees appointed when the Gloucestershire Referees association was first formed in 1892. He became Secretary of the Club, and took a seat on the Board of the Ground Company as the representative of the Club in 1893, when Sid Starr gave up this role to become Company Secretary. As such he played a prominent part in the early development of Kingsholm. He was made a Life Member of the Club. He also served as Secretary of the Gloucestershire County Football Union 1890-1900, was President in 1901-02, and was the County's representative on the committee of the Rugby Football Union 1900-09.

T. GRAVES SMITH.
(Capt. 1885-9.)

A photograph of Tom in 1902 [CC&GG]

As Secretary of both Club and County, he found himself on both sides of the argument in 1894 when the County punished the Club over the Shewell affair (see later chapter), and the Club appealed against the County's judgement. Tom wrote letters to himself to start with, and he must have been disappointed that these exchanges failed to resolve the situation. But he had other distractions in 1894 - he married Minnie Laura Butt, and his best man was Norman Biggs, a Welsh International and captain of Cardiff; and he joined the Dudbridge Iron Works Ltd, Stroud, where he became a Director until his retirement in 1919.

Tom was a member of the Institute of Mechanical Engineers, and was made a fellow of the Royal Society of Arts. In his later years, besides maintaining his love of rugby and Kingsholm, he served on the committees of the Cotteswold Naturalist Field Club and the Bristol and Gloucestershire Archaeological Society. He died at Stroud in 1935, aged 74.

MR. T. G. SMITH, Hon. Sec., of the Gloucester Football Club.

A cartoon of Tom Graves Smith published in 1891 [Magpie]

Further Development of Kingsholm, 1892-93

By THE TIME the pavilion was up in 1892, the Board were already pushing ahead with further development of the ground. A plan was drawn up for the area in front of the new pavilion. An enclosure was created, surrounded by a fence, with a gate to give access to the field of play, and steps to form a terrace for spectators. Having built the pavilion, Enoch Clutterbuck was invited to tender, and his offer to do the work for £35 was accepted.

It was found that the goal posts needed replacing, and in October 1892, £1 13s 6d was paid for new posts, but 10s of this was recovered immediately by selling the old posts to the local Gordon Wanderers club. Later in the season a further 16s was paid to J Lewis for further new goalposts and ironwork. In November 1892, it was decided to erect a flagpole at least 50ft high next to the new pavilion and just clear of the enclosure fence; tenders were sought, and the one from J & W Brookes Bros for £7 15s od was accepted. The following month, the Club requested the provision of stands (by which they meant uncovered terraces for spectators to stand on) on the cheaper (south) side of the ground, and the Company agreed to provide these for two-thirds of the length of the pitch. These facilities were further enhanced early the next season – in October 1893, the Ground Company agreed to purchase more seats and stands, which were supplied by Mr Madge.

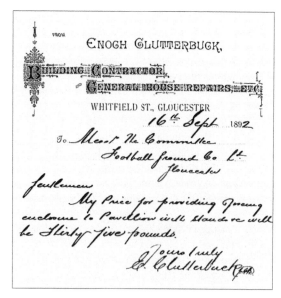

Enoch Clutterbuck's tender for the enclosure in front of the pavilion [Gloucester Rugby]

A cartoon of the St Marks Street side of the ground, drawn during the match lost 0-11 to Old Merchant Taylors on Boxing Day 1892 – note the spectators standing on a small bank and the end of the pavilion just showing on the left [Magpie]

Frosty weather threatened cancellation of the match against Newport on 17th December 1892, but the committee shied away from using salt. Instead, Mr Griffett was paid one guinea to provide hay. Harry Dyke, the groundsman, was paid 9s 1d for 3 days work in spreading the hay across the ground, and a further £4 was paid to a team of men for taking the hay off the pitch ahead of the match, and for putting it back afterwards. These measures were rewarded when the biggest crowd of the season poured into Kingsholm to see the match, paying £86 16s 6d in gate money. Newport won the game 2-0, by a try to nil.

Ten days later, a game was played against Kent Wanderers without the hay being removed. This was labelled an 'exhibition match', in which the visitors made off with the spoils. They not only won by a goal (5) to nil, but also took £7 3s 0d as their half share of the gate money. They also benefitted from expenditure of 3s 6d on beer and 2s 6d on whiskey to entertain them after the game.

There being no facilities at Kingsholm, the Ram Hotel was used on match days for changing, baths and teas, and a brake was used to transport the players to the ground. On 18th March 1893, 10s was paid to Mr Franklin for the brake he provided to transport the Middlesex Wanderers team, who won by a goal (5) to nil. Some teams appear to have warranted better teas than others. The Club paid £6 17s 0d to the Ram Hotel for tea after the match against Coventry (which Coventry had won 3-2, by a penalty against a try), whereas Leicester (having been beaten 12-0, with Gloucester scoring two goals and a try) were offered a more miserly tea, for which the bill from the Ram was only £3. On 15th April 1893, the Ram was paid £15 for baths etc for the whole season.

The Club earned much of its income from gate takings. An example of the income and expenditure for a match is the game against Swansea on 8th April 1893. Income amounted to £23 19s 0d, made up of £6 14 s from the 1s side, £16 8s 6d from the 6d side, and 16s 6d from transfers to the pavilion. Expenditure totalled £2 6s, made up of 1s on lemons, 12s 6d on gatemen, 8s on police, 10s for three men working on the preparation of the ground, 1s on delivery of bills, 2s 6d on beer and 11s on the expenses of Hughes, the Gloucester full back, for travel from Bristol. This left the Club with a profit of £21 13s.

The constitution of the Ground Company required three Directors to retire each year. When this became necessary for the first time it was decided in September 1892 that those who would retire at the forthcoming shareholders' meeting would be selected in alphabetic order, so Messrs Cummings, Dancey and Davis stood down, although they were all then re-elected. The Directors held keys to a private door into the ground, but it was found that unauthorised persons were obtaining entrance to the

ground this way, so new locks and keys were procured in November 1892. At the start of the following season, it took a Board decision to allow Mr Hanman, the Club Captain, to be loaned a key to the Directors' door for the duration of the season.

During the summer of 1893, further work was undertaken to improve the playing surface – 3,259 cubic yards of earth were used to infill so as to produce a more level surface, and 3,725 cubic yards were used to form a bank along the north side of the ground adjoining St Mark Street from Deans Walk to Kingsholm Road. This bank remains to this day as the base for the Shed and the Lions' Den.

As regards summer lettings of the ground in 1893, an advertisement was placed in the local press - 'This extensive enclosed pleasure ground to be let, with grand stands, turnstiles, and all facilities for fetes, circuses and all kinds of entertainments.' Lettings which would clash with rugby matches were not allowed – for example, J C Byett's offer to hire the gravelled corner of the ground for fair rides at Easter was declined. However, after the season was ended, Mr McCrea was permitted to hire the ground for fireworks displays on 1st and 3rd June for 5 guineas per night; he also hired the whole ground for £25 for a Military Sports and Fete on Whit Monday 1893.

A SNAPSHOT AT KINGSHOLM.

This is the earliest known photograph of Kingsholm, published in the Gloucestershire Magpie on 30th September 1893, and taken looking towards the south-east corner of the ground, with Worcester Street and St Marks Church in the background; it shows the low terraces for spectators along the southern side of the pitch which had been put in during the previous season [Magpie]

Several cricket clubs continued to use the ground on a regular basis. The agreement with the Young Men's Religious Society's Cricket Club was renewed at the same rent of £7 10s 0d, and that with the Police Cricket Club was also renewed for £2. The St Mary de Lode Cricket Club offered £5 for the season, but were told that they could have the Worcester Street side for £7 10s 0d, which they accepted. Both the Early Closing Cricket Club and the Post Office Cricket Club applied to rent a pitch at Kingsholm for the four summer months for five years at £20. However, the Board did not want to commit that far ahead, and were only prepared to conclude an annual agreement. We know that the Grocers' Cricket Club also played at Kingsholm, because they caused irritation by failing to return the key to the Deans Walk entrance.

The ground was also used for athletic meetings, as originally intended, this purpose having been included in the name of the Football and Athletic Ground Company when it was originally set up. In August 1893 the Gloucester Athletic Society held their annual festival on 'the new four lap track at Kingsholm. A novelty for an athletic meeting will be introduced by the inclusion in the programme of a promenade concert, dancing and fireworks' It was a big success.

In 1893, after two years of operations, the Ground Company declared assets of £6,279 3s 8d, and a profit of £159 15s 3d, as a result of which the Board decided to pay out £150 as a 5% dividend on the 3,000 £1 shares.

The advertisement for the athletics meeting at Kingsholm in August 1893 [Citizen]

More Trouble from a Frozen Pitch

GLOUCESTER WERE DUE to play Moseley at Kingsholm on Saturday 2nd December 1893. There was some doubt about the game going ahead because of freezing weather, but Gloucester telegraphed Moseley reassuring them that all was well and that they should travel. When the visiting team, and their supporters, arrived, it was to find an ice-bound ground, which they refused to play on. Gloucester suggested that they play a game of association football instead, to keep the crowd entertained, but Moseley were having none of that either. They left the field in disgust, muttering about a 'wild goose chase'.

By now some spectators were in the ground, most having paid admission at the turnstiles, but as usual others found less expensive means of entry. The crowd included a vociferous contingent from Moseley, and they were particularly aggrieved at having nothing to show for either their entry charges or the cost of their travel from Birmingham. When the match was called off the Gloucester officials were surrounded by fans complaining of the late cancellation and demanding their money back. The Treasurer of Gloucester, Mr C Robbins, recognised that he had a problem in that he had no way of telling who had paid and who had not.

He therefore suggested that all of the takings be donated to the Royal Infirmary. The majority of the crowd were not feeling that charitable, and let him know it in fairly direct terms.

So, Mr Robbins checked the counter on the turnstile, and discovered that 39 people had paid a shilling each for entry to the ground. He was faced with 54 people demanding their money back. They were growing increasingly hostile, and threatening to call the police. The innovative Mr Robbins then came up with a proposal that he would repay the entry charge to anyone able to produce a railway ticket to show they had travelled to the match that day. Many rushed forward and received their shilling back. But many still remained demanding their money, so the resourceful Mr Robbins took down their names, and promised they would be allowed free entry to the next home game.

Some were still not happy. Further action against the Club was threatened. One spectator threatened court action, and Moseley threatened an appeal to the Rugby Union if their demand for repayment of all their expenses was not forthcoming. But the situation had been effectively defused, and these threats came to nothing.

When the Rugby Union Closed Kingsholm

John Hanman, who was regarded by one and all as a perfect gentleman, was very popular with the players, and of whom it was said that no captain 'worked harder to keep the players one and all in perfect harmony, and no one has been more untiring or indefatigable in his efforts to lead his men on to victory' [Citizen]

IN DECEMBER 1893, the Gloucester Thursday team played a match away at Stroud. As usual the team included several players from the City Club. After the match, Walter Shewell, one of the Stroud players, mentioned to a couple of his Gloucester opponents, that he was planning to leave Stroud in search of work, and that he might come to Gloucester to try to find a job, in which case he would be interested in playing for Gloucester.

When they returned home from Stroud, the Gloucester players mentioned Shewell's hopes to the Gloucester captain, John Hanman, and he promised to see if he could help. Within days Shewell arrived on Hanman's doorstep. It so happened that Hanman was having trouble getting a team together for the match at Newport the following Saturday, and gratefully accepted Shewell's offer to play. Gloucester lost 0-29.

The problem was that Shewell was still registered as a Stroud player, and there was not much love lost between the clubs. Stroud complained to the Gloucestershire Union, claiming that Gloucester had broken the Rugby Union laws on transfers and professionalism. Most of the County Union officers were from the Gloucester Club, and Hanman was on the County Judicial Committee. Indeed Tom Graves Smith, as Secretary of the Club and the County Union, wrote letters to himself about the issue. Nevertheless, the County Union banned Shewell and the two Gloucester players who had talked to him after the Thursday match, let Hanman off, but fined the Gloucester Club ten pounds. The Club committee felt they had done nothing wrong (even if their captain had), were appalled to have their belief in amateur principles impugned, and therefore appealed to the Rugby Union to overturn the County's decision.

They quickly realised that this might make matters worse, because the Rugby Union was very concerned about professionalism

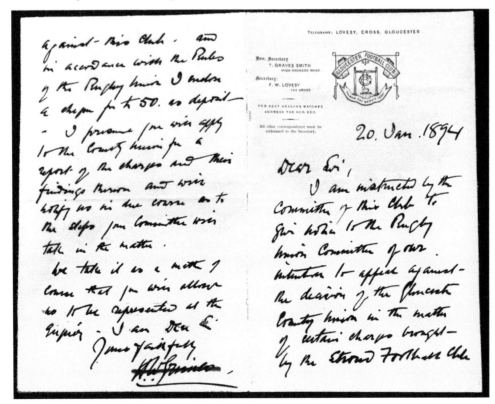

Letter from the Gloucester Club to the Rugby Union registering their appeal against the decision of the County Union [Gloucester Rugby]

Rugby Football Union.
Minutes of Committee Meeting held at the Queen's Hotel, Leeds, March 3. 94.

Present:- W. Cail (Chair) R.S. Whalley, J. Maclaren, E.T. Gurdon, G. Berney, H.L. Ashmore, C.A. Crane, A.M. Crook, H. Fuller, L. Hickson, B. Kilner, J.A. Miller, M. Newsome, T.M. Swinburn, Rev. G.T. Warren, J.W.H. Thorp, and G. Rowland Hill.

Minutes of the last Meeting were read and confirmed.

The report of the Sub Committee on the Gloucester and Stroud Club case was presented, which is as follows.
"That Gloucester Football Club and Ground be suspended from 5th to 24th March both included.
That Mr Hanman be suspended from playing Football during the remainder of this Season.
That the expenses of this enquiry be paid by the

Gloucester Football Club."
As the question has been decided under the Professional Laws and not under the Transfer Laws, the Sub Committee recommends the Gloucester County Union to relieve the £10. provided it has not been already handed to a Charity."

The apology of the Hunslet Captain to Mr J.A. Smith, Hon: Sec:, Scottish Union was read and was deemed satisfactory.

A discussion arose as to R.E. Lockwood and others being permitted to play for their Club on the day of the England v Scotland Match, if they declined to play for England. On this subject the following resolution was adopted.
"That in future anyone declining to play for his Country shall not be allowed to play for his Club or County, unless he receives permission from the Union Committee."
Letter was read from S. Hall a Swinton

The minutes of the RFU meeting recording the punishments handed out to the Gloucester Club and to the Club captain, John Hanman [World Rugby Museum, Twickenham]

amongst northern clubs, which would result a year later in the schism between Rugby Union and Rugby League. Gloucester withdrew their appeal, but the Rugby Union decided to look into the matter anyway, and found Gloucester guilty. Although the County Union fine and suspensions were rescinded, the Club was suspended, and no rugby was allowed at Kingsholm between 5th and 24th March 1894. John Hanman was suspended for the rest of the season.

This outcome was received with indignation in Gloucester, but there was no right of appeal, so the Club had to put up with the perceived humiliation and the suspensions. The players were frustrated by the lack of matches, although the break may actually have been a good thing in that their form was exceptionally good when they resumed playing. When Kingsholm reopened, the Club played three matches in four days, against Lennox, a team from London, on Easter Monday; against Runcorn, a northern club on tour, on the Tuesday; and against the Devon Nomads, a strong invitation side, on the Thursday. Gloucester beat them all, and for good measure slipped a Second XV game against Sandhurst into the vacant day on Wednesday. However, the closure of the Kingsholm ground did result in a loss of income, which the Club felt keenly, and measures were put in hand to generate additional income to make up for it.

John Hanman attracted some criticism for his part in the affair, although Club officials stoutly defended their captain throughout, and criticised players who expressed a contrary view as disloyal. Hanman

himself clearly felt the need to make some amends for his part in the affair, which he did by organising events to raise funds for the Club. During the Club's suspension, a soccer match was organised against Gloucester City AFC, which the soccer players won 6-1 on Budding's Field. The play was described as 'more amusing than scientific, as some of the Rugbyites could not, or would not, accustom them selves to the difference in the style of play. They were continually penalised for picking up the ball with their hands instead of using their feet and heads.'

Additional rugby matches organised to assuage the effects of the closure of Kingsholm included Club fixtures against E Fenner's XV and Castleford, and a County fixture, Gloucestershire and South Wales v Yorkshire. This last match in particular excited a lot of interest, and special excursion trains were run to bring spectators from South Wales, the Forest of Dean and Bristol. A crowd of at least 4,500 assembled at Kingsholm in fine weather to see a match in which 'never had so many leading lights in Rugby football appeared in this district at one time'. John Hanman was credited with working indefatigably to ensure the fixture came off, although he was not able to play because still suspended. Yorkshire were the reigning County Champions, and a wealth of internationals took to the field. It is perhaps significant that these matches involved northern and Welsh players, who had little sympathy with the RFU interpretation of the laws concerning professionalism.

Music and Songs

AT THE OPENING of the Kingsholm ground in 1891, the Engineers' Band entertained the crowd, and in the following years a band was engaged to play whenever there were big matches and big crowds. Singing was also a popular pastime with players and spectators. One refrain sung during the first season at Kingsholm was:

> But soon they'll be again to the fore,
> Sing, my boys, line up, Oh!
> See them play on the Kingsholm ground,
> Sing, my boys, line up, Oh!
> Work together, work with a will,
> Line up, again my boys, Oh!
> Who's afeared of any foe?
> Sing, line up, my boys, Oh!

After the match against Coventry in that first season, the teams repaired to the Spread Eagle for tea, but high spirits took over as they 'engaged in a tea fight', before moving on to the Oddfellows Hall for a smoking concert, during which one of the most popular songs was 'On the Ball':

> In the days to come, when we've left behind
> Our boyhood's glorious games,
> And our youthful vigour has declined
> With its mirth and its noble aims;
> We will think of the time, the happy time,
> And its mem'ry fond recall,
> When in the bloom of our youthful prime
> We kept upon the ball.
> Then kick off; throw it out! Form a decent scrimmage!
> Keep it loose – a splendid rush! Bravo! Win or die!
> On the ball, Gloucester! Never mind the danger;
> Now's your chance – steady all – Hurrah! We've scored a try
> Let all to-night then drink with me
> To the football game we love,
> And wish it may successful be
> All other games above.
> Then in one grand united toast
> Join player, friend and sub,
> And fondly pledge our pride and boast –
> Success to the Gloucester Club.
> Chorus – Then kick off, etc.

There was also impromptu music at matches – the report of a fixture against Penarth on 23rd April 1892 records that:

> Eventually Jackson raced round finely and scored in a fairly favourable position. A cornet player on the ground created immense amusement by tootling 'Ta-ra-ra-boom-de-ay' at this juncture, Jackson converted well, and play was subsequently in the centre for some minutes…and then Jackson with a second magnificent run from the 25 got in under the posts, the trumpeter signalling this with 'All Very Fine and Large.' On the try being converted the company were treated to a repetition of 'Ta-ra-ra-boom-de-ay.' The game had now been in progress 30 minutes and a rest was taken' (for half-time). 'The game was re-

started to the strain of 'Auld Lang Syne' from the leather-lunged musician. Jones got in in a forward rush. Jackson again converted, these two achievements being greeted with 'Maggie Murphy' and the 'Bogie Man' from the brazen instrument.

The entertainment even continued after the game, which was the last for the Club by their full-back, A F Hughes:

> The cornet player before mentioned reserved for 'A. F.' the musical honours of the occasion, accompanying him down Worcester-street with the proclamation 'See the Conquering Hero Comes.' This, we presume, was not because Hughes was the particular hero of this match, but was rather meant as a tribute of the praise which follows the popular player to Burton, and as an indication that he had preserved his grand form right up to the end of the last match with his old club mates.

In April 1897, before the match at Kingsholm, in which Gloucester took away Llanelly's unbeaten record for the season, Hinton's band 'discoursed a capital selection of music'. In the late 19th and early 20th centuries, Fred Rowland's Band took over these duties, sometimes advertised as his Military Band or his Augmented Band. They played, for example, at the England v Wales international in 1900, when even the Welsh press was impressed by the quality of the Kingsholm singing – 'when the chorus of 'Soldiers of the Queen' was taken up with gusto it rather recalled the scenes of typical Welsh gatherings, when the people sing under every circumstance'. Fred Rowlands entertained regularly throughout this period, and especially at big games such as when the South Africans and Australians visited in 1906 and 1908, and for the County Championship Final in 1910. Arthur Hudson reminiscing on these times many years later wrote 'I wonder how many people can recall Fred Rowlands and his band of instrumentalists who played in the streets and on the ground before games'.

At about this time, there was a song attributed to the Kingsholm supporters, known as 'We are the Glo'ster Boys', which went as follows:

> We are from Glo'ster, the pride of the west
> Some of the lads and some of the best
> We are respected wherever we go, where we come from nobody knows
> They call us the pride of the ladies, the ladies
> We spend all our wages, our wages, our wages
> We are respected wherever we go
> We are the Glo'ster boys
> Maggie dear, pint of beer, a Woodbine and a match
> A tuppence ha'penny stick of rock, we're off to the rugby match
> To see ol' Glo'ster score a try, the best try in the land
> We are the Glo'ster boys!
> We are the Glo'ster boys, we are the Glo'ster boys!
> We know our manners, we spend our tanners, we are respected wherever we may go
> And when you're walking down the Kingsholm Road
> Doors and windows open wide
> You can hear the people shout 'Put them bloody Woodbines out!'
> 'Cause we are the Glo'ster boys'

Victorian Ladies at Kingsholm

LADIES WERE ENCOURAGED to attend matches from the early days at The Spa, and the pavilion was reserved for ladies and members. When the Flamingoes visited from London in February 1876 for the first match at which admission charges were made, the ladies were reported to have 'mustered in full force in the pavilion', seats being provided especially for them. This was closely followed in March 1876 by the first serious injury to a Gloucester player, a fractured thigh sustained by Sydney Lane in a match against Ross-on-Wye. This was reported to have greatly upset the ladies present, and for some time their attendance at matches fell away as a result.

The first recorded instance of ladies playing on the Kingsholm turf was on 11th November 1895, when an exhibition soccer match was played at Kingsholm by two teams of lady players who were touring the country. It generated a lot of interest, and attracted a large crowd, despite appalling weather. However, the event also attracted a good deal of derision, as is evident from the report published in the Citizen the following day:

THE LADY FOOTBALLERS

When a lovely woman stoops to folly' there is no telling where she will end. We do not suggest that she has reached the nethermost depth of her possible degradation upon the football field. It may be argued that the line we have quoted above does not apply to the females who disported themselves on the Kingsholm Ground on Monday afternoon because they are not lovely but no matter! They were announced as the 'original' lady footballers. Their football is certainly 'original' enough to warrant this title, and it is to be hoped that these aborigines may disappear before an enlightened and advancing civilisation. If they could play football some sort of excuse for their appearance might be found, though 'the only art their guilt can cover' is not that of playing football. But with one or two exceptions they cannot, their notions of the game being elementary in the extreme and their attempts to play it fatuous. Of course, having regard to their sex, we must not expect them to come up to the standard of masculine form, though they invite comparison when they ask the public to pay for the privilege of seeing them perform. It must be remembered that the climatic conditions were all against a scientific exposition, pelting rain, muddy ground, and slippery, sodden ball being sufficient to test the stamina and skill of players made of much sterner stuff. But they evidently belong to the class known in football parlance as 'piano players'. Their movements were for the most part leisurely, their pace slow, their ability a negligible quality. They betrayed a natural anxiety to avoid hurting one another by charging, and a disinclination to fall in the mud. Nor did their costume make very appreciable addition to the freedom and ease of their movements. And let it be said that, so far as modesty is concerned, the most fastidious could hardly take exception to their attire. The blouses and 'bloomers' left nothing to be desired as regards decency, and would even have been picturesque had it not been for their stained and weather-beaten condition, which accorded well with the dishevelled hair and general appearance of the wearers, some of whose faces wore a look familiar to those who know what over-training, staleness and undue exertion will do for the features. We have made one or two exceptions to the charge of ludicrous incompetence. A noticeable one was the lady rejoicing in the sobriquet of 'Tommy'. She was really clever with some of her dribbles, and was much more agile and fast – if we may use the term without reproach in this connection – than her comrades, who trotted about in a rather aimless fashion, and indulged frequently and appropriately enough in 'miss' kicks. The game would, perhaps, have been more exciting if the goalkeepers had not been two mere men-things who most ungallantly kicked the ball away whenever the respective goals were in danger; and there might have been more fun if three ladies had officiated as referee and touch-judges. The next best thing, we suppose, to having ladies in this position is to have 'ladies' men', though we do not for a moment suggest that this was the qualification of either of the gentlemen who acted in these capacities on Monday. Thanks to the exertions of the masculine custodians no goals were scored by either side. The first portion of the game lasted half an hour; and when the second had been in progress fifteen minutes the rain became so bad that even the lady footballers could not stand it. It was getting dark too and the people – there was a big crowd, £55 being taken at the gate – were leaving the ground in droves. Those who were left cheered the bedraggled specimens of femininity as they made for the welcome shelter of the pavilion, 'Tommy' coming in for special recognition. Then the spectators dispersed, and probably agreed that getting wet served the players and onlookers right for being there. They had come to scoff, remained to do so, and did. Football is all very well in its place. The two do not harmonise. They are hopelessly incongruous. If anyone wanted convincing of that fact Monday's display at Kingsholm can have left no room for doubt upon the point. People do strange things for a living sometimes. Facing a pitiless storm and showers of merciless chaff in 'rational' costume, in order to kick a ball about for the amusement of the multitudes seems to me to be to us at once one of the most peculiar and irrational methods of gaining a livelihood.

This experiment was not repeated, and the emphasis remained firmly on encouraging support rather than participation by the womenfolk of Gloucester. Lady spectators were offered special membership rates by the Club and, even when there was a need to increase income substantially after World War One, they were still offered a lower rate. For the 1918-19 season, patrons were charged two guineas, ordinary members £1, ladies 10s, and players 1s. The ladies continued to be accommodated with the members, away from the 'popular' side, where behaviour and language were less genteel.

All Manner of Entertainments at Kingsholm, 1893-99

THE PRICE OF admission to matches at Kingsholm attracted some criticism. In December 1893, 'a member and ardent well wisher of the Club' wrote to the Citizen:

I am told that the financial condition of the Gloucester Football Club is in anything but a flourishing state ... I think that the principal cause may be found in the management adopting their 'high price' policy. I have always maintained, and have freely expressed my opinion to individual members of the committee, that only on very exceptional occasions should the charge for admission be higher than sixpence, and those exceptions, if I were asked to express my views, should apply only to such fixtures as Newport, Cardiff, Old Merchant Taylors, Broughton, and Runcorn, and those only if absolutely necessary. The committee can have but a very sorry idea of catering for the public if they continue this ruinous policy, as it will be sure to prove in the end. My advice is, adopt popular prices of admission, and by a little re-arrangement of the ground provide plenty of enclosed spaces and stand room, and then if those who come to see the game choose to pay extra for good positions let them by all means do so; but do not by prohibitory prices keep the football-loving public outside, for however much we may love our national winter game, we do not relish having to pay an excessive charge to witness it. So far as I am informed, in none of the great centres of football is a higher charge than 6d imposed, except when very big matches are played, and why Gloucester should remain almost, if not quite, unique in this respect I am at a loss to understand.

This plea fell on deaf ears, the main reason being the amount of rent which the Club had to pay to the Company for use of Kingsholm, and the Company insisted that the level of rent was necessary to sustain the development of the ground.

By February 1894, the Ground Company had achieved a lot by way of development of the ground, but had overstretched its resources to the extent of being overdrawn at the Bank by £761 11s 7d. The Board decided that it should investigate the possibility of an additional mortgage of £750/800, but it proved impossible to agree an increase on the original mortgage, so an extension to the Company's overdraft at the bank was arranged. Later that year, the Company paid £48 10s 10d on mortgage interest and £13 2s 6d on rates, and a reduced dividend of 2 ½%.

The financial situation added to the pressure to increase the Company's income, and tenders were again sought for letting out the ground for sheep grazing during the summer of 1894, with three tenders received for £10, £9 and £7 10s 0d. Despite this financial pressure, the Board were conscious of their first priority being to cater for sport, and for rugby in particular. The Board therefore declined a proposal that the City Corporation should move the Pleasure Fair from Barton Street to Kingsholm, the principal concerns being damage to the ground and that it was contrary to the purposes intended for the ground.

The charges for advertising at the ground were generating some resistance, and several advertisers were threatening to quit. The advertising agent, William Dancey, persuaded the Board to reduce the rents for advertisements on the fence along Worcester Street. Those from the City end up to the middle entrance were reduced to 15s - £1 per annum and those from the middle entrance to the St Mark's end were reduced to 5s - 10s, with further reductions if advertisers took spaces for a number of years.

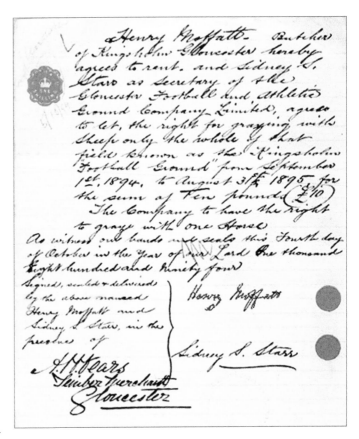

The contract let for grazing sheep at Kingsholm in 1894-95 [Gloucester Rugby]

From 1894, the ground was let for military drill training by the Gloucester Engineers on the same terms as for the Rifles, ie 5s for a single Company and 10s for the whole Battalion. There was a useful by-product of this letting in that the Engineers decided that they needed illumination of their activities, and acquired a 'Wells' lamp for this purpose. This was innovative technology - the 'Wells' lamp was the first really bright portable lighting designed for use outdoors. It consisted of a fuel tank containing paraffin, with a burner on a tall post above it. The burner was a blowlamp which incorporated a vaporiser to heat the oil before it went out of the nozzle. Pressure was sustained by a hand-operated stirrup pump, but the lamp could then burn for some hours before more pumping was required. Unfortunately the lamp broke down at Kingsholm, but Capt Ricketts of the Gloucester Engineers came to the rescue and fixed it. His offer to then rent the lamp to the Ground Company for 2s 6d per week was accepted, so the novelty of training by artificial light started at Kingsholm during the 1894-95 season.

This relationship with the Engineers expanded, and a legal agreement was drawn up permitting Richard Rogers of Cheltenham to rent 'Moffatt's Corner' at Kingsholm for engineering work by the First Gloucestershire Volunteer Royal Engineers. It also specified the right to hold foot drill on the whole field and granted sole use of one room under the pavilion. This was to apply from 1st May 1895 to 31st August 1897 for a rent of £10.

Although it was the need to acquire a rugby ground which led to the acquisition of Kingsholm, and the rugby club members who were the driving force behind the Ground Company, nevertheless the original

A Wells lamp [Wikipedia]

intention of the Ground Company, as reflected in the company name, had been to develop Kingsholm for athletics in the summer. The Board of the Ground Company regarded it as their duty to promote use of the ground by the Gloucester Athletic Club. It was agreed that Athletic Club members be allowed to train at Kingsholm before 10am and after 6:30pm at a cost of 2s 6d per member. The Athletic Club also wanted to hold 2 or 3 evening meetings, for which a charge of 4 guineas was set. When the evening meeting on 22nd June 1892 made a large loss, the charge was halved to 2 guineas. A deputation from the Athletic Club met the Board of the Ground Company in March 1893 to discuss holding their Annual Festival at Kingsholm in August – they were offered the whole ground for 2 days for £30, including a ¼ mile track.

By the following year, these arrangements were turning sour. In July 1894, the Athletic Club judged that the Kingsholm track was not in a fit state for their forthcoming Sports Day, but the Company Board disagreed and decided to hold the Athletic Club to their agreement. The Athletic Club suggested that arbitration be used to settle the dispute, offering Dr W G Grace, C Herbert & R H Wickham as arbitrators. The Board of the Company agreed the principle of arbitration, but rejected the Athletic Club nominations, and proposed that 3 local arbitrators be used – the Mayor of Gloucester, John Bryan and William Stout. The Athletic Club rejected these arbitrators, and proposed that each side appoint one arbitrator, who would then select an umpire. The Board stuck with their proposal, and threatened to go public by publishing the whole correspondence and an explanation if the matter was not settled by 31st July. It did not come to this – the Board compromised by agreeing to accept the Athletic Club proposal for arbitration if their officers would accept personal liability for the award, with a Director from each club as arbitrators, who could appoint a referee if necessary. By this time the date for the Sports Day had passed without the event happening, the Athletic Club had had enough, and offered £15 to settle the dispute. The Board still thought that they had been treated discourteously, but agreed to settle. Although the Athletic Club moved their event to the Spa, an offer from the Athletic Club of £2 10s 0d for the hire of seating from Kingsholm was accepted. Meanwhile Athletic Club training continued at Kingsholm, and an athletics meet went ahead on the ground, but organised by the Rugby Club.

In order to avoid this type of problem in 1895, the Ground Company proposed that the Athletic Club should themselves be responsible for preparing the quarter mile track for their Sports Day. Harry Dyke, the Company groundsman, would be paid by the Athletics Club for preparing the track at 3s per day for the five weeks running up to the event. There would also be a hire charge for the ground of £25, including use of the horse roller. However, the Board of the Ground Company were aware that they had refused several lucrative lettings during the summer in order to keep to their original objective of encouraging athletics at Kingsholm, and these problems with the Athletics Club proved to be the thin end of the wedge which ended with Kingsholm becoming almost exclusively a rugby ground.

With an eye on securing a share of the money being made by the Ground Company from the more profitable of their lettings, the Club asked for a change to their tenancy agreement, so that they could let the ground for purposes other than rugby during the rugby season. The Board of the Ground Company were reluctant to accept such a diminution of their income, and refused this request. Following the refusal, Messrs Stout & Robbins from the Club attended a Company Board meeting in October 1893 to press the Club's case. The Board still declined to alter the existing agreement, but offered a provisional or supplementary agreement, whereby the 2 secretaries of the Club and the Ground Company could agree lets of the ground during the rugby season, but all contracts were to be in the name of the Ground Company. Gross gate money would be shared equally, but would be banked by the Ground Company, and payment made to the Club only if their £275 rent had been paid. No expenses would fall to the Club, and the Ground Company would be responsible for making good any damage.

In 1894 the terms of the tenancy were further amended to allow the Club to have the ground from 1st September to 20th April, and for the rent to be payable in three instalments (£90 on 1st November, £90 on 1st January, and the balance on 20th April). This revised tenancy agreement is reproduced in full at Appendix K. Throughout this discussion it is apparent that all the participants saw the Ground Company as a temporary expedient, and that the Club would eventually own the Kingsholm ground, although it would be many years before this came to fruition.

Despite this unanimity of purpose, and the number of individuals with close ties to both Club and Ground Company, territorial disputes could get quite trivial at times. In October 1893, the Club claimed £1 from the Ground Company for work undertaken in picking up stones from the field of play. Although the state of the ground was the responsibility of the Ground Company, the Board of the Company refused to pay on the grounds that they did not want to set a precedent for the Club to incur expenditure on the ground without the prior approval of the Company, and then expect the Company to pay up.

The Company also kept to a hard line in their dealings with neighbours. The Football Club reported that Mrs Dutton of Deans Walk had complained about spectators standing on her wall to watch matches, thereby damaging it, and suggested that the fence round the ground be raised or canvas screens erected. The Board declined to respond, arguing that they did not feel responsible for protecting adjoining properties, and advised that Mrs Dutton should seek a police prosecution to resolve the situation.

The Company Board also decided that Mr Stephens be asked to pay 1s per annum for the right to light into his warehouse overlooking the field. He declined, so the Company erected boards in front of his window. They later went further, and employed a local builder to brick up Mr Stephens' window. They were similarly resolute when Mr Allen complained of damage to his garden next to the Vinegar Works from people going across it to get into the ground - the Directors took the line that it was his responsibility to stop people getting onto his property. Likewise they initially dismissed a claim from Mr Allen for £1 10s od as compensation for his crops being eaten by sheep escaping from the field. They pointed out that his was the only property on the other side of the River Twyver without its own fence, but he kept arguing his claim, and the Company eventually paid him 10s to settle the issue.

Financial pressures underpinned these decisions, as they did when the Board decided that the auditing of the Company accounts for 1894 would now take less time than when the Company was started up, so the fee paid to the auditor, Mr Coombs, was halved from two guineas to one. Meanwhile income from the sale by the Club of season tickets for the 1894-95 season were 257 at 10s, 692 at 5s, and 136 at 3s, giving a total income of £321 18s od from 1,085 members. This enabled the Club to pay their £275 rent in full, but their accounts showed a deficit of £25 9s 10d at the end of the season. The otherwise miserly Board of the Ground Company sent them a cheque for this amount to save them from starting the following season in debt.

Lettings in 1895 featured the St Mary de Lode flower show at two guineas. The Post Office Sports Day brought in seven guineas, and the Gloucester Harriers were charged five guineas for use of the ground for a ten mile race. The All Saints School treat brought in a further one guinea, but they were the last to get this bargain rate – it was resolved not to let for less than two guineas for any future event. Sanger's Circus rented the ground as usual in July 1895, and a polo match between Gloucester and Stroud was played as an experiment to gauge the level of interest – it was a success to the extent that the Ground Company made a profit of £3 14s 6d.

Perhaps the biggest draw of the summer was Auguste Gaudron and his balloon. Gaudron was an interesting character, variously referred to as 'Captain' Gaudron and 'Professor' Gaudron. Born in Paris, he came to England to work for a balloon manufacturer, married the boss's daughter, and set up his own company, and toured the country, and the continent, with his display team. He came across Dolly Shepherd working as a waitress at Alexandra Palace, and persuaded her to become the first lady parachutist, advertised as 'the Parachute Queen'. In 1908, he designed and flew the Mammoth balloon from Crystal Palace in London to Meeki Derevi in Russia, taking 36.5 hours to fly 1,117 miles, a world record. Gaudron died in 1913, and is buried in Highgate Cemetery, where his grave is topped with a magnificent stone balloon.

Although he suffered no mishap at Kingsholm, this was not always the case. In France on one occasion he was dragged along the ground for three miles, and when at last a railway bridge halted his balloon, a signalman rushed out with a pickaxe, and hacked at the balloon, saying 'I want to kill the lion'. Scarcely had the bruised aeronaut got clear of the rails when an express train rushed by. And on another occasion at Trieste, his attendants let him go without his parachute, and, seated on his swing under the balloon, he sailed away 6,000 feet over the Adriatic. He climbed the net in order to turn the balloon over and let some of the gas out of the neck, the danger being that it would deflate entirely. However, he half emptied it, and descended at speed into the sea, where he swam about for half an hour before a passing steamer picked him up.

He was paid £30 to appear at Kingsholm for the 1895 Whit Monday fete, when he leaped from his balloon and parachuted down from a height of 1,000 feet. The balloon was valveless, and had a neck five feet in diameter, and a capacity of 12,000 cubic feet. His parachute weighed 23 lbs and was attached to the balloon by a cord, the breaking strain of which was 90 lbs. This was designed to snap when Gaudron dropped from the rope swing on which he sat under the balloon. He never descended from a height of less than 1,000 feet, needing about 150 feet for the silk parachute to open.

Other attractions at the fete were Lieutenant Chard's dog circus, the Paddock troupe of trick bicyclists, a number of variety artistes, the Artillery and Engineers' Bands, and fireworks. With this line-up pulling in

Gaudron's balloon at Kingsholm, watched by Messrs Reardon and Bingle, Secretary of the Gloucester Club [Gloucestershire Archives]

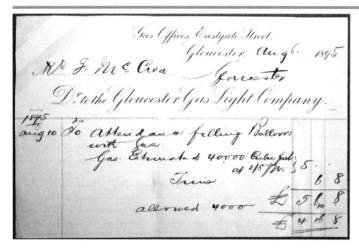

The invoice for the gas for the balloon [Gloucester Rugby]

the crowds, the fete brought in a total of £251 14s 3d against expenditure of £204 6s 8d. Encouraged by this, Mr Reardon also put on a balloon ascent, which profited the Company to the more modest tune of £2 0s 10d. But Gaudron was engaged again to perform at Kingsholm as the main attraction at the August Bank Holiday fete. On this occasion he offered to take passengers up in his balloon on a tether for 2s 6d, and in free flight for £5. Tickets for entry to the fete were 6d, and the event turned a good profit with income of £206 12s 4d against expenditure of £166 1s 10d.

Mr McCrea was employed to manage both of these events, and his success resulted in his becoming regularly involved in organising events at Kingsholm. He hired the ground for pony races, and agreed a rent of £5 with the Company Secretary, which almost led to Sid Starr's resignation.

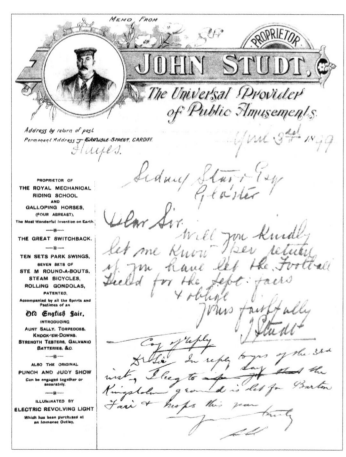

Studt hoped to return to Kingsholm in 1899, but he was disappointed [Gloucester Rugby]

After four years with only cold water available at Kingsholm, the Company Board agreed in September 1895 to a request from the Football Club to heat water on training nights and match days, and Mr Gurney was contracted to install a heating furnace, for which he was paid £8. The Company balance sheet showed a surplus of £96 8s 4d on the previous year's working, of which £75 was distributed as a 2 ½ % dividend, with the remainder put into the depreciation account. Effectively the dividend was reduced because of further ground improvements - £19 14s 0d was spent on improving the entrance at the Deans Walk corner, and the levelled area of the ground was significantly increased.

In 1896, the Barton Fair transferred to Kingsholm – Mr Studt, who ran it, was offered the half of the ground on which the Thursday Rugby Club played for £150, or the much smaller 'Vinegar Works Corner' of the ground for £40 – he chose the cheaper option. Because this fell within the rugby season, half of this hire charge was counted against the Club's rent.

By 1897, McCrea felt that the hire charges at Kingsholm were too high [Gloucester Rugby]

This was a bad year for Mr McCrea – his events were disrupted by a smallpox epidemic in Gloucester, and he made a loss on the August Bank Holiday Fete, so he was required to pay only £5 of his £25 debt to the Company. It was also a poor year for the Company. The epidemic also hit the Company's income through cancelled events, and although the balance sheet for 1895-96 still showed a profit of £61 15s 11d, this was deemed insufficient to allow any dividend to be paid to shareholders.

In the first five years of ownership of Kingsholm, the value of the land had increased in value, so, towards the end of 1896, it was proposed that this could be used to raise capital by increasing the mortgage. Hatton offered to put the mortgage up to £3,200 at 3 ¾ % - the Company Board agreed that this offer be accepted to the extent of £650 being added to the £2,500 mortgage, making a total of £3,150 (on the understanding that the odd £150 might be paid off at any time convenient to the Company). However, Hatton reported that his co-Trustees were only prepared to increase the mortgage to £3,000 at 3 ¾ %, and this is what was eventually agreed, with the deed for the new £500 mortgage signed in November 1896. As a result the half-yearly interest payments by the Ground Company on the mortgage increased from £50 to £56 5s 0d.

In 1897, the ground was declared to be in excellent condition for all athletic purposes, and interest in hiring it, and revenues from lettings, reached a new peak. The Company did have to fix one problem, when a tap in the Vinegar Works Corner leaked water over the pavement in Worcester

Street – the Ground Company was taken to task by the Corporation's delightfully named 'Inspector of Nuisance'. That summer saw the usual sports days, flower shows, fairs, Sanger's Circus, school treats, sheep grazing, and fireworks, but cricket was no longer played regularly on the ground, the Board taking the view that the grass needed time to recover during the summer months. These hirings contributed to the Company making a profit of £158 10s 3d in 1896-97, on the basis of which a dividend of 5%, costing £150, was paid. There was confidence in the future prospects of the Company, and the Club was also doing sufficiently well to purchase a further 100 shares in the Ground Company.

In 1898, agreement was reached between the Ground Company and the Club on improvements to the Pavilion on the north side of the ground at an anticipated cost of £55. The Club agreed to forego their share of the rent for the Barton Fair as their contribution to these costs. A contract was let with Messrs Gurney Bros who estimated £57, but ended up charging £60, for moving back the fence in front of the Pavilion, running three steps of terracing from one end of the St Marks Street side right through to the other (again on the north side), and extending the side fence of the Pavilion to make up the length taken off in front. This marked the start of the terrace which was later to develop into the famous 'Shed'.

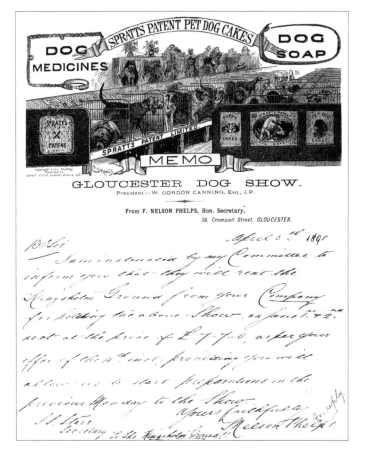

The Gloucester Dog Show was held at Kingsholm in 1898 [Gloucester Rugby]

The popularity of the games at Kingsholm and the newspaper coverage which resulted, led to the accommodation for the press being doubled, so that they occupied all of the front seats in the Pavilion. Additional rental income came from Messrs John Stephens & Co who used a corner near the Vinegar Works, 30yds x 18yds, for storing bricks, timber, etc, at the rate of £1 per week.

The minutes of the Ground Company Board meeting on 1st March 1899 record that:

The Chairman suggested to the Board that he – the Chairman – thought the time had arrived when they might well discuss the advisability of cancelling the supplementary agreement between the Football Club & the Ground Company made in 1895. He said it would be well within the recollection of the Board that the supplementary agreement he alluded to was arranged at the time the Football Club was financially weak and in low water – and the agreement was to the effect that the Football Club should take half gross proceeds of any and all circuses, shows, entertainments, etc held on the ground during the football season, the Company to bear all expenses appertaining to these shows, etc. Mr Vears said he need not remind the Board what this meant – each member knew as well as he did – that more than once the Company's half had been more than swallowed up in putting the field back in order after these shows, etc. The Company always had a warm corner in their hearts for the Football Club and wished to see them prosperous. In fact, the one guiding wish of every Director had been, and was, that one day the Ground might be entirely in the hands of the Football Club. The Club now were moving in that direction, they were already very large shareholders and were still buyers of shares. And he – the Chairman – did not think they would be in anyway losers financially by this agreement being annulled, because what the Club lost from half the proceeds they would as the largest shareholders gain by an increased dividend. The Club he felt sure would remember that about the same time this agreement was made, the Company also granted them some £25 or £26 to put right a deficit the Club had on that years working. And Mr Vears also said he felt sure his brother Directors would agree with him that they – the Directors – had a duty also to perform towards the shareholders who had not had a too rosy a time of it in the way of dividends. The Club was now financially strong and could also well afford to consider the paying of a reasonable dividend to all shareholders. After a full and general discussion in which the Board quite supported the Chairman's views, it was decided in the absence of the Football Club's representative that the Chairman should have an interview with Mr H W Grimes before taking any further steps in the matter.

In March 1899, A V Hatton decided to withdraw from the mortgage on the ground, and transferred his interest to Messrs Poytress and Pates. This change caused the Directors of the Ground Company to review the terms of the mortgage, and they decided that the 3 ¾ % interest being paid was too high, and that less interest would be charged by a Benefit Society. By the end of the year they had made the necessary arrangements, and on 19th December 1899, the previous mortgage plus interest was paid off. The whole £3,000 mortgage on Kingsholm was transferred to the City of Gloucester Working Men's Conservative Benefit Society, for whom Jimmy Boughton acted as solicitor. The 3% interest on the new mortgage was payable in half-yearly instalments on 19th June and 19th December, which brought these payments down to £45 including tax.

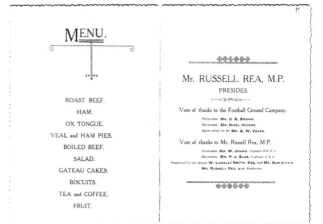

Right Programme for the tea hosted by Russell Rea MP to celebrate the opening of the gymnasium [Gloucester Rugby]

September 1905. The presence of the great and the good of Gloucester, who made speeches galore, and Fred Rowland's band, made it quite an occasion. Harry Dancey, the architect, presented an ornamental silver key in a case to A W Vears, the Chairman of the Ground Company, who in turn passed it on to Russell Rea to keep as a souvenir of the occasion. Russell Rea then formally handed over the building to Councillor C E Brown, President of Gloucester Football Club. The opening ceremony and the facilities provided in the gymnasium were reported in detail in the Citizen; this report can be read in full at Appendix L.

As can be seen on the plans, the original design of the gymnasium included a balcony overlooking the ground, described as an additional grandstand. This was not included in the original construction, the intention being to add it later. Indeed the question was raised at the Ground Company AGM on 6th October 1905, when Mr Grant urged the Directors to erect the balcony at an estimated cost of £75. The Chairman, Mr Vears said that this work had not been undertaken because they did not have enough money to pay for it, but that the matter had not been lost sight of. Although the proposal for a balcony was raised again in subsequent years, it never came to fruition.

The builder, A J Dolman was paid for his work in instalments - £180 on 2nd August 1905, £300 on 2nd September, £200 on 27th September, £75 on 27th October, and £63 1s 8d on 21st February 1906. The total cost of the gymnasium was £1,140-16-5. This was made up of the £818 1s 8d paid to A J Dolman; £127 10s 0 for hot water etc paid to Woodward & Co; £86 8s 9d paid to Turner & Pritchard, plumbers and sanitary; £70 15s 0d to cover the costs of Harry Dancey, Architect & Clerk of Works; £15 8s 0d to cover the legal costs of the solicitors, Madge & Grimes; and £15 16s 5d on bank charges for a temporary overdraft during the building work.

In order to raise more funds, the Ground Company issued a further 150 shares in the Company (raising the total share capital in the Company to £3,150); these were sold at par to the Gloucester Football Club. On 2nd January 1906 the Directors also took out an additional mortgage of £1,000 with the Gloucester Conservative Benefit Society at 4% per annum (taking the total mortgage to £4,000).

The hopes of additional revenue from lettings of the main room in the gymnasium were disappointed, largely because the Gloucester Corn Exchange was available for a rent of two guineas, which undercut the charge for the gymnasium, half of which had to be paid to the Club during the football season.

The provision of changing rooms in the gymnasium brought to an end the previous arrangements, which had involved the home team changing in rather cramped accommodation in the White Hart, before walking across the road in their playing kit, blazers and caps. Meanwhile their opponents had changed at the Ram Hotel in Southgate Street, before being transported to the ground in a wagonette.

The gymnasium is the oldest building still standing at Kingsholm. It is now called the Lions' Den, and contains offices, a function room and the Glo'ster Boys Bar, home of the Gloucester Players' Association. On the walls of the main room are the annual honours boards of the Club and many team photographs, and in the Glo'ster Boys' Bar are many more displays illustrating the past glories of former players.

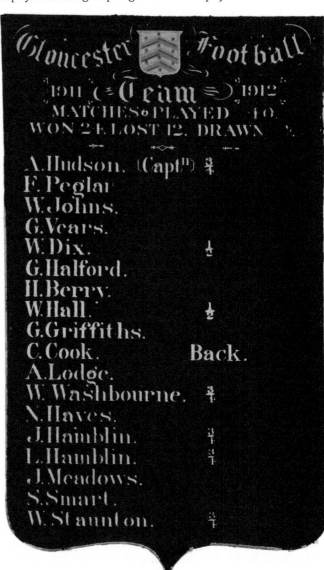

One of the honours boards displayed in the Lions' Den [Malc King]

Southern Hemisphere Visitors

New Zealand

THE FIRST ALL Blacks side to tour in the Northern Hemisphere came to play Gloucester on Thursday 19th October 1905, welcomed by the headline 'The Colonials at Kingsholm' in the Citizen. The event was the cause of much interest and excitement in the City, even though everyone expected Gloucester to be pulverised. The touring party arrived in Gloucester on the Monday preceding the match, and stayed at the Ram Hotel, venturing forth to train at Kingsholm on the Tuesday and Wednesday. They expressed themselves particularly impressed by the facilities in the gymnasium which had been opened the previous month.

Most of the large works in the city shut down to allow their employees to go to the game, schools closed early, and demand for tickets was immense. A temporary stand was erected behind the goal posts at the Worcester Street end, but the Gloucester committee had learnt from their experience of hosting the international match in 1900, so expenditure on extra facilities was kept to a minimum for this game.

The All Blacks throw in at a lineout, with the Vinegar Works in the background on the left and the Cathedral on the right] [CC&GG]

The crowd in front of the gymnasium is shown on the left of this photograph; ahead is The White Hart on the far side of Worcester Street, in front of which is the end of the temporary stand [CC&GG]

A scene from the game looking across to the south-east corner of the ground, with houses on Worcester Street and St Marks Church visible in the background [CC&GG]

The match was blessed with a fine day, and a large crowd had gathered even before the gates were opened. Special excursion trains brought spectators from far and wide, including Stroud, Cheltenham, Swindon, and the Forest of Dean. As the Citizen put it 'thousands of people who ordinarily would not walk across the road to see a first-class match between English or Welsh teams will travel miles to see the, at present, all-conquering heroes from down under'. Hinton's band entertained the crowd whilst they waited. The High Commissioner for New Zealand and local dignitaries occupied the front rows of the grandstand, and by kick-off, the crowd was estimated at 8-10,000.

Although Gloucester were by no means disgraced, the match did indeed prove to be men against boys. The home side was unfortunate in suffering several injuries, which rendered them a man light for periods of the match, during which they conceded several scores. But the All Blacks helped themselves to ten tries in total, without reply, and ran out easy winners by 44-0 in front of a crowd who were mightily impressed by their speed and skill, the like of which had never before been seen at Kingsholm.

The game produced record gate receipts and total income came to £569 4s 4d, a record for a Club match. Expenditure amounted to £98 19s

8d, leaving a credit balance of £470 4s 8d, of which £329 3s 0d (70%) went to the New Zealand tourists and £141 1s 8d (30%) was retained by the Club. Two of the Club's officers, S W Bingle (Secretary) and Walter Worth (Treasurer), had taken on most of the burden of organising the whole event, in thanks for which the Club paid each a gratuity of 5 guineas.

Expenditures included £15 10s for the hire of a stand 17 feet long from J Romans. A bill for £8 10s from Charles Romans covered the hire of 700 chairs, 9,800 feet of forms, and fixing 1200 seats. Alfred Dolman was paid £2 4s 9d for a variety of work, including the erection of 4 tiers of staging from the end of the seating recently built in front of the gymnasium. The Gloucestershire Constabulary provided 30 policemen for 3 hours at 1s per hour, which amounted to £4 10s 0d plus travelling expenses.

After the match the Mayor and the City High Sheriff entertained both teams and other guests to tea at the Guildhall. The guests then visited the Theatre Royal to see a performance of 'Hamlet' by the Benson Company.

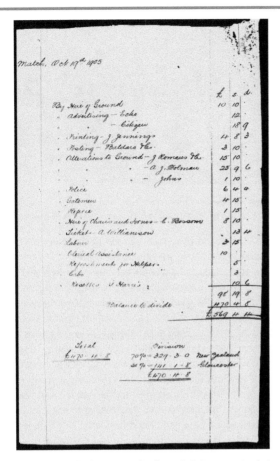

The accounts for the New Zealand match [Gloucester Rugby]

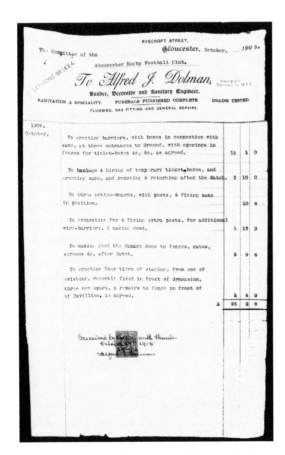

The invoice for the additional stand [Gloucester Rugby]

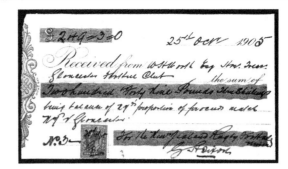

The receipt issued by the New Zealand RFU for their share of the match takings [Gloucester Rugby]

South Africa

New Zealand having overwhelmed a lot of club sides on their tour in 1905-06, there was some attempt to strengthen the local opposition when the South Africans toured the following season. It was the County rather than the Club which faced up to the Springboks at Kingsholm on Saturday 3rd November 1906. However, the plan was not working very well - after eleven matches, mostly against county sides, the Springboks arrived in Gloucester unbeaten, and with a record very similar to that of the All Blacks. The visitors set up camp in the Bell Hotel, Gloucester.

Arrangements for the match were again left in the capable hands of the Gloucester Club officials, Messrs Bingle and Worth, who followed the pattern set for the All Blacks game. The County paid £20 for the hire of the ground, plus £1 for the rent of an office at the ground, and £6 representing two days wages for Harry Dyke to prepare the ground for the match. An extra stand was hired for £10, and this increased the ground capacity to 12,000 - 14,000. There were some 1,200 reserved seats, all of which were sold in advance. Fine weather helped to bring in a large crowd. Some were waiting for the gates to open three hours before kick off, the ropes were soon lined seven or eight deep all round the pitch, and the bank at the Deans Walk end was packed to capacity.

Right from the start of the game Gloucestershire were under pressure, the power and pace of the visitors threatening to overwhelm the home side, who saw little of the ball. Despite heroic defence by Wood, Hudson and Smith, the Springboks ran in three tries during the first half, converting one of them. The second half was a similar story, with Gloucestershire finding few opportunities to attack. The spectators were amused when Hudson and Loubser went for the ball near touch and crashed into the touch judge, all three ending in a heap. South Africa scored two more tries, converting one of them, kicked a dropped goal and ran out winners 23-0, a score line which did not flatter their superiority. Their speed, skill and teamwork impressed, although the home side were

The crowd in front of the pavilion [CC&GG]

Members of the South African party sitting in the front row [CC&GG]

credited for their plucky resistance. The strength of the Springboks up front gave them a wealth of possession, and they had the pace outside to exploit it. Although several players were knocked out in the course of the game, these were all declared accidental, and the South Africans were heartily cheered on leaving the field.

A lineout during the South African match with the posts at the Deans Walk end of the ground in the background [CC&GG]

The County Union hosted a dinner at the Bell Hotel after the match. J R Poole made a *'cinematograph photo of the game in progress'*, which was shown on the *'bioscope'* at the Gloucester Palace of Varieties the following week. Income from the match was £703 6s 1d, and expenditure was £118 7s 3d, leaving a profit of £584 18s 10d, the best yet for a match at Kingsholm. Aside from the internationals, this also proved to be the most profitable match of the tour for the South Africans.

Australia

The first visit of the 'Wallabies' to Kingsholm on Thursday 1st October 1908 was the second match of the tour, and again the County was selected as the opponents in order to provide stiffer opposition. The visitors failed to arouse the same enthusiasm amongst the Kingsholm faithful as the previous appearances of the All Blacks and South Africans, and there was an outcry against the charges of admission. The minimum price on the gate was 1s, which was the same as the County charged for the South African game, but the Club had only charged 6d for the All Blacks match.

The Wallabies stayed at the Ram Hotel, and visited the cathedral on the morning of the match, before turning up to a sunny Kingsholm described in the Citizen as 'Phew! Did you say county cricket or football? The sun at any rate must have declared for cricket, for old King Sol blazed

The crowd between the pavilion on the left and the gymnasium on the right; in the centre of the front row are Fred Lovesy and Gordon Vears with their wives [CC&GG]

forth in full summer radiance. Just right for the Colonials, of course, just their football weather, but very trying for the county.'

The Australians had the upper hand from the start, and took their chances rather better in a somewhat messy first half. They turned round one goal and two tries to the good. Gloucestershire started the second half in better style, but Berry was injured and the ambulance men took him off to repair a gash in his head, although he returned on the wing when Neale was knocked out and had to leave the field of play permanently. Soon after two more players were laid out as a result of heavy tackles, but resumed after a delay. Gloucestershire came close, but it was the Australians who scored the only points of the half with a converted try, and ran out 16-0 winners. The locals went home grumbling about two of the Australian tries being from forward passes, whilst Gent had been denied when blown up for a similar offence. The press agreed that the County had suffered the worst of the refereeing decisions, but there was no question that the better team had won.

Extra stands had been erected by J Romans, but the ground was not filled to capacity, and the total takings of £350 were well down compared with the matches against South Africa and New Zealand.

After the match, Mr Russell Rea, MP for Gloucester, entertained the teams and officials to high tea at the Guildhall. This was rather rushed because the Australians were dashing back that evening to their base at Newton Abbot. Time was still found for the great and the good to make their speeches. Mr Rea explained that 'it had been Spartan fare because he had been strictly told that they were restricted from the ordinary, long, stodgy, continued dinners which English hospitality made customary'. Of the Australians he declared that 'they were not only ordinary sportsmen but were regarded as Paladins and champions in the 'gentle' game'. The Australian captain responded by acknowledging that his team had not played well, but declared that 'it was not only that their play had been defective but that Gloucestershire had played extremely well. It was a strenuous game for strong men and not for the weak and effeminate, and he did not believe in it being played as a means of livelihood.'

A lineout during the Australian match [CC&GG]

The French make an Appearance

Shortly after the Wallabies had made their first appearance on the ground, Kingsholm had its first taste of French rugby when Racing Club de France opened their Christmas tour with a match against Gloucestershire on Christmas Eve 1908. The visitors arrived in Gloucester at noon, and were met at the railway station and taken to the Ram Hotel, where they "partook of lunch". Thus fed and watered the Frenchmen made their way to Kingsholm, where a large crowd greeted them warmly. Smartly attired in pale blue and white striped jerseys, they came onto the pitch to the strains of the "Marsellaise", almost a century before Philippe Sant Andre was regularly extended a similar courtesy.

Gloucester rugby fans were soon taking note of the strong showing in the scrums and the desire to give the ball plenty of air, which, over the years since, have become recognised as particular attributes of the French game. Nevertheless it was Gloucestershire who showed more penetration and they had notched up four tries before half time, when they led 14-0. Racing Club failed to last the pace in the second half and, although the French domination of the scrums continued, the home side ran in five further tries to win easily, 39-0.

The gate produced £53 15s 9d, from which a guarantee of £20 was paid to Racing Club. Other expenses were 5s for the referee, £1 3s 0d for the gatemen, and 2s for Dyke and Wheeler, the groundsmen.

A team including at least some Gloucester players visited Paris in the early 1890s, but there is just a photograph to record the event and no details are known of any matches played, but the Gloucester Club made successful visits to France in 1911 and 1912, first beating Stade Toulousain 18-13 and a year later beating Stade Francais 13-3. However, the first Club match against a French side at Kingsholm did not take place until the French Universities defeated Gloucester 17-0 on 29th March 1966, and the first visit to Kingsholm by a French Club side was Begles who won 21-20 on 18th September 1975.

Taken at the match against Guy's Hospital on 16th October 1920, which Gloucester won 6-3, this photograph shows in the background the new stand, which was a covered standing terrace on the south side of the ground, with an open terrace alongside [CC&GG]

In August and September 1920, the Club funded the erection of a new stand, paid for in two instalments of £500 and £465 to the builder, Wright Anderson. This at least provided protection from the weather for many of the spectators on the south side of the ground, but it was standing rather than seated accommodation. The Club spent a further £607 18s 3d on repairs and renewals to existing stands and fencing.

During the 1920-21 season, there were extended negotiations between the Club and the Ground Company as to what new agreement between them should be put in place more permanently. This resulted in the Club agreeing to pay annual rent of £250, an additional £250 towards the cost of putting right dilapidations and repairs, and half of the rates (which amounted to £121 4s 3d in 1923).

The highlights of the 1920-21 season at Kingsholm were county matches. Gloucestershire won a group game there, beating Devon 15-3, and returned to Kingsholm for the semi-final against Surrey, which they also won comfortably 21-3. Having a home draw for the final, the County again chose Kingsholm, where they defeated Leicestershire 31-4. The following season, they beat Cornwall 34-3 in a group game at Kingsholm, and when the semi-final was drawn 8-8 away to Surrey, they brought them back to Kingsholm for the replay and won 30-0. Gloucestershire won the final against North Midlands at Villa Park to become champions for the third season in succession.

In June 1921, the Ground Company gave permission for the Club to improve further the accommodation at the ground. As a result £78 4s 6d was spent on extra seating in the pavilion on the north side of the ground, £120 on renewing the terracing to the side of the grandstand on the south side, and £64 2s 6d on new terracing at the Worcester Street end on the east side. In fact the Club was doing so well financially, that it could not only afford to pay for these improvements, but also revive its aspiration to own the Kingsholm ground outright. With this in mind, the Club continued to buy up any shares in the Ground Company which individual shareholders were prepared to sell.

The transfer to the Club Trustees, Arthur Fielding and John Brookes of Ground Company shares previously owned by J W 'Down 'Em' Bayley, a distinguished Gloucester player whose playing career spanned 1878-86 [Gloucester Rugby]

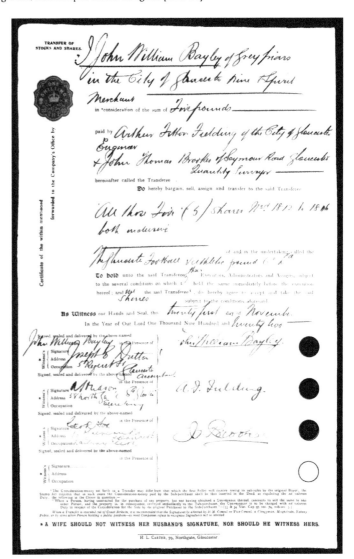

Arthur Hudson

ARTHUR HUDSON WAS born in Gloucester in 1882, and grew up as a soccer player. Indeed his first association with Kingsholm was playing soccer there for the City Albion club, which rented a pitch on the part of the ground now given over to the car park. This proximity to rugby may have triggered his interest, and in 1902 he switched to the handling game. He soon became a regular in the first team as either wing or centre, although it was as a wing that he would really make his mark. Contemporary reports speak of Arthur being the hardest of men to tackle, running with his knees held high. He made 260 appearances for Gloucester and scored 236 tries (including 41 tries in the 1905-6 season). He captained the club for 5 seasons from 1908 to 1913. Arthur also made 28 appearances for Gloucestershire, captained the county, won the county championship in 1920, and scored 9 tries in 8 games for England between 1906 and 1910, including four in one match against France in Paris.

He started work as a clerk with the Midland Railway, but eventually gave this up to run his own sports outfitters shop. This started as a partnership instigated by Duncan McGregor, a member of the 1905 New Zealand touring side, with Arthur's name being used to promote the business, and Arthur's sister working in the shop. The business prospered, and when McGregor returned to New Zealand, it became a Hudson family concern, which Arthur later passed on to his son, Gordon, and then to his grandson, John, the present owner.

A distinguished playing career was interrupted by WW1, when Arthur joined the Royal Navy, and served on submarines. When ashore he played rugby for Devonport Services, the Navy and the Combined Services. On several occasions he brought a Royal Naval Depot side up from Plymouth to play at Kingsholm. He continued playing after the war, but, in 1920, he was injured playing against Yorkshire in the county championship final, and that finished his playing career.

In 1919, he became Assistant Secretary of the Club, and the following year stepped up to be Secretary, a role which he went on to combine with Treasurer and Fixture Secretary for many years. He also became a Director of the Ground Company. He took a close control of Club affairs and finances, and liked to tell people that he ran the Club *like a business*. Arthur's pivotal role in effecting the prosperity of the Club was regularly acknowledged by the President, Dr Arnold Alcock, and Chairman, John Brookes, with whom he worked closely through most of the 1920s and 1930s. Arthur took pride in being able to report a 'healthy balance sheet', and 'The Doc' reminisced in later years about 'the genius displayed by Mr Hudson in the management of the affairs of the club'.

During the Second World War, when the Kingsholm ground was made over to the wartime authorities, it was Arthur who kept a close eye on what was going on. He did his best to safeguard the Club and Ground Company interests, which smoothed the way for the eventual resumption of rugby. When peace finally returned, the Club wanted to pay an honorarium to Arthur for all his efforts during the war years. Arthur was grateful for the offer, but insisted that the money be used to start a fund to develop a Memorial Ground, as a permanent tribute to the rugby players

Arthur Hudson [Gloucester Rugby]

who were killed in action. This magnanimous gesture engendered a warm response and several years of fund raising resulted in the purchase of the Memorial Ground on Tuffley Avenue, which remains in use by junior clubs to the present day. Arthur remained a trustee of the Club and the Memorial Ground until his death.

In 1951, Arthur reminisced on the occasion of the 60th jubilee of the Kingsholm ground: 'Looking back over 50 years as a player and official, I do not begrudge one minute of the time I have devoted to Rugby. To me it has been a labour of love; it has given me some of my richest memories.'

Arthur remained as Club Secretary right through to 1962, thereafter becoming Team Secretary, continuing as a Life Member and Vice-President, and assuming the mantle of the 'Grand Old Man of Gloucester Rugby'. It was claimed that he did more for Gloucester rugby than any other member of the Club. He also served on the county committee.

Arthur's other main sporting interests were athletics and tennis. He was Secretary of the Gloucester Athletic Club, which he also restored to financial security, and he ran 20 tennis courts on his land at the Chestnuts, Estcourt Road. He died on 27th July 1973, aged 90, by which time he had been proud to see his son, Gordon, become Captain and later Chairman of the Club.

John Brookes

John Brookes [Gloucester Rugby]

JOHN T BROOKES never played rugby for Gloucester, but he was a very enthusiastic supporter of the game, and gave the Club the benefit of his managerial skills. These had been developed as Works Manager at the Gloucester Railway Carriage & Wagon Works Ltd. He was first elected onto the Club committee in 1906, but came to prominence in the administration of the Club as Secretary, before being appointed Trustee and Vice-President. In 1916, he purchased shares in the Ground Company, and subsequently became a Director of the Company, initially as one of the Club representatives on the Board.

In 1922 he was elected Chairman of the Club, and established a formidable partnership with the Club Secretary, Arthur Hudson. The pair of them operated at the helm of the Club, steering it on a very successful course for the next 17 years. John set the policies, which ensured that the Club continued to develop, and Arthur kept a tight control of the finances. During the 1920s, John revitalised the policy under which the Club actively sought to purchase any shares which became available in the Ground Company. This soon led to the Club owning a controlling interest, and thus secured the Club's control of their ground. This provided the foundation from which the Club could confidently embark on further development of the ground.

The Club suffered terrible tragedies when two players, Sid Brown and Stan Bayliss, died in successive seasons in the mid-1920s, as a result of injuries sustained whilst playing for Gloucester at Kingsholm. There was another major setback in 1933, when the main stand burned down, but an emergency recovery plan resulted in a new and better stand being built in a matter of weeks, which remained in place until 2007. John's competent and positive hand on the tiller was important in ensuring that the Club continued to prosper through these difficult times, and the ground developed enormously during his period in charge.

He served on the committee of the Gloucestershire Rugby Union for many years before being elected President in 1937, the sixth representative of the Gloucester Club to be so honoured. He was also the auditor of the County Bowling Association.

John was regarded as an exemplar of the qualities required of a Chairman – he combined a sociable and friendly character with a collective management approach, business acumen, and a rational and careful strategy. When he died suddenly of pneumonia in 1939, the tributes to him spoke of 'a man of character and integrity' and 'a happy and hearty comrade', and reflected warmly his long and unstinting sense of service to the Club.

WB of the Citizen recorded that:

Of the many officials of the Gloucester Club with whom I have been intimately acquainted, no one was held in higher esteem than 'Genial John', a firm friend, keen lover of rugby, splendid administrator, and popular with everyone. A loveable character, Mr Brookes enjoyed a joke even against himself, and he was always good company on away matches, never forgetting to supply himself with a bag of peppermints to dispense to members of the party.

At the Club AGM following John's death, Arnold Alcock said:

We have all read and heard many remarkably stirring tributes to the memory of Mr John Brookes, but those of us here possessing his friendship, loving his personality and admiring his qualities, know how really true and eloquently sincere were those words of memory. This Club will profit by his work and example, which will live for a long time.

The All Blacks Return

THE SECOND ALL Blacks tour included a match at Kingsholm on 24th September 1924, but this time against the County team. Although this was designed to provide stronger opposition for the tourists, there still seemed little hope for the home side against a New Zealand side which

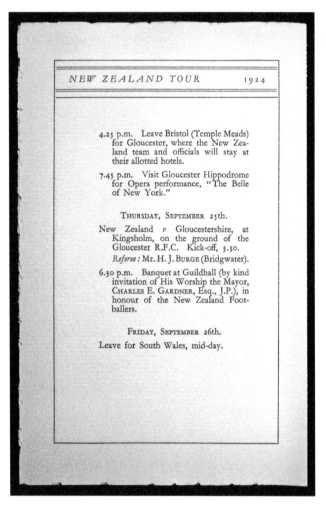

NEW ZEALAND TOUR   1924

4.25 p.m.   Leave Bristol (Temple Meads) for Gloucester, where the New Zealand team and officials will stay at their allotted hotels.

7.45 p.m.   Visit Gloucester Hippodrome for Opera performance, "The Belle of New York."

THURSDAY, SEPTEMBER 25th.
New Zealand v Gloucestershire, at Kingsholm, on the ground of the Gloucester R.F.C. Kick-off, 3.30.
Referee: Mr. H. J. BURGE (Bridgwater).

6.30 p.m.   Banquet at Guildhall (by kind invitation of His Worship the Mayor, CHARLES E. GARDNER, Esq., J.P.), in honour of the New Zealand Footballers.

FRIDAY, SEPTEMBER 26th.
Leave for South Wales, mid-day.

The itinerary for the All Blacks visit to Gloucester [Gloucestershire Archives]

OFFICIAL SOUVENIR PROGRAMME 2d.

Printed and Published under the auspices of the Gloucestershire Rugby Football Union

**KINGSHOLM
GLOUCESTER**

Grand Rugby Football Match

New Zealand

VERSUS

Glo'stershire

Thursday,
September 25th, 1924

KICK-OFF 3-30 P.M.

NEW ZEALAND FIXTURES
1924-25.

Sept. 13   Devon.
  „   18   Cornwall.
  „   20   Somerset.
  „   25   Gloucestershire.
  „   27   Swansea.
Oct.   2   Newport.
  „   4   Leicester.
  „   8   North Midlands.
  „   11   Cheshire.
  „   15   Durham.
  „   18   Yorkshire.
  „   22   Lancashire.
  „   25   Cumberland.
Nov.   1   IRELAND.
  „   5   Ulster.
  „   Northumberland.
  „   Cambridge University.
  „   15   Harlequins.
  „   20   Oxford University.
  „   22   Cardiff.
  „   29   WALES.
Dec.   4   Llanelly.
  „   6   East Midlands.
  „   11   Warwickshire.
  „   13   Combined Services.
  „   17   Hampshire.
  „   27   Blackheath.
Jan.   3   ENGLAND.

THE FIRST ALL BLACKS.
The 1905 All Blacks had their line crossed only nine times in thirty-three matches. They scored 215 tries, their chief scorers being W. J. Wallace (77 goals and 2? tries), J. Hunter (41 tries), G. W. Smith (19 tries), and R. G. ...eans (17 tries).

The programme cover for the New Zealand match [Gloucester Rugby]

Many former heroes for Gloucestershire turned up to see how their successors fared against the All Blacks; shown here are, from left, G Romans, G L Jones, J Oates, W T Pearce, G Holford, T Bagwell, J Stephens, A J Gardner, B Parham and W Leighton. Of these, 'Jummer' Stephens and Bert Parham had first hand experience of taking on the All Blacks at Kingsholm, having played for Gloucester against the 1905 tourists [CC&GG]

The crowd packed in on the Tump [CC&GG]

was building a formidable reputation. Hours of incessant rain produced a sodden pitch, which served to even things up a bit. It may also have discouraged some from attending, but advance ticket sales were excellent, and the weather did little to dampen the enthusiasm of the 15,000 spectators packed into Kingsholm.

New Zealand scored a try early on and, although it was backs-to-the-wall stuff for Gloucestershire, they conceded nothing further before half time. Despite being a man down in the second half, Gloucestershire went on the attack, only for the All Blacks to break away for a second try, which sealed the match 6-0. George Nepia, the All Blacks captain described Kingsholm as 'a Taranaki cow-yard, old style, and everyone splished, splashed and sploshed after the ball wherever it was. We learned that the talk about effete Englishmen was so much talk. They could take it, and give it too.'

This photograph taken during the fire, shows how dangerously close the big top was to the stand [Citizen]

must go on as soon as possible. Bertram Mills himself announced to the Citizen that: 'it was an amazing escape; as a result of the outbreak it will be necessary to cancel the 2:30 programme, but the 5:30 show will be given in full'. The circus had escaped relatively lightly, but Kingsholm no longer had a main stand.

This calamity did not rule out future circus visits – in 1934, Chapman's Circus were offered the site for £15, but said that they could only afford £10 for a day's hire, and this was accepted.

Gordon Hudson, a teenager at the time, spoke to Pete Wilson about this incident nearly sixty years later and, recalled:

Father [Arthur Hudson] was the Secretary then. He saw some smoke coming up and he thought it was Johnny Stephens' factory which was a factory making pickles and so on behind Kingsholm – it was a well known Gloucester landmark and the smell was as well. He went

down and of course the stand was on fire, they were spraying the top, but up she went. A terrible blow – that was a horrifying moment.

A New Stand Arises from the Ashes

IN THE IMMEDIATE aftermath of the fire and as he sadly contemplated the scene of devastation at Kingsholm on 9th September 1933, the Citizen interviewed Arthur Hudson, who said:

> The first I knew of the fire was when I saw huge clouds of smoke from my shop window. I could not tell what caused it, but instinct seemed to warn me that the Football Ground was involved. When I got down here the stand was a blazing inferno. Although the stand is insured it will be a heavy blow to the Club that such a happening should have taken place at the outset of the season.

The first thing the Club did was to send a letter of appreciation to Superintendent Windebank for the magnificent efforts of the Fire Brigade in controlling the fire, and then they immediately started work on a recovery plan. On Monday 11th September, two days after the fire, an emergency meeting was held at Kingsholm. Present were the Club committee and Ground Company directors, along with the Fire Insurance Company's Assessor, Mr Baker, a representative of Davies Bros (Wolverhampton), Mr Dent & Mr William Jones. All were agreed that the remains of the grandstand should be totally condemned, and discussion quickly moved on to what structure should replace it. By the time a second emergency meeting was held the following day, a tender had been received from Davies Bros for dismantling the wreck of the burned stand, and estimates had been sent to the Insurance Assessor by Davies Bros for the steel work, and by William Jones for interior work, on the new stand. Mr Leah was appointed as architect for the new structure.

The new season kicked off against Moseley on 16th September 1933, only a week after the fire, and matches continued at Kingsholm whilst the demolition and construction work was underway. In order to tide the Club over while the new stand was under construction, an offer was accepted from the County Cricket Club for the loan of portable stands. In fact gate takings for this period were not much down on the same matches the previous season. However, in light of the changed circumstances, the Club committee rescinded their previous decision to take over the remaining mortgage on the ground from the Ground Company.

On 26th September, at a further emergency meeting of the Club committee, the architect, Mr Leah, presented a plan of the ground, the stands and a tracing of the pitch. After studying this, it was agreed that the new stand should be erected 17 feet back from the line of the previous stand. Mr Leah was instructed to obtain tenders from potential builders of the new stand. The insurance company's assessor, Mr Baker, made an offer of £2,884 in settlement of the claim on the old stand, and this was accepted. It was agreed that the Club should pay Davies Bros for dismantling the remains of the old stand, and that the salvage would belong to the Club. In due course tin sheets salvaged from stand were sold for 5d per sheet to Messrs Stephens, and Mr Dalloway paid £63 for the salvaged ironwork.

On 3rd October, the architect's plans for the new stand were approved by the Club committee, and the tender from William Jones for the building work was accepted. On 16th October a planning application was submitted for the new grandstand to be built of steel, asbestos-covered, and with block stairs. It must have seemed a bit like shutting the stable door after the horse had bolted, but on 17th October the Club decided to buy three Minimax fire extinguishers.

Work on the new stand continued apace, day and night shifts being worked to erect the steel framework as quickly as possible. On 4th November the Citizen reported that:

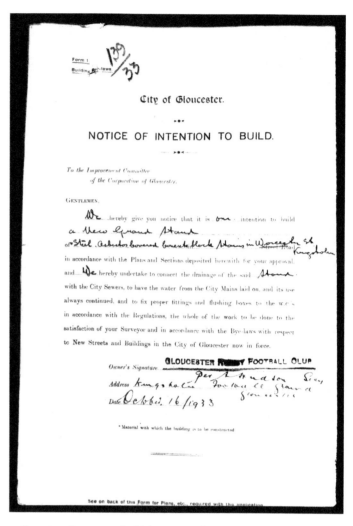

The notice of intention to build the new grandstand [Gloucestershire Archives]

> So far as spectators are concerned the new grandstand at Kingsholm will be ready for the County match next Saturday. There will be seating accommodation for 1,330 people, and in front of the stand there will be room for about 1,500 people to stand, most of whom will be under cover. Remarkable progress has been made in erecting the stand, as it is now barely eight weeks since the old stand was burned down. Day and night shifts were worked to erect the steel framework, and the floor has already been laid. Carpenters have been busy this week, and the asbestos roof is in position. Although slightly smaller than the old one, the new stand is more substantial, and spectators will find that they have been provided with more leg room. A difficulty has been the two open erections on either side of the new stand. These have to be moved back several feet bodily in order to give spectators in the new stand a clear view of the whole of the field. They have to be placed on concrete foundations, but this it is hoped will have been carried out by November 11.

The work was indeed completed and the new stand was opened on 11th November, only nine weeks after the fire had burned down its predecessor. The accommodation provided met with the approval of the Citizen:

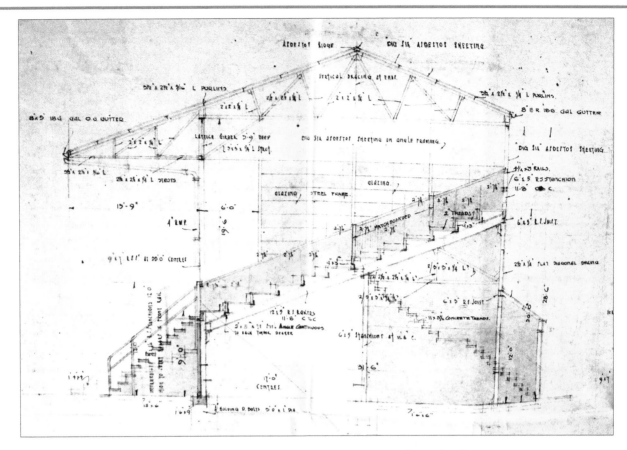

The architect's plans for the new grandstand [Gloucestershire Archives]

This view of the new grandstand was probably taken from the scoreboard ladder on the Tump [John Hudson]

In the planning of the new stand the comfort of the spectators has been one of the chief factors to be borne in mind and careful attention to detail and clever designing of the whole has resulted in splendid results having been achieved. The seating in the new erection has been arranged so that patrons are accommodated in the centre section, and other spectators in wings on either side. There are three entrances at the back of the stand and three front exits. In the stand are dressing-rooms, a ladies' cloak room, and a Press box. The main contract for the work was placed in the hands of Mr. William Jones, general building contractor, of Worcester-street, Gloucester, who spared no endeavour to provide a thoroughly good stand in the shortest possible time. When it is remembered that the actual work of erection was confined to five weeks, it will be realised that the contract was placed in very good hands. The same can be said of Messrs. Davies Brothers and Co., Ltd., Crown Works, Wolverhampton, who were responsible for the structural steel work and of the Gloucester Stone Co., Ltd., Barnwood, who very materially assisted matters by supplying over 500 reinforced units for the terracing and steps. These were specially designed in consultation with the architect, and were delivered to the general contractor in record time.

Despite the short timescale for construction of the new stand, it would last a lot longer than its predecessor, and remained in use until 2007, when it was finally demolished to make way for the present stadium. The new stand was insured for £2,500, for which the annual premium was £6 5s 0d, and it was described on the policy as being built of concrete, brick and asbestos on a steel framework, with timber seating on a concrete and timber terrace. At the same time, the gymnasium, baths and offices, brick and timber built and tiled, were insured for £2,000, at a premium £2 10s 0d.

The new stand was first occupied at the county match between Gloucestershire and Somerset, for which the entry charges were:

New Grand Stand Reserved Seats	- Centre 4s, Wings 3s
' ' ' Unreserved	- Centre 3s 6d, Wings 2s 6d
' ' ' Enclosure	- 2s 6d
Old Stand	- 2s 6d
Worcester St Side	- 1s 6d
Deans Walk	- 1s

Tom Voyce

ANTHONY THOMAS VOYCE was born in Gloucester and educated at the old National School. During his playing career he was selected in a wide variety of positions, but he was such a good player that he succeeded in every one of them. At school, he initially made his mark on the wing and at centre, but was selected for England schoolboys at fly half. The Great War then intervened and he immediately signed up as a private in the Glosters, but was later commissioned, passed out from Sandhurst, and became a Captain in the Buffs. He was selected for an Army trial as a forward. During the war he sustained injuries which affected his eyesight for the rest of his life, but, whilst it later prevented him from driving a car, it does not seem to have detracted in any way from his ability to follow the ball and hunt down opposing backs on the rugby field.

On return to civilian life, he made his first appearances for Gloucester in 1920, back on the wing. However, an injury to 'Tart' Hall before the start of a game caused Tom to be switched to wing forward at the last moment. He made such an impact that he not only carried on playing there for Gloucester, but was also selected at wing forward for the County and for England, all in his first full season of senior rugby. He revolutionised the role of wing forward by putting the emphasis on moving quickly away from the pack and causing mayhem amongst the opposition backs. This led to him being dubbed as the 'father of all wing forwards'.

He went on to play 28 matches for Gloucestershire and to captain the Club for 3 seasons, 1924-27. He won 27 England caps between 1920 and 1926, including two back-to-back grand slams, played for the Barbarians, and toured South Africa with the British Isles team in 1924. Wavell Wakefield, the England captain, said that he always wrote Tom's name first on the selection sheet, and he described him as 'a wonderful inspiration to any side; Tom had that personality and mental, competitive outlook that makes up a truly great player; and he was a shining example to others in that he was determined to put something back into the game for all the pleasure he had out of it.'

Tom was always willing to assist sport in any form, and organised a couple of special matches at Kingsholm in aid of local cricket. In 1922,

Tom Voyce about to score for England against Wales; Tom has signed the photograph [Gloucester Rugby]

The scene along Worcester Street, with the Kingsholm ground on the left, when the floods caused the home fixture against Newport to be switched to an away game on 22nd March 1947 [Gloucestershire Archives]

The flooding inside the ground looking towards the Tump [Journal]

stand of £1,400, but Government restrictions would not let them build it. Consequently, it was likely to go up in cost by the time they could build it, probably to £1,600 or more.

While this was going on, the severe weather during the 1946-47 winter meant that rugby was suspended for several weeks, and the Club suffered substantial financial losses. Snow and straw was cleared from the pitch to allow the Cardiff match to go ahead on 8th February. This revealed that large parts of the ground underneath were frozen, but 5,000 spectators were already in the ground and the two teams agreed to play despite the conditions. Cardiff won a fast and exciting game 12-11. On 15th March the fixture against Guy's Hospital was played in a snowstorm and Gloucester won 11-3. But those were the only Club games played between 18th January and 29th March.

When the thaw eventually arrived, Kingsholm flooded. The water was deepest in the north-west corner of the pitch, where there was a significant dip. Consequently this was later built up to alleviate the problem and to give a more level playing surface.

However, the County had managed to play their Championship match against Middlesex on 1st March. This game had been scheduled previously at Twickenham and Richmond, but postponed twice because of frost on those grounds. It was sign of the times that the Gloucestershire team had planned to travel up to London on the day of the match rather than the night before 'owing to the difficulty of finding food and accommodation'. Desperate to get the game played, Middlesex agreed to come to Kingsholm, where they lost 17-24. This resulted in Gloucestershire travelling to Lancashire for the final of the County Championship, where they fought out an 8-8 draw. Some 19,000 packed into Kingsholm for the replay on 26th April 1947, paying entrance charges varying between 1s and 7s 6d, but the raucous home support could not prevent Lancashire winning the title 14-3.

The financial situation for the Club was exacerbated in March 1947, when the RFU announced that no mid-week matches should be played in deference to the Government's wishes under the National Economy Emergency. When it came to replacement of the goalposts, only wooden posts were available, because tubular iron posts required a Ministry of Supply permit, which was impossible to obtain.

In September 1947, Australia returned to Kingsholm and beat a combined Gloucestershire and Somerset side 30-8. Ticket prices at Kingsholm ranged from 2s to 10s, and the tourists were welcomed enthusiastically by a crowd of 15,000, who were kept in good order by the sixteen policemen hired for the occasion. Mr Outridge provided the teas, quoting £5 for 55 plain teas, and £7 10s for meat teas. The Club went for the expensive option, which was thought appropriate for a special occasion

such as this. The result of this profligacy was a dispute with the County Union. The tea was reported to be excellent, but the County objected to the size of the bill. There had also been a breakdown in communications and the Australians had not understood that tea was provided, although there had been no shortage of volunteers to eat what they missed. The Club responded by complaining about the lack of publicity and advertising of

Bill Hook kicks a goal against Lydney in the first match of the 1947-48 season, with the west end of the Shed in the background [Gloucester Rugby]

the match by the County, which had detracted from the match takings (of which the Club received 15%). The County Union subsequently refused to order teas for their matches at Kingsholm, but the Club did not want Kingsholm to get a bad name with visiting teams, and went ahead and provided them at their own expense.

During 1948 wire fencing was installed all around the ground, with three small gates and one large one. Insurance cover for the south grandstand and terrace was £7,500, for the north stand (the Shed) £2,000 and for the east stand and terrace (Worcester Street) £1,000. In the insurance policy the stands on the south side were described as being constructed in brick, asbestos and steel, with timber seating on concrete and timber terracing. The Worcester Street stand was described as being constructed in iron and steel. For the 1948-49 season, the insurance cover for the south stand was increased to £11,625 at a premium of £25 6s 3d.

Ken Daniell (89 appearances for Gloucester, 1945-50) recalls:

Regarding the ground in the top games, ie Cardiff and County games, seats were put round inside the rails to accommodate the large crowds meaning all the players were very close to the crowd. There was always lots of banter, some good, some bad, when the ball went out of play.

Restrictions on building materials and labour continued to constrain the Club's ambitions for Kingsholm during 1949. Although an extension to the main stand and development of the Social Club were planned, in the event new works were confined to concrete steps to form terracing on the Tump at the Deans Walk end of the ground and in front of the gymnasium. The main stand was painted for £658 by Messrs Bailey Naylor, a new boiler in the gymnasium was procured for £159 18s 3d, and more concreting and fencing was put in behind the south stand, but a lack of labour prevented concrete being laid in the car park. In November 1949 it was decided to complete the improved enclosure of the ground with a concrete wall to replace the corrugated iron fence along the Deans Walk boundary, and with 60 yards of fencing at the Worcester Street end. To the considerable relief of female spectators, a ladies' lavatory was installed on the north side of the ground for the first time.

Bob Timms scoring at the Tump end, on which the first concrete steps had been built in 1949 [Gloucester Rugby]

In December 1949, Kingsholm was awarded the second England trial, which attracted a crowd of about 10,000, doubtless bolstered by the presence of a local hero in Tom Price, although Bill Hook, the Gloucester full back, had to cry off. There was not much to choose between the teams, and the Probables were judged fortunate to win by as much as 13-6. Receipts from the match amounted to £1,009 8s 6d, and expenditure came to £235 15s 7d, leaving a profit of £773 12s 11d. The 20% share which was paid to the Gloucester Club came to £154 14s 7d.

M R Steele-Bodger, who captained the Possibles in this game, later wrote, when President of the RFU:

Kingsholm – what a wonderful name for that ground – surely the most renowned of all the club grounds in England! Apart from the rather painful time when I broke my nose there in an International trial game I have none but the happiest memories of Kingsholm, both as player and selector. The atmosphere and the welcome are real and sincere.

The Memorial Ground

DURING THE SECOND World War, the Club Secretary, Arthur Hudson, had kept a careful eye on what was being done at the Kingsholm ground, and tried to defend the interests of the Club and Ground Company as best he could. When Kingsholm had reverted to being a rugby ground again in 1946, the Committee felt that his selfless work should receive proper recognition, and unanimously agreed that Arthur should be presented with an honorarium of £150 for his services to the Club since the start of the war. Arthur would have none of it, in that he appreciated the gesture, but would not accept any personal remuneration for his role in safeguarding his beloved Kingsholm. Rather he proposed that the money be used to start a fund to provide a ground for local clubs as a fitting memorial to those players who had lost their lives during the war.

Arthur's proposal went down well with the Committee who resolved:

That a Memorial Fund be inaugurated to commemorate the memory of the players of the Gloucester Rugby Football Club who have made the supreme sacrifice in the two Great Wars;

That this memorial should take the form of a fund to purchase a playing ground for the use of Clubs of Gloucester & District Clubs at the discretion of the Gloucester Rugby Football Club and its Trustees;

That £500 be placed in the Memorial Fund as the Club's first subscription; and

That the profits of the programmes for the season be transferred to the Fund.

The Memorial Ground Fund was officially launched at the Club's AGM in June 1946. It was envisaged that the ground would be large enough for five or six pitches. The North Gloucester Combination of local rugby clubs had been struggling to find sufficient pitches for many years, and were delighted that the Gloucester Club were going to help. The Trustees appointed to run the Memorial Fund were the Club President, Arnold Alcock, and the Vice-Presidents, Tom Voyce and Arthur Hudson.

When the plan was made public, it was greeted with widespread enthusiasm and willingness to contribute. Collections were made at matches (for example, £9 4s was raised at a match with the Gloucestershire Regiment, and £50 16s 8d at the Boxing Day match against Old Merchant Taylors), and donations started to flow in. Donors included both individuals and other rugby clubs. These included £100 from Mr & Mrs Fred Byard, £10 from Mr Chorley Williams, 2 guineas from Newport RFC, 5 guineas from All Blues RFC, £5 from Fieldings, and 2 guineas from Mr George Baggage, President of Bristol RFC. Many former players, including Tom Millington, Fred Wadley and Tom Voyce, also contributed. Sums, generally in the range of £7-£10, were raised from programme sales at each match, and the total from this source for the 1947-48 season amounted to £350 10s. The County Union agreed that profits from their match programmes should also go into the Fund, and made a further donation of £75. In January 1947, a snowfall threatened the Cardiff match, but Mr W Cannock and his lorry came to the rescue in covering and then clearing the pitch; he refused the payment of £5 offered for his services, insisting that it should instead be put into the Memorial Fund. At the end of each season the Club looked at its balance sheet and decided how much it could afford to put into the Fund; in 1947 and 1948 this was £200. By the time of the Club AGM in 1949, the Fund stood at £3,086.

A site at Barnwood, on land owned by the Gloucester Corporation, was initially considered for the new ground, but that fell through, and by 1948 the Club was seeking alternative suggestions. Several options were pursued over the subsequent couple of years, including sites at Hempsted, Longlevens and Longford, but none of them came to fruition.

When the Club AGM was held in July 1952, the Fund had grown to £4,800, and Dr Alcock was able to announce that they had finally succeeded in obtaining a ground, eight acres in size, temporarily used as allotments, and located just off Tuffley Avenue, adjoining the Wagon Works ground. He declared that 'it would please those fine young men, whom we honour more than anything, to know that the future of playing fields for the younger generation in Gloucester is assured.' The trust deed was signed on 16th September 1952 by Messrs Alcock, Voyce and Hudson, and occupation of the ground was announced the following month.

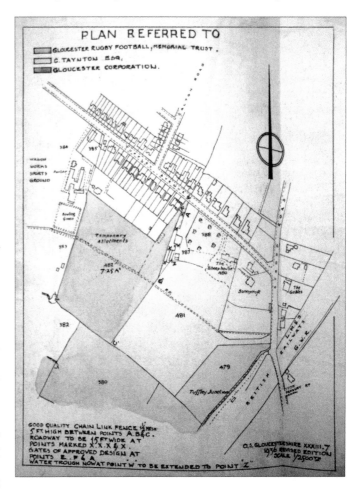

This map shows the ownership of the land at the Tuffley Avenue site including the temporary allotments purchased by the Club [Gloucester Rugby]

It took another two years to clear, level and fence the ground. Four pitches were laid out. However, costs were mounting, and in 1954 the Club loaned an additional £500 to the Trust. They hoped to start playing on the ground in 1956 or 1957.

However, there was a hitch in 1955, when a planning inquiry looked into an application for planning permission on land adjoining the

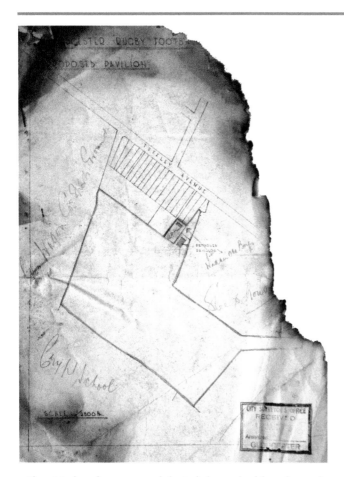

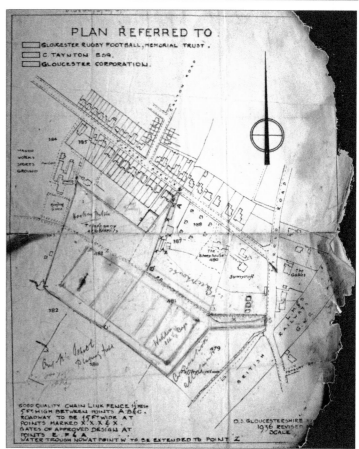

The original purchase was extended to include some land formerly owned by C Taynton. This formed part of the plot containing 'The Sheep House', and may well be the same land which was recommended for purchase by the Club in 1891, but which was then dropped in favour of Castle Grim at Kingsholm [Gloucester Rugby]

The layout of the Memorial Ground in 1962 [Gloucester Rugby]

Memorial Ground. They heard that this land and the Memorial Ground had been scheduled for educational purposes in the City Development Plan of 1951. The City Planning Department said it was still planned to build three schools and a college on the whole site, although this probably would not happen for a further ten years. It was claimed that the Rugby Club knew that their tenure might be short-term when purchasing the ground in 1952, although the Club denied this. Fortunately this threat fizzled out, but progress on developing the ground continued to be slow.

In October 1961, the Club's Memorial Ground sub-committee considered tenders for changing quarters, but the figures being quoted of £9,000 - £10,000 were seen as prohibitive. Tenders were also sought for concrete walls to replace the fencing. It was decided to approach the Playing Fields Association, the RFU and the Ministry of Education for grants or loans, and finally the ground came into use.

Sign at the entrance to the Memorial Ground in 2015 [Malc King]

To this day, Old Cryptians and Widden Old Boys RFC play on the Memorial Ground and have their clubhouses there.

Celebrating Sixty Years at Kingsholm

The Great and the Good Reminisce

'THE DIAMOND JUBILEE of the Twickenham of the West' was the title of the special supplement of the Citizen published in September 1951 to mark the start of the 60th season of matches at Kingsholm. The 50th anniversary had fallen during the war years, when nobody felt like celebrating, but they made up for it ten years later with a plethora of reminiscences.

WB (Bill Bailey), the doyen of Citizen rugby reporting and now well into his 80s, was brought out of retirement to lead the way in the special edition:

When the whistle shrills for the kick-off in the customary opening-of-season clash between Gloucester and Lydney, it will, coincidentally, signalise the start of Gloucester Rugby Football Club's 60th year on the now famous enclosure. These 60 years, studded with unforgettable examples of triumph over adversity … of courage and initiative on and off the field … of rousing battles and thrilling victories interwoven with heart-breaks and set-backs … have earned for Kingsholm and the Club an ineffaceable place in the history of rugby. Sixty years ago a small band of pioneers stood on the open spaces that was once Kingsholm and dreamed of building one of the finest rugby stadiums in the West. The path was not easy. Many vicissitudes were experienced. Many disappointments and blows were endured. But in the end the dream of the pioneers and worthy generations of successors came true. Kingsholm, the West's own Twickenham, is not only one of the finest grounds but one of the greatest rugby bastions in the country. Throughout the length and breadth of the British Isles, and in far-flung outposts of the world, Gloucester is famous for its Rugby Club and Kingsholm enclosure.

WB [Citizen]

Others were invited to pay their own tributes to Kingsholm. The President of the Rugby Football Union, H Cleaver, declared that:

This is surely the time to acknowledge with grateful thanks the foresight of those rugger enthusiasts in Gloucester who in 1891 secured the Kingsholm ground, and to those officials and members who, as the years went on, bought and paid for it so that it became the home of the Gloucester Football Club for all time. Not only have they served the Club but they have served the boys of Gloucester, giving them the opportunity by using their own efforts, of playing

for their town and club, which should be the ambition of every boy in Gloucester who takes up the grand old game of amateur Rugger.

H Cleaver [World Rugby Museum, Twickenham]

Tom Voyce (171 appearances for Gloucester 1918-28, England and British Lions) pitched in with:

The thrills of victory and defeat…the Herculean battles against odds…the subtle change of tactics which tipped the scales…the roars which have shaken Kingsholm to signalise an outstanding feat and, above all, the grand comradeship which shines like a jewel in the history of Gloucester rugby. These are but a few of many corners in my own particular treasure house of memories of never-to-be-forgotten years on and off the field of play.

Tom Voyce [Gloucester Rugby]

Dai Gent (146 appearances for Gloucester, 1903-12, and England international) maintained:

To me, Kingsholm is the best club ground in the country; yes, and in the world! The Kingsholm ground was for seven years part of my being, and has ever since been the core of the memories of my active playing days. This is the ground to give the home side an advantage, that every real Rugby man the world over knows and which the many Gloucester men that I met in New Zealand asked after at once. Perhaps they would not all have felt quite the same affection for it now, with its added stands and other amenities, all so different from what it was in my days, with just one small homely stand; the dressing room for the players in the little inn opposite the entrance; the walk from the inn to the ground in our caps and blazers, and the little run about on the sacred turf before the kick off. All this is a long time ago, though, but there still stands this almost hallowed ground, Arthur Hudson still watches over it, and its name is still Kingsholm. May its traditions continue, and may those young fellows who play on it be conscious, at least now and then, of their goodly heritage.

Dai Gent [World Rugby Museum, Twickenham]

'Doc' Alcock (England and President of Gloucester), recorded his favourite memories:

I like to remember the great match against the team of Capt W S Donne, the then president of the ERU, which Gloucester - captained by Tom Voyce — just won after a most exciting game. Many thrilling games at Kingsholm, notably perhaps some of those against Oxford University, which stand out in my memory as the most brilliant. They were unrivalled in skill, open play, team-work and good sportsmanship. Of individuals imprinted in my memory stand out 'Father' Dix and his cheeky tries (how seldom a scrum half scores now!); Tom Millington and his deadly tackling and versatility in playing in any position in the back division; and Tom Voyce and his amazing try against Newport when he received the ball in the centre of the field and without wavering ran straight through the Welsh side and put the ball down between the posts. In more recent times my memory is thrilled with the match winning of Harold Boughton and Willie Jones. The latter I regard as the best handler and kicker of a Rugby ball I have ever seen. And I do not think I shall forget Charlie Crabtree picking the ball off the ground at full-back and scoring against Leicester. I look back with pride on many team achievements … that unexplained atmosphere, good fellowship and sportsmanship

'Doc' Alcock [Gloucester Rugby]

in Gloucester Rugby circles … the outstanding service of Arthur Hudson … the loyalty of officials, committee and supporters … the conscientious referees. And I like to look forward to the time when we shall be allowed to carry out all the improvements we envisage to make Kingsholm the best equipped ground in the British Isles.

Arthur Hudson (268 appearances for Gloucester, 1902-20, England, and Secretary of the Club) contributed:

Kingsholm has provided me with a rich harvest of 50 years of memories, for I have seen it grow from a meadow with a barn which served as a stand to the present magnificent stadium. I like to remember the scores of fine players, officials and committee members who have helped to make the Club what it is to-day … the great struggles and magnificent feats … the humorous little incidents which form an integral part of the history of the club and ground.

Gloucester players changed in the White Hart and the visitors in the Ram in Southgate Street, from where they travelled to Kingsholm by wagonette. In those far-away days it was not unusual for the Club to be hard up. In fact, officials and committeemen were required to act as guarantors to the bank. Revenue at the first match at Kingsholm came to only a few pounds. On February 6 1949, when the famous Cardiff side were visitors, the gate receipts were £831. The attendance at that game was 15,000 — a club match record — although over 20,000, the highest ever, saw the England and Wales boys international in 1947. Biggest receipts came from the Services internationals during the war when over £10,000 was raised for charities. One match alone produced £2,100.

Arthur Hudson [Gloucester Rugby]

It is intriguing to go through the records to note how few games have been cancelled owing to the weather. As a result of the great flood in 1947 — when Kingsholm was invaded by water for the first time — our home match with Newport was switched. But a great fall of snow one Christmas in the early 1920s nearly caused cancellation of the meeting with the Old Merchant Taylors. On that occasion, however, we beat the elements. Snow covered Kingsholm to a considerable depth and I had the shock of my life when I came back from a visit to Hereford to see how much was on the ground. An SOS was sent out and within a short time hundreds of people carrying shovels made their way to the ground. These spade commandos worked hour after hour clearing the ground and their work was completed to enable the match to start only 15 minutes late. This was a magnificent achievement and an example of the fine spirit of Rugby followers. Looking back over 50 years as a player and official, I do not begrudge one minute of the time I have devoted to Rugby. To me it has been a labour of love; it has given me some of my richest memories.

The Jubilee Dinner

WHEN IT CAME to the actual anniversary on 10th October 1951, of the first match at Kingsholm in 1891, a dinner was held the following evening to mark the occasion. It was attended by many heroes of Kingsholm, past and present, as well as representatives of the leading English and Welsh clubs who had been regular visitors to the ground.

The Programme for the Jubilee Dinner [Gloucester Rugby]

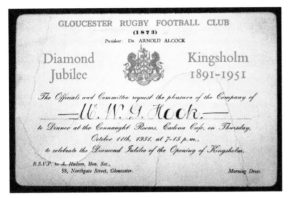

The invitation to the Jubilee Dinner which was sent to Bill Hook (Gloucester, Gloucestershire and England) [Bill Hook]

There was an abundance of speeches. The President of the Gloucester Club, 'Doc' Alcock, told of his pride at presiding at the jubilee dinner of the Club in 1924, and now at the jubilee dinner for Kingsholm. He recalled 'when finances were so low that they thought of selling the whole of the Kingsholm ground's frontage in Worcester Street for shops', a threat which he said was averted thanks to the efforts of Arthur Hudson.

The Mayor of Gloucester, W J Smith, complimented the Club on consistently bringing credit and honour to the city - 'we in the city are proud of the fact that, win or lose, the game is played in the grand sportsmanlike manner which one always associates with rugby football.'

Dai Gent, the former Gloucester captain and international, observed that 'you have at this very representative gathering more famous people in British rugby football than I have seen assembled at the same table for a very long time'. He also claimed that 'Kingsholm was not far behind the

Cathedral in spreading the name of the city in various parts of the world.

Charlie Williams and Walter Taylor, the only two surviving members of the Gloucester team which had beaten Burton in the first match at Kingsholm 60 years previously, were both present at the dinner. Two representatives of the Burton club were also among the guests. Charlie was asked to reminisce, and said:

> Looking back it's hard to realise that Kingsholm was opened as long as 60 years ago. I still retain vivid memories of the players' trip by horse brake to the ground … incidents during the game with Burton … and the celebration dinner. Since then the club has built up a magnificent record. To me it has left a legacy of golden memories of grand games … fine colleagues … and a wonderful spirit of sportsmanship. I am proud to have filled a small niche in such a distinguished company of sportsmen.

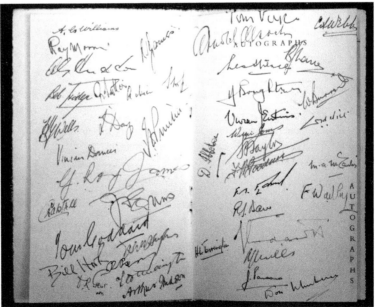

Autographs collected at the Jubilee Dinner [Gloucester Rugby]

Frustration in the Fifties

AS THE 1950S got under way, the country was starting to get back on its feet, and there were hopes that improvements could finally be made at Kingsholm, but the frustrations were set to endure for a while yet. In 1950, a Nissen hut was considered as a tea room, but this idea was dropped in favour of building a room under the main stand. The Supporters' Club was given permission to put a hut on the ground for recruitment and interviews with members. Officials and players were allocated parking spaces in the car park, from which, if they chose, they could watch matches, and in 1951 this privilege was extended to a disabled pensioner.

J V Smith (Stroud and England; President RFU) played at Kingsholm in this period, normally as an away player, but also at home for Gloucestershire and once as a guest in the Gloucester side. He recalls that:

Kingsholm was a ground I particularly liked playing at. It was a very heavy ground, very heavy. You had to be fit to play it. I always remember when I went down with the Army team to play against Gloucester, Brigadier Aslett, who was the England centre three quarter selector said, 'you're going down to Kingsholm and I'm telling you, as an old player, that ground will test you in the last ten minutes. If you're not fit, you won't last'. It was true. I have seen sides, in the last ten minutes, wilt because the forwards at Gloucester put them under pressure. I was a sprinter and athlete anyway, so I loved playing on that ground.

In 1951, the Club committee renewed their efforts as regards development of the ground. The grounds committee met with Mr Morgan, the City Architect, who had agreed to provide advice in a private capacity. In order to make progress he advised against a new build, and recommended a phased approach, with a social room being provided in the short term, and space being left for further extensions when the necessary permits could be obtained. He recommended Mr Ravenhill, who had recently retired from his department, to draw up the necessary plans. This advice was heeded, although Tom Voyce wanted the addition of a skittle alley. Mr Ravenhill came up with two options, estimated at £15,700 and £11,700, and when pressed for a minimalist option of a social room only, estimated that at £4,000, but he was gloomy about the prospects of obtaining the necessary licences and permits for any of these options.

At the Clubs' AGM in 1951, there was a commitment to a long term policy of ground improvements and an increase in seating accommodation, with the first priority being given to the provision of a social club and tea room for the use of players and members, and £16,000

was set aside for these various schemes. However, throughout 1951 and 1952 the Club was continually frustrated by plans being turned down, no matter how much they were watered down. Mr Ravenhill was paid £50 for his work, but at the Club AGM in June 1952, Mr Balchin, the Treasurer, reported that 'the committee are sorry to report that many improvements which they had hoped to carry out with regard to the additional comfort and amenities of members and players have had to be postponed because of inability to obtain licences for the work'.

A Festival of Britain hockey tournament was staged in 1951, which included the Indian Gymkhana side playing at Kingsholm. They were welcomed at Gloucester Central Station by Tom Voyce as Chairman of the sports and entertainments committee, and Mr B J Cooke, the organiser of the tournament at Kingsholm. They first played on the evening of Wednesday 20th June, and proved far too fast and quick-thinking for their opponents, Somerset, and won 4-0. The crowd was estimated at 600-700. After the match, the Mayor welcomed the teams to a hockey ball at the Guildhall. Indian Gymkhana played two further matches on the Friday, beating Bristol University 2-1 in the afternoon and drawing 1-1 with South Wales in the evening. Their star performer was Qayyum Khan on the left wing, who had represented Pakistan at the Olympics.

In November 1953, the Club returned to the charge in trying to achieve an extension to the main grandstand; the preferred option was to extend at both ends, but the fallback position was to build only at the Worcester Street end. Davies Bros came up with an estimate of £4,395 to build two steel framed extensions, each 80ft long (flooring, seating, brickwork and foundations would be extra), but this was again put on hold.

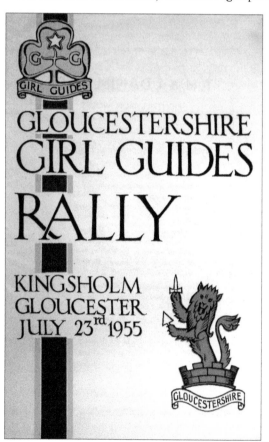

[Gloucestershire Archives]

Cricket being played in front of the Worcester Street stand in 1959; note the small hut next to the front of the south stand, where tickets were sold for transfers into the grandstand [Gloucestershire Archives]

In April 1954, three quotes were obtained for refurbishment of the Worcester Street stand, and the lowest, from William Jones, was accepted. This was costed at £1,195 for a new fence, repairs and painting, and £102 for a concrete path at the rear. Finally a plan came to fruition, this work on the Worcester Street stand being completed during the summer of 1954.

Around this time boys were employed for the first time to retrieve balls kicked off the pitch during games. Garth Cromwell reminisced:

Mervyn Hughes who was Club President asked my father whether my brother, Godfrey, and I would be the ball boys at Kingsholm because they were losing so many balls. So that was our claim to fame – the first ever ball boys at Kingsholm. We did it for four to five years. We used to be paid the princely sum of 2s per game and when you went in to get your money from Bertie Balchin [Club Treasurer] if the balls weren't recovered you didn't get paid. Most of the balls got kicked over the stand and finished up in the gardens of St Marks Street, and then after the game if any balls were missing you'd go round and knock on all the doors until you found the garden the ball was in.

In June 1955, approval was finally given for plans for the new social club, a quote was accepted from William Jones & Son for £1,775, and work on the foundations commenced in August. However, progress was very slow, and it took far longer to build than the three months originally estimated. Eventually it was finished, an alcohol licence was obtained, and furniture purchased – twelve armchairs for £3 9s 6d each, six ordinary chairs for £2 4s 6d, and three round formica-top tables for £5 2s 6d. It was opened for an experimental period from Easter 1956, and a formal opening was held on 12th May. It did not get off to an auspicious start – only one player turned up at the opening, and six days later there was a robbery when £15-worth of cigarettes were stolen, although the culprits were arrested and charged.

In December 1959, the capacity and admission charges for the various parts of the ground were as follows:

- on the south side, at the western end, an open terrace holding 1,075 at 6s;
- on the south side, in the centre, a grandstand holding 225 at 15s in the centre, and 550 at 10s in each of the wings, and a terrace in front (capacity not given, but estimated as 1,500 when the stand was built in 1933) at 5s;
- on the south side, at the eastern end, an open terrace holding 1,000 at 6s;
- on the western side (the Tump), an open terrace holding 4,000 at 2s 6d;
- on the northern side, at the western end, a covered terrace (the Shed) holding 3,300 at 4s;
- on the northern side, at the eastern end (in front of the gymnasium), an open terrace holding 1,000 at 4s;
on the eastern side (Worcester Street), a covered terrace holding 1,000 at 4s.

This adds up to a total capacity of about 14,200.

Summer lettings of the ground continued; for example, in 1959-60, £50 was charged for the Liberal fete and £75 for the Jehovah's Witnesses, but events such as these were less numerous than in earlier years, because more emphasis was placed on preserving the quality of the playing surface, and on the ground being available for players to use for training.

Despite all the inhibitions on developing the ground during the 1950s, the unique atmosphere of Kingsholm made it a memorable place to play rugby, as a couple of the players from that era recall:

Mike Baker (180 appearances for Gloucester, 1948-59) recalls: 'It was a great thrill to run out on the pitch at Kingsholm; I still feel the tingle in the back of my neck. Playing for Gloucester is very special.'

Bob Timms (150 appearances for Gloucester, 1958-66) recollects: 'It was always a great honour to run out onto our Kingsholm turf. Every time you went out, it was an unbelievable feeling.'

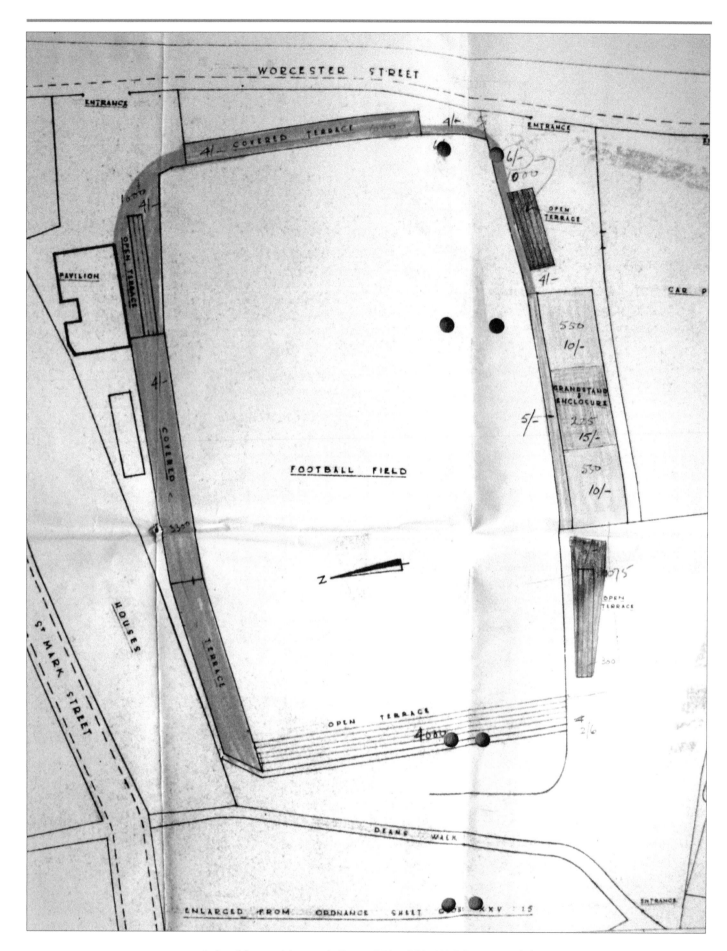

A plan of the ground drawn up by Dancey & Meredith in 1959 [Gloucester Rugby]

Mervyn Hughes

MERVYN HUGHES WAS an open side wing forward who played 44 matches for Gloucester, 1937-39. He was a Welsh trialist and Oxford blue who also turned out for Chepstow, London Welsh, Cardiff and Gloucestershire. He was Chairman of Gloucester RFC for 22 years, President for a further 16 years, and was one of the great figures of Gloucester Rugby in the post-war era.

Harold Mervyn Hughes was born on 12th July 1913. He played for Chepstow as a schoolboy and in 1930 represented that club against Gloucester United, before going on to study divinity at St David's College Lampeter. He went up to Oxford in 1934 and appeared regularly for the first XV during the 1934-35 season although missing his blue that season. On 7th November 1935 he was 'outstanding' in an Oxford University side which lost 9-10 against the All Blacks, who fielded virtually their best team. And he did play for Oxford in the 1935 and 1936 varsity matches.

He joined London Welsh before coming down from Oxford, and soon made his mark there. In a match against Harlequins he was described as 'an outstanding figure – he seemed faster than the fastest Harlequin back, which was saying something', and his prospects looked good - 'H M Hughes, the Oxford wing forward, looks one of the most promising players of his type in the British Isles'. In 1936-37 he appeared in the final Welsh trial, switched his club allegiance to Cardiff and made his debut for them against the Barbarians.

Mervyn was ordained a deacon and appointed to St Catherine's Gloucester in October 1937, and the following month made his debut for Gloucester against his old university at Kingsholm. He was ordained a priest in September 1938 and played regularly for Gloucester and Gloucestershire throughout that season. At this time he was one of three clergymen playing for the Club, the others being England international, Kit Tanner, and fellow Oxford blue, Bill Phillips.

He continued to play for Gloucester during the early part of the war, and his last major match was in November 1940 at Kingsholm for Wavell Wakefield's XV v Tom Voyce's XV, one of the wartime charity matches. During the war he organised rugby matches for his regiment, but an injury to his knee whilst playing in one of these games ended his career on the field.

After the war, he joined the Gloucester Club Committee and was elected Chairman in 1949, a post he held for 22 years, during which time he oversaw many improvements at Kingsholm, both to the fabric of the ground and to the performance of the Club on the field of play.

The story goes that when a vacancy needed filling in the living at Hucclecote, the Bishop of Gloucester consulted the Churchwarden and showed him a list of possible names. The Churchwarden, a fanatical Gloucester supporter, spotted Mervyn's name and declared him the only acceptable candidate, so the appointment was made. Mervyn liked to admit that when his predecessor at Hucclecote handed over to him, he advised that Mervyn should replace this troublesome Churchwarden, advice which Mervyn eventually put into action by mutual consent some 21 years later. His clerical career prospered, and he was appointed a canon, but more senior religious responsibilities in no way diluted his devotion to the Gloucester Club.

His love of rugby and Gloucester was evident to all, and he let neither his position within the Church, nor within the Club, interfere with his fanatical support. He often travelled with the team to away games, acting as pianist for the team when they stopped at a pub for a beer and a song. He enjoyed a fine reputation for heartily joining in the bawdy rugby songs, although he used to fall silent as the coach got closer to home.

Canon Mervyn Hughes [Gloucester Rugby]

His explanation was that he felt it improper for a canon of Gloucester Cathedral to sing such songs within the boundaries of his diocese.

The advent of Sunday matches was not welcome to him, but when the committee decided to go down this path, he assured them that he would not be obstructive in any way, but that he himself would not be coming to Kingsholm on a Sunday. He was very popular with the players and was usually asked by them to tie the knot when they came to be married. This of course allowed them to blame him for any subsequent restrictions which marital responsibilities placed on their availability for rugby, but he always took such banter in good part.

Mervyn eventually retired as Chairman in 1971, having already been elected a Vice President in 1965, and was made a Life Member in 1976. He succeeded his good friend Tom Voyce as President in 1979 and presided over the Club during the turbulent years leading up to the introduction of the professional game. During that period sponsorship revenue increased hugely and the first hospitality boxes were built on the ground. Strict coaching regimes were introduced leading to the appointment of the Club's first professional Director of Rugby in 1993.

As a staunch advocate of the amateur game, he undoubtedly viewed some of these developments with concern, whilst being determined that the Club should maintain its position in the top tier of rugby in the country. He retired as President in 1995, but continued to support the Club at every level. Attending 1st XV, United and Colts games, it was evident that he could never have too much Gloucester rugby. He died at his home in Upton St Leonards in February 1998.

Canon Mervyn Hughes declared:

The working man supported the Club as you could see if you were at Kingsholm. It gets tremendous support. And there's never been any sort of distinction between class or colour or anything else. With creed, you never asked him his religion except when you took him to hospital!'

Problems with Visiting Teams

Apartheid Comes to Fortress Kingsholm

SOUTHERN COUNTIES WERE due to host a match with South Africa at Bournemouth on 28th January 1970, but the tourists were attracting a lot of anti-apartheid demonstrators, and the police advised that the ground there could not be adequately secured. The RFU requested that the match be switched to Kingsholm, and the Gloucester Club agreed. There were considerable differences of opinion within the Club and within the wider Gloucester community about this decision.

On the evening before the match, two hundred and fifty anti-apartheid demonstrators marched through the streets of Gloucester, with the former Gloucester and England full-back, Bill Hook, to the fore carrying a "Springboks Out" banner. Other slogans on the numerous banners included "Dr Vorster, get out of Gloucester" and "Don't scrum with the Springbok scum". There was also a demonstration outside the Queen's Hotel in Cheltenham, where the Springboks were staying. These various demonstrations were noisy but peaceful. Later that night a "Welcome Springboks" slogan was painted on the gate and walls of Palace House, the home of the Bishop of Gloucester, who had been very critical of the match taking place in the City.

One of the demonstrations against the game [Journal]

There was also controversy over schoolboys attending the match, after tickets were sold in schools, only for the Education Officer to intervene and rule that pupils must not go to Kingsholm. The match being on a Wednesday, it was a normal school day, so it would be reasonable to expect that pupils should attend school as usual. However the explanation given for refusing permission to attend the match was that if boys had been permitted to miss lessons for this purpose, then the school authorities would also have had to allow boys to go to the demonstration against the match.

On the day of the match, there was a silent, and chiefly middle-aged group, who merely wished to stand up and be counted as being opposed to apartheid. There were also hundreds of students who came to Gloucester from Aston, Birmingham, Bristol and Cheltenham, and they were far from silent. They all assembled in the Park and speeches were made. The police surrounding the demonstrators were amused to hear the police pay claim being supported. The demonstrators then set off to march to the ground.

There was plenty of noise, tension and banner waving, but no violence, and the demonstrators were stopped by a three-deep line of police manning barriers across Worcester Street, whilst the teams, officials and supporters were guided into the ground via Sebert Street. Shortly before kick-off the strong contingent of police outside the ground linked arms and pushed the demonstrators back to make a bigger entrance for spectators. Behind the main stand at the ground 500 police, bussed in from all over the south of England and South Wales, were stretching their legs and drinking cups of tea. Gloucester Fire Brigade positioned a water tender near the stand in case of fire. The police had set up their headquarters in the social club at the ground. Although there was some pushing against the police, whose main difficulty was getting all the spectators into the ground, local residents appeared to view the demonstration as entertaining rather than threatening.

The police had time to enjoy a meal inside Kingsholm [Journal]

Once the game had kicked off, the demonstrators outside the ground marched back through the City centre, some returning later to Worcester Street, and others going to Gloucester Central Police Station, where a few of their number had been taken after being arrested on the ground. About forty demonstrating students had gained access to the ground using forged tickets. Two were arrested when found to be in possession of smoke canisters, others were ejected from the ground for chanting "Sieg Heil", and three were arrested for running onto the pitch during the match.

Despite the Tump being closed off, some 14,000 were present inside the ground to watch the rugby, which was the biggest crowd at Kingsholm since 16,000 had watched the previous South African tourists in 1960, when there were less stringent restrictions on crowd size.

As for the match itself, the Springboks came and saw and conquered 13-0, but they had to put in some hard graft against a Southern Counties side who put up a much better show than expected. There was little constructive rugby in the first half, which was scoreless. The Springboks scored early in the second half, but it was only in the last ten minutes that they increased their advantage.

During the match, one demonstrator ran onto the pitch and stood by players as they went into a scrum giving a black power salute. As two policemen rushed him off, a man came from the far side on to the field, quickly followed by another, but they were soon herded away. Others on top of the Shed kicked in a small section of the roof, which angered the crowd below and caused minor injury, but their dangling legs were fortunately just out of reach of the hands reaching up to pull them down.

Well over 100 policemen formed a solid cordon around the players as they shook hands and walked off the field, but there were no incidents.

A scene from the game, played in front of packed stands but an empty Tump
[Journal]

The Citizen reported that after the match "something new for Gloucester was the sight of 100 young people sitting in the middle of Kingsholm Road, holding an impromptu discussion on apartheid, the evils of British Imperialism, and the role of the working class in such demonstrations". The day was regarded as a success by all concerned - spectators enjoyed a reasonable game of Rugby, the demonstrators made their point, and both groups praised the 690 policemen present, who found the applause they received from the demonstrators a novel but welcome experience.

Fijian Independence Celebrated Wildly

DURING A 14-MATCH tour arranged to celebrate the granting of Fijian independence, Fiji played their second match at Kingsholm on Independence Day itself. The Fijian High Commissioner attended. On a damp, grey, drizzly afternoon, it was a sell-out and there were reported to be 20,000 packed into the ground.

The Citizen reported that "the Independence Day celebrations in the South Pacific must have been tinged with more than a little regret when news filtered through that their touring rugby side – some say the most entertaining in the world – had been beaten by Gloucestershire". There were actually a couple of Somerset men drafted into the Western Counties

AFTER attending Fiji Independance Day celebrations in London the Fiji High Commissioner, His Excellency Josua Rabukawagh flew to Staverton and was escorted to Kingsholm to watch the Fijians play the Western Counties. Above he meets members of the Counties team before the match and below the Deputy Mayor, Ald. Freda Wilton mets the Fijians.

[Journal]

side. The match was perhaps the most violent ever seen at Kingsholm, and the Western Counties suffered multiple injuries at the hands of the over-exuberant Fijians, who were heavily penalised for their misdemeanours and consequently lost 13-25.

Kingsholm in the Seventies

IN 1970 THE Worcester Street stand needed re-roofing, the cost of which was estimated to be about £800. The money was raised with £450 from the "200 Club" account, and by asking the Memorial Ground Trustees to repay their outstanding loan of £300. Around this time, the popularity of squash as a sport was growing fast, and in May 1970 the players put forward a proposal that squash courts should be built under the main stand. By the end of that year detailed plans for three courts had been drawn up, but competing demands for Club funds meant that they never came to fruition.

In March 1971, a capacity crowd of 18,000 packed into Kingsholm on a cold and windy day to watch the final of the County Championship. They had high hopes of success for the home side, despite Surrey's multi-national array of stars. Surrey were captained by Bob Hiller, which added to the entertainment, since he had a booming voice to go with his booming boot, and frequently employed it in repartee with the inhabitants of the Shed. His side also dominated on the field, rarely letting go of the ball as they built an 11-0 lead by half-time. A penalty by Eric Stephens briefly revived the hopes of the home crowd, but Surrey responded with a final try to secure victory 14-3.

We have the benefit of the views of the opposing full backs in this match about the Kingsholm experience:

Bob Hiller may have triumphed this day, but he still said of Kingsholm:

I've played Rugby in South Africa, New Zealand, Wales and other odd spots where the supporters are a bit fanatical, but I'd rather play at any of those places than at Kingsholm. Brother, that crowd is unique!"

Despite defeat in this match, Eric Stephens (221 appearances for Gloucester, 1961-74, and President of the Club, 2013-16) has fond memories of the ground stretching back generations:

It was a tremendous experience to run out and play at Kingsholm. It made you feel very proud and it was just the ultimate as far as I was concerned. Kingsholm means so much to me and my family, as both my grandfathers played there for Gloucester. I recall my grandmother telling me of spending her honeymoon there on Boxing Day 1899 following her wedding at St. Paul's church on Christmas Day. Personally I have enjoyed many happy hours at Kingsholm both

on and off the pitch, and I look forward to many more.

And at least his grandmother had the pleasure of spending her honeymoon watching a fast and entertaining game, which her new husband's team won 16-3 against Old Merchant Taylors.

The conversion of sterling to a decimal currency in 1971 was used as an excuse to increase prices right across the country, and Kingsholm was no exception, there being a substantial hike in admission charges. The price for a patron season ticket, which included entry to the social club and car parking on the ground, was set at £7.50p. Season tickets for wing stand seats went up from £3 15s (£3.75) to £5, and for ground entry from £2 to £3. Pensioners saw their wing stand seats go up from £1 15s (£1.75) to £2, and for ground entry from 15s (75p) to £1. Prices for old players went up from £1 15s (£1.75) to £2 for wing stand seats, and from 15s (75p) to £1 for ground entry. Season tickets for current players were increased from 10s (50p) to £1, but included the car park and social club. Junior tickets went up from £1 15s (£1.75) to £2 for wing stand seats and from 15s (75p) to £1 for ground entry. Gate admission prices for individual games went up from 5s (25p) to 40p for centre stand seats (OAPs and juniors 25p), from 4s (20p) to 30p for wing stand seats (OAPs and juniors 20p), and from 3s (15p) to 20p for ground admission (OAPs and juniors 15p). The price of programmes went up from 6d (2 ½ p) to 3p.

In October 1972, New Zealand returned to Kingsholm for the opening match of their tour. Having beaten Gloucester and then Gloucestershire on previous visits, they were now pitted against Western Counties, at least nominally. In fact the home side was Gloucestershire under another name, being composed entirely of Gloucester and Bristol players.

A temporary stand was erected for the match, which provided an extra 600 seats, and allowed a capacity crowd of 16,000 to give a rousing reception to Ian Kirkpatrick's All Blacks. But it was as nothing compared to the roar which greeted the home side when they took the field. The Western Counties label made no difference to the Kingsholm crowd who chanted "Glawster" in support of them throughout the match, but it produced no miracles. The All Blacks powered their way to a 21-0 lead by half-time, and, despite Mike Burton scoring a try to lift the home supporters, Bryan Williams ran in a hat trick for the All Blacks, who finished 39-12 winners.

Income from the match was £6,817, including gate money of £6,354-90, and programme sales of £392-90. Expenditure was £1,332-36, including £460-50 for the temporary stand, leaving a profit of £5,484-64.

OFFICIAL PROGRAMME   FIVE NP

WESTERN COUNTIES
(GLOUCESTERSHIRE & SOMERSET)
v.
NEW ZEALAND

KINGSHOLM GROUND, GLOUCESTER
SATURDAY, OCTOBER 28th, 1972
Kick-off 3.00 p.m.

[J Jay]

Out of this, £1,022-55 (15% of the gross gate) was paid to the RFU, and a similar amount accrued to the Club. The remaining excess of income was equally divided between the Gloucestershire and Somerset County Unions - £1,719-77 to each. After the match, a civic reception was hosted by the Mayor of Gloucester, Mr Alf Rich.

Bob Duff, the All Blacks coach said:

The ground was probably one of the best we have ever played on, and that applies to New Zealand as well.

Bill McLaren (BBC rugby commentator) reflected:

I covered the Western Counties v New Zealand Match at Kingsholm in 1972. I at once felt at home. The crowd were so totally involved; they weren't just there because it was the thing to do in Gloucester. They sought to live every moment with their chosen representatives. They were not mere spectators; they were ardent supporters, adherents.

During 1972 there were proposals to improve and increase the standing accommodation at Kingsholm. It was suggested that a retaining wall be built in the south-west corner of the ground, between the Tump and the grandstand, so that the level of the soil could be raised. However, this idea foundered in the face of doubts as to whether the expenditure would be worthwhile for the number of additional spectators, and a belief that future demand would be for seats rather than standing places. Another proposal was to improve the standing room on the Tump, but the estimated cost for this of £3,000 plus crash barriers, ruled it out as uneconomical. And there was also a plan to move the changing rooms from the gymnasium, and to build new ones under the main stand; plans were drawn up, but ended up being shelved for the time being.

The first match played by the Gloucester Club was on 4th October 1873, and to mark the centenary, Don Rutherford gathered together an International XV consisting of a formidable array of rugby stars to play at Kingsholm on 3rd October 1973. A large crowd turned out to watch their team celebrate their history and were rewarded with one of the best games of rugby ever seen on the ground and with a magnificent 24-14 victory for the Club.

Tony Brown (captain of Gloucestershire County Cricket Club) wrote:

Kingsholm is certainly no place for the faint-hearted – player or spectator. If it's been like that for the past hundred years I can't imagine anyone in Gloucester ever allowing it to change.

Other changes were in the air in December 1973, when the Club Committee agreed in principle that mini-rugby could be played before the kick-off in First XV games at Kingsholm. There was also a lot of discussion about Sunday games. It was decided to go ahead, with admission by programme, and the first Sunday fixture at Kingsholm was against Bristol on 3rd February 1974, which Gloucester won 7-3 thanks to a try from Stuart Dix and a dropped goal by Bob Redwood. Also in 1974, a new heating and hot water system was installed by R Fowke for £2,650. Summer lettings continued, and on 1st June 1974, the ground was hired to the City of Gloucester Festival Committee for £100, and Army motor cycling teams and gun crews put on displays.

The 1974-75 season saw more success for the County side, much of it associated with Kingsholm. They opened their campaign there with a 14-3 win over neighbours Somerset, which set them on the way to winning a tough south-west group, before returning to Kingsholm in February 1975 for the semi-final against a Warwickshire side which had romped through to this stage and started as favourites. Some 12,000 spectators raised the roof at Kingsholm as they were treated to one of the best performances they had ever enjoyed from their County side. Gloucestershire totally dominated their opponents up front and ran them ragged behind in completing a 28-3 annihilation.

It was no surprise that Gloucestershire, making their sixth successive appearance in the County Championship final, chose to return to Kingsholm to play against Eastern Counties, who were visiting the ground for the first time. They were treated to some vile West Country weather and a huge crowd, conservatively estimated at 15,000. The spectators were not able to enjoy a lot of constructive rugby in the muddy conditions, but their afternoon was enlivened by periodic bouts of fisticuffs, and they were able to cheer their team on to a 13-9 victory which was more convincing than the score suggests.

Peter Butler (317 appearances for Gloucester, 1972-82, and England international), who played a major part in these County successes, comments on his own experience of playing at Kingsholm:

The first time it was trepidation, but once you've made your mark you feel that you belong, and you're contributing, and you're part of the whole thing,

and reflects on the impact which Kingsholm had on visiting teams:

Nobody liked going there. I watched the faces of the guys who came to Kingsholm and they didn't want to play rugby against these real hard nuts.

In October 1975, work started on bricking over the side of the clubhouse facing the pitch (now the Lion's Den). This was paid for by the 250 Club, which had raised £750 during the previous year.

In December 1975, England took on the South in a trial match at Kingsholm. The Citizen reported "partisan they may be, but the Kingsholm crowd is as knowledgeable as any in the country, as they readily showed when this shambles of a second England trial was staged at Kingsholm". Local pride had been dented with the omission of the Gloucester full back, Peter Butler, and this was highlighted when Alastair Hignell, playing in that position for England, missed a series of kicks at goal. As the Citizen described it – "despite Hignell being a favourite when playing for Gloucestershire, his failures gave the Kingsholm faithful too good an opportunity to miss in reminding the selectors of the error of their ways by chanting "Butler, Butler" each time a kick went wide". An undistinguished game finally ended with David Duckham scoring in the corner to win the game 11-3, but that just left time for a last derisive "Butler" chant from the crowd when Hignell missed the conversion.

Nevertheless, Alastair Hignell recalls his visits to Kingsholm with real affection:

My after-dinner stories always involve coming to Kingsholm because the level of banter and the level of rugby expertise as well and knowledge and humour, is just fantastic. I tell the story that the thing about the Gloucester supporters is that they really do hate people from Bristol. They absolutely abhor full backs because they can see them and get them in their line, and they are always standing on their own and they can shout insults at them. They don't like anybody outside the forwards really, you know, any backs at all are fair game for the Shed.

You'd run down in front of the Shed, and it would sound as if it was the venue for the world gobbing championships - there was always 'rr – rr – oi – oi!' And they always used to greet me with this fantastic thing 'ere, Alice!'. You know, I couldn't understand why a short fat bloke with a beard should be called Alice by the Gloucester supporters. Maybe that says something about the Gloucester men, or maybe it says more about the Gloucester women!

I'd get 'oi Alice, go back to cricket!' and then a bloke would say 'you're no bloody good at that either!' And the first time you kick the ball into touch – 'oi, that's your second mistake! Your first was coming 'ere!' So, it was lovely banter from the crowd and yet it was hostile – it was always very, very hostile. Of course, some people don't like playing in front of that but I just used to love it, just like Rollitt – I wouldn't go around waving my fist in the air, I wasn't that big or brave – but I loved the atmosphere because there was this real intensity and this real love for the game and this humour as well."

The rampant inflation experienced in the British economy in the 1970s was reflected in admission charges at Kingsholm, which were increased in 1975 from £8.50 to £10.50 for patrons, from £6 to £7.50 for a season ticket in the grandstand wings, from £3.60 to £4.50 for ground entry, and from £1 to £1.50 for the car park. In 1976, one extension to the social club was completed, and the following year, approval was given to plans for a further extension to the lounge in the social club at an estimated cost of £4,000. Fences surrounding the ground were replaced with walls. Also in 1976, the boundary wall alongside Worcester Street was built, and four years later a wall was built round the car park by D R Moore, with £7,500 coming from the social club and £1,500 from the County Council. With these expenditures, and others such as a tour to America and improvements to the playing surface, not to mention the underlying problem of inflation, the Club made a loss in 1977 of £6,785, so entry

The scoreboard erected on the Tump in 1978 by J F Hopson at a cost of £2,144; Messrs Whitbread Flowers Ltd were charged £500 per annum for the advertising space at the top [John Davis]

Lavery (Cheltenham), and A J Turton (Cheltenham) for the English side. Scotland's effort was hampered by the loss of their captain, and England scored three goals to a dropped goal to make the final margin of victory 15-3.

These sides met again on 1st April 1970, the crowd of 7,000 at Kingsholm was boosted by the inclusion as England full-back of Mike Redding, who played fly-half for his club, Gloucester All Blues, and full-back for his school, Sir Thomas Rich's. They were enthralled by a sparkling game played under floodlights on a chilly evening. Snow resumed falling soon after the start, but both teams showed a real determination to play handling rugby. With the wind behind them in the second half, England turned round Scotland's 5-3 advantage at half-time to run out 13-5 winners.

Kingsholm was then treated to a series of encounters between England and Wales at under-19 level. On 29th March 1972, a crowd of 10,000 found much to applaud in a methodical and skilful performance by an England side which recorded only its second win in seven encounters at this level against the Welsh with a comfortable 16-0 victory. Despite a sunny day, only 5,000 turned up for the next match between these sides two years later on 6th April 1974, when Wales gained their revenge in an ill-tempered, disappointing game 15-9. The tables turned again on 13th April 1976, when a penalty goal by Marcus Rose settled the issue in England's favour, although this solitary score hardly did justice to a fast and keenly contested game.

Ireland's first visit to Kingsholm for an under-19 international on 6th April 1977 attracted a crowd of about 6,000. An England side, full of confidence from a 26-19 victory over Wales the previous week, made a shaky start and were perhaps fortunate to be 11-7 ahead at half-time, but their powerful pack took control in the second half and they ran out convincing winners 37-7.

Later that year, on 7th December 1977, the Australia Schools (19 Group) tourists visited Kingsholm to take on the South West Schools side which contained two Gloucester representatives, Baker and Calver. Despite persistent rain, the young Australians stuck to their slick passing and fast running game and scored six tries against four penalties as they ran up a 28-12 score line.

The next 19-Group match at Kingsholm on 4th April 1978 saw England take on Scotland. In a game which was marred by two serious injuries, England came out of the blocks faster and scored three tries to lead 12-3 at half-time, but seemed to lose their ambition in the second half, managing to score only one further try in winning 16-3.

On 23rd January 1995 the Australian Under-18 side came to Kingsholm for the last game of their tour, not only unbeaten on this tour but also undefeated by a European side for more than twenty years. The England Schools side rose to the occasion and coped with the wet and windy conditions better to record a memorable 30-3 victory.

Coppers at Kingsholm

FOR MORE THAN a hundred years, there was a police presence at Kingsholm on match days, with the Club responsible for paying for those on duty inside the ground. For example, the police submitted a bill for £15 for their presence at the 1900 international match at Kingsholm, and £6 4s 4d when New Zealand visited in 1905, the Gloucestershire Constabulary provided 30 policemen for 3 hours. The largest police presence at Kingsholm came in 1970, when the visit of the South Africans provoked a large anti-apartheid demonstration. Police and demonstrators descended on Kingsholm from far and wide, but the presence of 690 police allowed the match to go ahead. This match aside, the police attendance on match days steadily reduced over the years, but only ceased after the game went professional and the Club took sole control of security on the ground.

The bill for policing the 1900 international... [Gloucester Rugby]

...and for the All Blacks game in 1905 [Gloucester Rugby]

Over the years many a policemen has played for Gloucester, the most eminent being (position / appearances for Gloucester):

David Ainge (back/98)
Sid Dangerfield (back/136), captain of County & British Police
Ron Etheridge (back/184)
John Fidler (second row/286), captain of British Police
Jerry Herniman (number 8/46)
Richard Jardine (centre/313)
David Jones (second row/49)
Simon Morris (centre/111)
Cyril Thomas (hooker/357)
Alan Wadley (forward/56)
Jack Watkins (prop/157), captain of Gloucester, County & British Police

Police teams have also played at the ground, the most notable matches involving the British and English police teams. In January 1953, the British Police played the RAF at Kingsholm, and returned some twenty seasons later in September 1972 to take on Gloucester. For this encounter the Police selected Gloucester's Jerry Herniman who regularly trod the beat at Kingsholm.

Jerry Herniman, who played 46 games for Gloucester, recalls life on the other side:

> I played against Gloucester sides three times at Kingsholm. The first made little impact on me, I was playing for Bristol Colts against Gloucester and to me at that age it was just another stadium. Of course the crowd was rather sparse but I do recall rather biased comments from those that were there.
> My second ordeal at Kingsholm was when I played for the British Police. The pre-match chat was all about what an intimidating venue we were being thrown into and how physical the game would be. Come the game time, personally I found the atmosphere inspiring. The crowd were very vociferous and of course I was subjected to a good deal of good humoured banter but the hairs on the back of my neck were aroused none the less.
> My final encounter was when I was called upon at the last minute, literally ten minutes before kick off, to step in and guest for Bath. As you can imagine, even in those days Bath were subjected to a good deal of hostility and the atmosphere was terrific. I did receive an

amount of rather aggressive comments from the old lags in the crowd who thought that I had deserted and joined Bath.

Walking the beat at night I would often check Kingsholm and found the atmosphere rather ghostly when empty. However one night I heard a rather odd noise coming from the changing room area. On investigation, and suspecting something sinister, I found Ken Whitten, known to all as Ski, who was the United baggage man for many years, sound asleep and snoring loudly on the treatment couch.

Gloucester Rugby Heritage has particular cause to be pleased that Kingsholm was part of Jerry Herniman's beat. When checking the ground on another night he came across a skip into which had been thrown numerous team photographs. He rescued them and has subsequently donated many to the Gloucester Rugby Archive and has kindly allowed us to copy the rest.

Police international matches were played at Kingsholm in 1973 and 1975, when the English Police took on their Welsh counterparts. The English side included Gloucester players, Richard Jardine and John Fidler in both 1973 and 1975, and Simon Morris in 1975, but the Welsh won both encounters, 16-12 and 15-6.

In October 1989, the British Police returned to Kingsholm to play a match against Gloucester in celebration of the 150th anniversary of the Gloucestershire Constabulary. At the time the Police were particularly well represented at international level by England and Lions stars, Dean Richards, Wade Dooley and Paul Ackford, but unfortunately none of them were available for this match. The Police discovered that coming to Kingsholm under strength was not much fun as Gloucester ran in fourteen tries, with Derrick Morgan leading the way with a hat trick. The Police responded gamely with three tries of their own, but went down 15-68.

[Gloucester Rugby]   *[Gloucester Rugby]*

The Roles of Ladies at Kingsholm

JUST AS THE Great War changed perceptions and attitudes for ever as regards the roles of men in society, so the parts which women played in the Second World War changed their expectations and ambitions. This certainly applied to Miss Violet Pegler. She had a good Gloucester Club pedigree, her father, Fred Pegler, having played 239 games for the Club, 1902-13. He took his daughter to her first match at Kingsholm when she was aged 5. She became a regular spectator along with a small group of women friends, and played touch rugby whilst in the Army during World War Two. She also represented the Army at hockey. In 1948, she advertised for players to start a ladies' rugby team, sufficient numbers came forward and Sidney Dangerfield, a Gloucester player, was recruited as trainer. Violet requested assistance from the Club, and suggested that mixed games be played at Kingsholm as curtain raisers before big matches. Her proposal came before the Club committee, but did not get very far. The President of the Club, Dr Arnold Alcock, declared that he "considered it inadvisable from all points of view" and that was the end of the discussion.

By 1972, Tom Voyce was President of the Club, and he met with a group of ladies who requested permission to stage a match against the Club team at Kingsholm. Tom reported to the committee, and some members expressed disquiet, but the match was eventually agreed on the understanding that it would be touch rugby involving only light contact, and with the proviso that the Club "would not be responsible for injury or accident". The match went ahead between the players and their wives and girlfriends, and "Ladies v Players" matches were repeated several times during the mid-1970s. In 1986, Mrs Marilyn Bayliss was given permission to organise a Ladies v Entertainers match at Kingsholm in aid of hospital charities.

Although the Club paid for professional catering after matches from early in its history until well after the Second World War, the attractions of cutting costs eventually resulted in the formation of a ladies' committee to provide meals after the match on a voluntary basis. This arrangement did not always go smoothly – in 1961 the whole ladies' committee felt so put upon that they resigned en masse. However, replacements were found, and the arrangement continued, but it became increasingly difficult to recruit volunteer ladies for these duties during the early 1980s. In 1983 a washing machine was installed in the ladies toilet for players' kit. By the 1983-84 season the demand for meals had grown to the point where the ladies' committee put their feet down and would only agree to provide them for players and officials. When the demand for meals for sponsors grew, the ladies' committee again declined to take on the additional work. By the end of the 1992-93 season the ladies' committee had been disbanded, and the Club reverted to a commercial contract for all catering requirements. However, the first catering contract was awarded to Di Long, a long term stalwart of the ladies' committee and wife of a former player, because she and her team were prepared to do the job at below commercial rates.

The Gloucester-Hartpury Ladies squad [Martin Bennett]

Gloucester–Hartpury Ladies in action at Kingsholm [Martin Bennett]

During the early 1990s, the number of women playing rugby in England grew very quickly, and many rugby clubs formed women's sections. Several women's teams were formed in the Gloucester area, but none directly associated with the Gloucester Club. Student teams were the first to make the breakthrough in terms of playing competitive games of women's rugby on the hallowed turf of Kingsholm. In May 2004, Kingsholm was the venue when the University of Gloucestershire triumphed by a massive 82-17 against their Worcestershire counterparts.

But the first Gloucester Rugby women's team only appeared on the scene with the formation of Gloucester-Hartpury Ladies in 2014. They played most of their matches at Hartpury, but made history on 7th March 2015 by becoming the first women's team representing the Gloucester Club to play at Kingsholm. The match was played immediately after a Premiership game between Gloucester and Northampton and was a semi-final of the Women's Junior National Cup, in which Gloucester-Hartpury defeated Teddington Antlers 24-0.

The Eighties

Tony "Spreaders" Spreadbury (International referee):

Kingsholm was and still is one of my favourite grounds. I first refereed there, Gloucester v Stroud, back in the early 1980s and had to hold up play as I swallowed a fly! Those were the days when the sponge man ran on with a bucket of water, which was already contaminated! When the RFU took over responsibility for appointing referees, the names of the match officials were added to the match day programme, and after the name the letters RFU were added. However, when I refereed at Kingsholm they added Tony Spreadbury – Bath!

"Spreaders" performing at Kingsholm [Gloucester Rugby]

In 1980, the Ground Company still owned Kingsholm, although, with nearly all the shares in the hands of the Club, it no longer had an active role. It started that year with four vacancies on the Board, but two were filled when the Board appointed Doug Wadley and Peter Ford as Directors, and the Club then filled the remaining two by nominating Terry Tandy and Alan Brinn. The general committee of the Club had by now grown to an unwieldy 29 members, and it was therefore left to the more select development sub-committee to generate sources of revenue, mainly for building and refurbishment.

In 1980, this sub-committee decided to make more use of the space under the main grandstand, and John Horner, a building surveyor who had played on the wing for the Club, was invited to produce designs. He had previously produced plans for squash courts and changing rooms under the main stand, which had been shelved for want of funding. His new plans to provide facilities under the main stand linked to a refurbished social club, included changing rooms, medical room, ground equipment store, toilets, lounge bar, committee and players' bar, dining room, kitchen, office and committee room. These plans were put to the committee and met with approval. As ever, funding was a problem – the cost was estimated at £150,000, and the Club had only £20,000, so the plans could not be implemented straight away. Nevertheless, planning permission and a low interest loan were sought, and the development sub-committee looked into the possibilities for sponsorship, debentures, brewery loans, lotteries and a manpower scheme for building.

Confidence was slightly dented when a loss of £11,228 was reported for the 1980-81 season, but this proved to be just a blip. Gate receipts were down that season because all of the John Player Cup matches had been played away, and there was significant expenditure on a brick wall built to provide a more substantial boundary around the ground. Meanwhile the Social Club was prospering, making a profit of £9,610 in 1980-81.

In general the years from 1981 were lucrative for the Club, each season producing a healthy balance sheet, culminating in a profit in the 1985-86 season of £33,478, a record for the Club. As this era of relative prosperity emerged, it allowed priorities to change, so that letting of thee ground in the summer was no longer regarded as essential to balance the books. Indeed in 1981 all such requests were refused in order to allow work on the pitch to proceed uninterrupted between seasons.

John Watkins (389 appearances for Gloucester, 1969-83, who captained the Club to victory in the John Player Cup in 1978 and is a member of a very select group of players who have won with England in both New Zealand and South Africa):

Kingsholm was the place. You always loved it. Saturday or Wednesday night was brilliant. You'd get down there and you knew there was going to be seven or eight thousand, which was a good crowd then. That was the place to be, I think, Kingsholm.

Contributing to the finances were representative matches hosted by Gloucester. The early 1980s saw several international sides visit Kingsholm. In October 1980, the stands were sold out for the visit of Zimbabwe to play the County, and gate receipts amounted to £2,680-20; Gloucestershire won the match 21-12.

Australia played the South and South West Division on a freezing cold Tuesday evening at Kingsholm in December 1981. Indeed the kick-off was brought forward because the Arctic conditions threatened to make the pitch ever less playable as the game wore on. Nevertheless the tourists drew a crowd of 11,000, who paid £6,189-00 for the privilege. A collection for charity was also taken and raised £419, which was equally divided between the local Salvation Army and the Penlee Lifeboat Appeal.

By the end of the match the surface was rock hard and there were plenty of walking wounded, bruised by the ground as much as the opposition. Australia won 16-3. After the game the players were entertained with a reception at the Gloucester Guildhall, where the

Australians commented that they were used to playing on hard grounds at home, but not on a skating rink.

The County side were seen more than usual at Kingsholm during the 1980-81 season, thanks to their long run in the County Championship. In November 1980 they clinched the South West group with a comfortable 18-3 victory over Somerset at Kingsholm, and returned a week later for the quarter-final against Buckinghamshire, which was won 19-0. Having defeated Warwickshire 3-0 at Bristol in the semi-final, Gloucestershire decided to return to Kingsholm for the final. Initially they were rebuffed, Gloucester giving priority to their fixture against Bridgend, but eventually the Club was persuaded to cancel this. On a foggy day it was just about possible to see a crowd of 10,000, who paid £4,244-20 at the gates. They were shocked when Northumberland scored two tries in the last five minutes to turn a 3-6 deficit into a 15-6 victory. They celebrated this success in their centenary year with their "Blaydon Races" anthem ringing around Kingsholm.

The Club match against Moseley on 4 December 1982 was televised, which brought in additional revenue and was regarded a sufficiently special event as to warrant a new set of jerseys to be supplied by Bukta Ltd and a marching band to be engaged to perform beforehand. Gloucester won the match, 15-13, with tries from Richard Mogg and Nick Price.

Phil Blakeway (139 appearances for Gloucester, 1971-85, and England international) said:

How can you not enjoy playing in that atmosphere down there at Kingsholm. It was a great place to play and a great privilege. It was a great feeling to walk outside when you'd won. When you lost, you just wanted to sit in that changing room and not come out. But it meant so much to the people in the area. I remember Colin Smart saying, when he played for Newport "everybody else used to hate coming to Kingsholm" he said "absolutely hated it because everybody there hated us, the ball boys hated us, the crowd hated us. We knew we were in for a real ***** afternoon."

Of course Gloucester players had similar feelings about playing on many of the grounds set in the valleys of South Wales, where the supporters were equally hostile, it always seemed to rain and any promising move was soon brought to a halt by a sharp whistle blown by a referee who had walked to the ground.

Season ticket prices and entry charges were increased almost every season. For example, the 1982-83 season saw ticket prices set at £25 for patrons, £15 for the grandstand wings, and £12 for ground entry. Charges at the gates on match days were £2 for the centre stand, £1.50 for the wings, £1.20 for ground entry, and 50p for the car park, with half price for OAPs and Juniors. Despite these increased prices, membership was growing. Revenues from advertising, both on hoardings around the

ground and in the match-day programmes, were also going up, local firms were persuaded to sponsor home fixtures, and deals were done with kit manufacturers. The success of the team on the field in both cup and merit table competitions made the Club a more attractive proposition for all those providing these sources of funding.

By this time the social club had been refurbished externally with wooden cladding, and it was decided to make some internal changes by doing away with the skittle alley and converting that space into additional bar area and cellar. Mickey Booth, the Club coach, requested that lights be installed on the back of the stand so that the players could train in the car park when the pitch was too wet, and these were installed during the summer of 1982, when 100 seats in the grandstand were also replaced at a cost of £13 per seat.

It was estimated that some £140,000 would be required to put amended plans for development under the main stand into effect. The Club were in the fortunate position of being able to choose between offers from two brewers, Bass and Whitbread, and decided to accept a loan of £90,000 from Bass at 6% per annum (in 1984, this rate of interest was reduced to

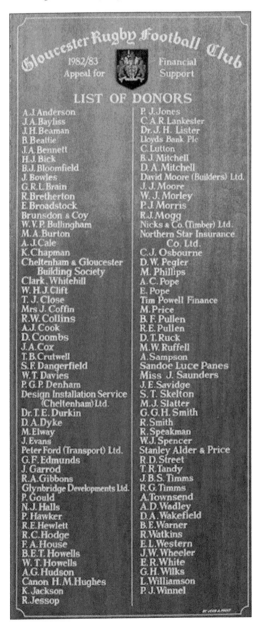

The Board listing Donors to the Appeal Fund, which is still on display in the entrance to the Lions' Den [Malc King]

2%). It helped that the Club returned a profit of £15,783 for the year ended 31 May 1983, and the social club made a profit of £5,762. The Club also appealed to individuals and companies to make interest-free loans of £250 and £600 respectively. These went into an Appeal Fund, which had raised over £15,000 by June 1983. Initially it was decided not to publish the names of those members who had loaned money, but when the Fund was closed at the end of 1983, a board was put up at Kingsholm recording the generosity of those members who had contributed and listing their names.

All these factors allowed the redevelopment of the main grandstand on the south side of the ground to go ahead. John Horner drew up yet another set of revised plans and a tender for this work was accepted for £121,000. A ticket office was built on the eastern end of the clubhouse closest to Worcester Street. The existing social club was rebuilt and refurbished, so that it still housed a bar extension, a cool room and beer store where the skittle alley had been, but the lounge bar was extended further and a new lobby and ladies toilet were added.

John Horner (50 appearances for Gloucester, 1969-74, and designer of many of the buildings at Kingsholm):

I played for Gloucester from the late 1960's to early 70's and I now travel to Kingsholm as a season ticket holder. I still get butterflies in my stomach at the top of Estcourt Road after all this time, such is the power of this special ground.

There was a new build to connect the social club with the main stand and a suite of rooms under the main stand. The facilities provided here were a function and dining room, a tea room, a kitchen, another beer store, a committee and players bar, a committee room, home and away changing rooms, and small rooms for the referee and doctor. Many of the Club's honours boards were removed from the old gymnasium and used as suspended ceiling panels in the committee and players bar (they would later be restored to their former home in what is now the Lions' Den). Under the western end of the stand was still room for the groundsman's store, and at the back of the stand was a men's urinal, which, for the sake of propriety was later fitted with western-style saloon swing doors.

It took a while at the start of the 1983-84 season for the Kingsholm faithful in the Shed to get used to their heroes appearing from the other side of the pitch rather than running out down the steps under the clock on the old gymnasium. A special match against Cardiff was organised to celebrate the opening of the new facilities on 21 September 1983, but Cardiff did most of the celebrating on the field with a 26-10 victory.

The clubs of Gloucestershire competed in a knockout competition, and County Cup Finals were often played at Kingsholm even after Gloucester had ceased to enter the competition. Although having a deserved reputation as being very hard fought if somewhat dour games, better suited for the afficionado rather than the casual spectator, they attracted large numbers of partisan supporters. For example, the 1983 final, in which Berry Hill beat Lydney 9-6, attracted a crowd of more than 6,000, a record for such a match, with gate receipts of £4,675·30. Two years later, Kingsholm once more hosted the final, which Berry Hill again won, 10-9 against Coney Hill, and gate takings were £4,536·70. These amounts of entrance money comfortably exceeded those taken at divisional and county games around that time.

Kingsholm figures even more prominently in the history of the clubs closer to home in and around Gloucester. The relationship between the 'City' club and the profusion of other rugby clubs in the district

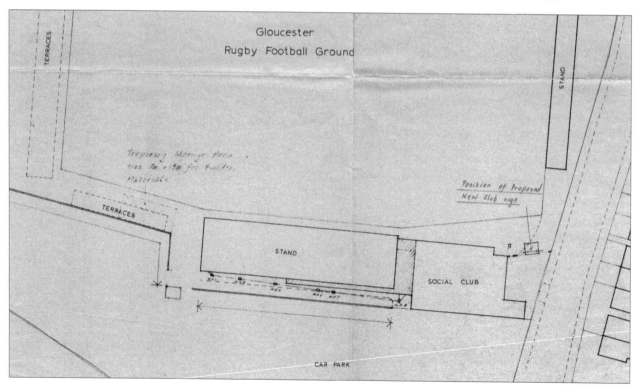

The site plan showing the extension to the social club in 1983 [John Horner]

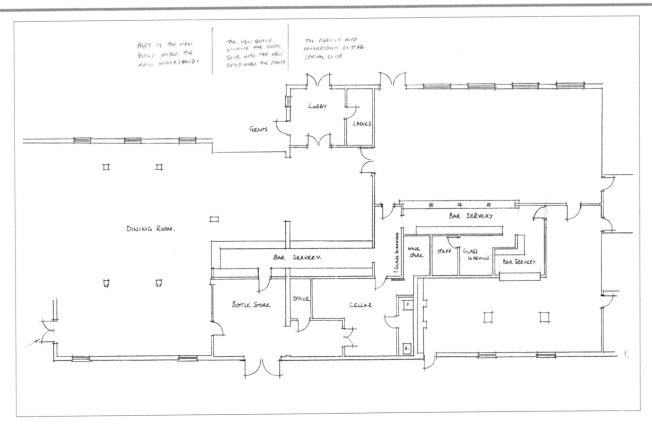

PART OF THE NEW BUILD UNDER THE MAIN GRANDSTAND.

THE NEW BUILD LINKING THE SOCIAL CLUB WITH THE NEW BUILD UNDER THE STAND

THE REBUILT AND REFURBISHED EXISTING SOCIAL CLUB

LOBBY

GENTS

LADIES

DINING ROOM.

BAR SERVERY

BAR SERVERY.

GLASS WASHING

WINE STORE

STAFF

GLASS WASHING

BAR SERVERY

BOTTLE STORE

OFFICE

CELLAR

A plan of part of the 1983 development [John Horner]

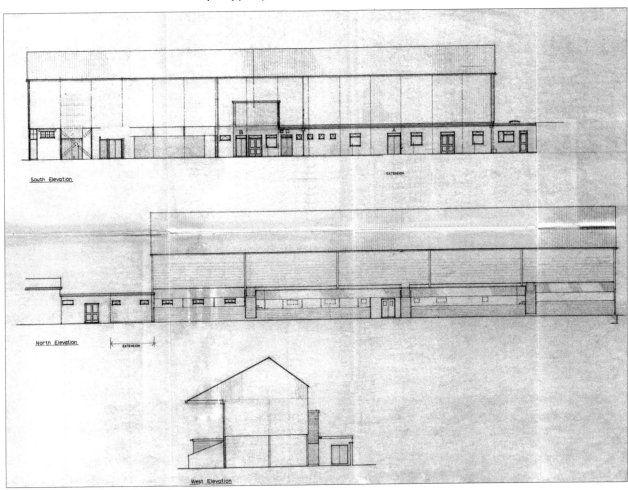

South Elevation

B

A

EXTENSION

North Elevation

EXTENSION

West Elevation

Front and rear elevations of the social club build in 1983 [John Horner]

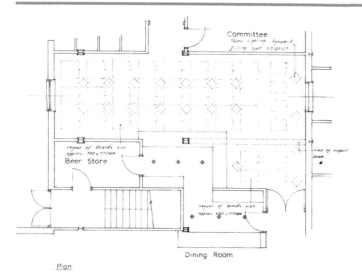

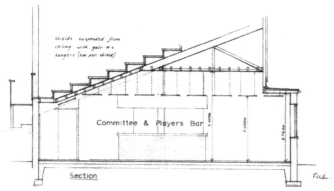

The plans for another part of the new build completed in 1983 under the main stand, showing the committee and players bar with a ceiling of suspended honours boards [John Horner]

has been an integral part of the success of rugby in Gloucester. The Gloucester Club has never run more than two senior teams, relying upon the availability of players from other clubs to make up numbers when necessary. The Club accepted that it had a responsibility and an interest in fostering and supporting rugby in the local clubs, and encouraged the formation of the North Gloucestershire Combination, which has acted as the umbrella organisation for local clubs for more than a century. The proud history of the Combination has recently been recorded in Martin Slatter's excellent book "Pride of the West". There were inevitably tensions when local clubs 'lost' players to Gloucester, especially when this occurred at very short notice, but overall these arrangements were mutually beneficial and were codified in a series of formal agreements.

Kingsholm has always been the mecca for the rugby mad citizens of Gloucester and the ambition of every player in the district has been to play on the hallowed turf. They could achieve this in a number of ways. Throughout the amateur era, any player could take himself and his boots along to Kingsholm at the start of each season to participate in trial matches. Many a star-studded playing career took off in this way, and whilst others might not have made the grade, they had tried and were able to treasure the memory of running out at Kingsholm. Matches were also played between the Club's second XV, Gloucester United, and a team representing the North Gloucestershire Combination. And Kingsholm has long been made available for the finals of the Combination cup competitions, which has allowed players to perform at Kingsholm playing for their own clubs.

These finals are well attended and continue to be held at Kingsholm to the present day. The centenary season of the Combination

culminated in the three cup finals being played at Kingsholm on the same day, 6th May 2012, with the Senior Combination Cup being won by Old Centralians, the Junior Cup and the Glanville Cup for third teams being won by Coney Hill. Of course the centenary dinner of the Combination was also held at Kingsholm, described by Martin Slatter as "the spiritual home of the city's smaller clubs", with Willie John McBride and Mike Burton as the main speakers.

In 1983-84, the format of the County Championship was changed and Gloucestershire appeared in Division One. Having defeated Surrey and Northumberland away, Gloucestershire came home to Kingsholm for the match which would decide the division. They duly defeated Yorkshire 23-6, and returned a fortnight later to take on Middlesex in the semi-final. The crowd was certainly up for this match and the Citizen declared that "the County's adherent and partisan devotees gave Kingsholm the cup tie atmosphere which visiting supporters secretly admire and outwardly loath". Middlesex built a 12-0 lead, but then the fervour and intensity of the home pack set Kingsholm alight. John Fidler and Malcolm Preedy were reckoned to have run further with ball in hand than the whole three-quarter line, and it was just enough to eke out a win by 13-12. Finals were now played at Twickenham, but many of the Kingsholm faithful were there in a crowd of 26,000, which saw Gloucestershire defeat Somerset 36-18.

In 1981, a Club shop had been mooted for Kingsholm, but was not thought possible until a responsible member could be found to run it. By June 1982, that person had been identified in David Foyle, and the Club committee granted approval in principle, but it still proved difficult to achieve. By September 1984, Allan Townsend had taken over the search for a suitable site, and finally a year later the shop opened, run by Nick Price, assisted by players, and for the first season it was agreed that all profits should go into the fund for the end-of-season tour.

In 1984, Auckland came to Kingsholm to play Gloucester, but the ground was shrouded in thick fog. Officials suggested that the game be called off, but Auckland would have none of it and Gloucester were happy to play too. Auckland were reported to have won, but accounts of the match are extremely sparse because almost nothing could be seen by those on the sidelines.

The Auckland President later explained their insistence on playing:

What you probably don't realise is that this is one of the four or five most famous purely rugby grounds in the world. When we announced the tour itinerary to the players, and told them they were coming to Kingsholm, they all stood up and cheered.

Dave "Spanner" Spencer (113 appearances for Gloucester and now organiser of the Cherry Pickers, the team of former Gloucester players who relive their glory days in matches to raise money for charity) played in the game and remembers it well more than thirty years later:

We all got on with it and kept playing, along with the entire crowd, who stayed put right to the end, cheering on all evening, in their own special way, their beloved "invisible" Cherry and Whites. This one match stood out and epitomised to me how important Kingsholm was not only to the players but also of course the fanatical and inspiring Gloucester supporters.

In January 1985, international rugby returned to Kingsholm, when Romania played the South and South West, who won 15-3. The muddy conditions on a Tuesday evening helped to level the gulf in ability between the teams, and the final score failed to reflect the one-sided nature of the match. Although the referee earned a lot of credit for doing his best to allow play to flow, the game was not much of a spectacle for the 7,000 spectators, but £9,667 was taken on the gates.

By 1985, the Club was felt to be in fairly good shape financially, although there was still £53,932 outstanding on the loan from Bass. This debt constrained the Club to minor projects such as the erection of boards over the turnstiles to advertise future matches, which were installed by Signet Signs at a cost of £1,928. In 1986, the Youth Opportunities scheme allowed the fence around the perimeter of the playing area to be replaced, with the Club paying £2,000 for materials, but the manpower coming free. The fence on the northern, St Marks Street, side of the ground was also replaced, and a container installed behind the Worcester Street stand to house the groundsman's tractor, thus allowing a new scrummaging machine to be stored in the garage under the grandstand. This container remained in place until 2005, when it had to be removed to make way for the new Worcester Street stand. Also in 1986, John Horner was engaged again to renovate the social club.

New and unforeseen demands for redevelopment of the ground were now looming as a result of changes in the legislation covering sports grounds. In 1985, a fire destroyed the wooden grandstand at Valley Parade, the home of Bradford City FC, with the loss of 56 lives, and many more injured. The Gloucester Fire Officer soon arrived to inspect Kingsholm and recommended some work, which was put in hand for the start of the next season. The Bradford tragedy was investigated by the Popplewell Inquiry, which led to the Safety of Sports Grounds Act (1986). This legislation placed new responsibilities on sports grounds across the country, but had particular pertinence for grounds with wooden stands, such as Kingsholm.

In August 1986, the Club applied to the local authority for a safety certificate in accordance with this Act, but this was refused, and the County Council wrote a report to explain their position. In November 1986, the police, fire service and building inspectors and legal departments of the County Council were all represented at a meeting at Kingsholm, and were unanimous in telling the Club that all the recommendations in the report had to be implemented in full. This meant that a substantial amount of work was required at Kingsholm before a safety certificate could be issued.

Although the Club briefly flirted with the notion of restricting attendances at Kingsholm to below 10,000, which might have allowed them to opt out of the requirements of the Act, this idea was soon discarded, and an architect and structural engineer were employed to draw up the necessary plans. A sub-committee was formed of Terry Tandy, Gordon Hudson, Reg Collins and Peter Ford with full powers to act on these issues for the Club. By March 1987 a plan for alterations to the grandstand was in place, and in June the committee toured the ground with John Fidler, who was carrying out the necessary work. John was a second row who had made 286 appearances for Gloucester, 1972-84, as well as winning representative honours with Gloucestershire and England.

The social club after the 1986 renovations [John Horner]

Arthur Russell, reporter for the Citizen:

It has been said that nowhere in the world, including New Zealand and Wales, is there any town or city which can provide greater enthusiasm for our great game of rugby than the Gloucester crowd of fanatical supporters. Many may dispute this, but the fact remains that Kingsholm followers know what they want; the mediocre will not suffice.

Following another disaster at a football stadium in 1989, when 95 Liverpool FC supporters died at Hillsborough, Sheffield, further requirements to improve safety were imposed on sports grounds. Compliance with these recommendations and the Safety of Sports Grounds legislation, was an expensive but essential requirement. For Kingsholm to comply, the Club initially estimated that it would cost about £200,000, with an additional £20,000 having to be found for improved maintenance procedures. However, this proved to be a huge under-estimate, and in 1993 the money actually spent on Kingsholm to meet the requirements of the Ground Safety Regulations was calculated to have been in excess of £600,000.

The first effect of these regulations at Kingsholm was that "The Tump" was no longer deemed safe, and it was roped off to prevent spectator access. A proposal for a new build at that western end of the ground first emerged in 1987, but it took three years to put the finance in place and to complete the construction.

Meanwhile, the difficulty of finding committee members willing and able to manage the growing commercial activities of the Club resulted in a contract being let in 1988 with a sports management company, Sport in Business, to run the Club's sponsorship and advertising activities for three years.

When the major clubs withdrew from the County Championship in 1985, Gloucestershire and Kent proposed a Divisional Championship, and this was put in place by the RFU for the 1985-86 season. Gloucester supported it by agreeing to release their players and were immediately rewarded by being selected to host one of the first Divisional fixtures at Kingsholm. This was between the South West and the Midlands on 14th December 1985. Although played on a Saturday, the match excited little interest, and the small crowd soon turned to jeering the poor efforts of the South West team, although the selection of ten Bath players doubtless served to heighten their scorn. The Midlands won 19-9. Only £3,425·75 was taken on the gates. But if this was thought to be a poor return, the next Divisional match scheduled for Kingsholm in 1987 turned out even worse. The ground was frozen and the game was switched to Torquay, which proved to be a financial disaster for the South West, since it was their only home game of the 1987-88 season, and a paltry £1,700 was taken on the gate from 800 spectators.

In December 1988, the South West defeated London 20-13 at Kingsholm, but only 4,623 spectators turned up, with gates receipts coming to £9,297·92. The Divisional Championship continued to struggle to generate much enthusiasm amongst supporters, as Kingsholm hosted further matches in 1990 and 1991, when the counter-attraction of World Cup rugby on the television was blamed for a paltry 102 spectators attending. Further matches were staged at Kingsholm in 1992 and 1993, before yet another sparse crowd saw the South West lose 11-16 to the Midlands on 25th November 1995 in what was to be the last Divisional game at Kingsholm before an unloved competition was put out of its misery.

David Frost, chief rugby correspondent for the Guardian, wrote:

For those of us who have to travel a long way to get to Gloucester Rugby there is something of a distant fortress about Kingsholm. It is no use coming to Kingsholm expecting to find the sophistication of the metropolis. It is no use imagining that you will see passing for passing's sake. You must accept Gloucester Rugby on Kingsholm's uncompromising terms. If you can do this, a visit to Kingsholm can be a rich and rewarding experience. It can be a reminder to those of us from other parts that the truths of the game remain unchanged; that hard, forward play, for instance, is still the surest basis for victory; that no game is worth playing unless you do your utmost to try to win it. Perhaps, then, the image of the fortress is no bad thing. It is as well that the truths of the game, together with so much else of value that makes up the heritage of Gloucester Rugby, should be held in such safe keeping.

The Final Years of Amateur Rugby at Kingsholm

IN NOVEMBER 1989, Guilor Petch Design Partnership drew up plans for a new build on the Tump. This included fourteen hospitality boxes with concrete terracing below and in front, at an estimated cost of £409,694·94. The Club again looked to Bass for funding, and a supplementary agreement was announced in January 1990. This consisted of a loan of £200,000, interest-free, for ten years, a sponsorship package of £10,000 for the remainder of the 1989-90 season, and one of £25,000 for each of the following three seasons. John Fidler Construction Ltd was again selected as the contractor for the building work. The hospitality boxes were completed for a final cost of £462,960·70, and the new facilities were opened at the start of the 1990-91 season. The first two companies to occupy boxes were Norville Optical and the Original Holloway Society, both long established Gloucester institutions.

By this time the contract with Sport in Business was expiring, and thought was given to employing a commercial manager in-house to run this part of the business. But in the event it was decided to combine the sponsorship and advertising responsibilities with the letting of the hospitality boxes and in April 1991 this was all contracted out. The company selected was Mike Burton (Sports Management) Limited. Mike

The standing terrace below the hospitality boxes [John Horner]

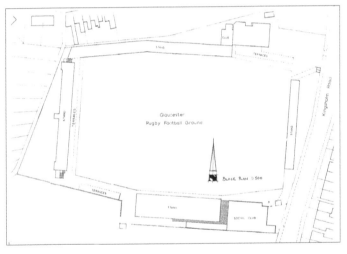

Plan showing the siting of the first hospitality boxes built on the Tump in 1990 [John Horner]

The initial construction of hospitality boxes at the Deans Walk end [John Horner]

The first hospitality box at Kingsholm was let to the Norville Optical Company. From left: Terry Hopson, former Gloucester player who was then employed by Norville Optical; Frank Norville, Chairman of Norville Optical; and Peter Ford, Chairman of the Gloucester Club [Gloucester Rugby]

was a Gloucester legend, who had made 365 appearances for the Club, 1964-81, and had also earned representative honours with Gloucestershire, England and the British Lions. However, he wrote a book soon after he stopped playing, for which he was paid, and, under the old amateur regulations, that made him a professional and had therefore precluded him from any involvement with the Club for many years.

Mike enjoyed an early success under his new contract by persuading Tewkesbury Press to sponsor the final match of the season against Harlequins to the tune of £4,000, a Club record for match sponsorship. As regards the hospitality boxes, to start with local firms rented a box for the season, but they were then offered a discount for the next five years if they paid up front. Many accepted these terms and the boxes were largely funded in this way. Long term loyalty to the cause has been proven by some of the companies who first occupied boxes on the Tump, since they remain in them to this day.

When the contract with Mike Burton's company ran out in 1994, it was renewed for a further season, but by 1995 his businesses were proving so successful across the sporting world, that he no longer had sufficient time to devote to the Gloucester Club and he relinquished the contract, recommending that the Club appoint a full-time commercial manager. Over this period, the profits of the Club had almost doubled from £65,021 for the 1992-93 season to £125,785 for 1994-95.

The need for the Club to respond to the fast pace of change which was underway in Rugby Union had been expressed in an article in the Citizen in July 1991, entitled "Kingsholm Need for Paid Management". In it the Club Treasurer, Doug Wadley, was quoted as saying

Rugby in its modern form needs real professionalism on the commercial and managerial as well as the playing side. If we want to stay in the top flight of clubs we need to consider a paid administration and executive. We have already built Club offices and will be appointing a part-time clerical assistant. We also constantly hear of players moving club for better incentives so we are committed to a major tour this year which will cost around £40-50,000, and we are looking at a medical scheme for the players which will cost approximately £15,000. In addition we have ongoing ground safety programmes.

With costs rising steeply, the Club put up admission prices for the 1990-91 season – by 35% for standing on the terraces, which was way above the rate of inflation. For 1991-92, the Club Committee felt they had to recommend a further increase of 50%, but this proposal met with a hostile reaction from the membership, and was thrown out at the Club's Annual General Meeting.

Peter West saw many games at Kingsholm across more than fifty years following the Second World War, often as commentator and

starting with the County Championship final against Lancashire in 1947. Interviewed in 1991, he enthused:

To come down to Kingsholm, to find it a temple to rugby, with the passion and the fervour, and the knowledge of the crowd, albeit a bit prejudiced – they like to see Gloucester win and I don't blame them - it was a revelation. The great thing about Gloucester Rugby is that it is THE game in Gloucester. Gloucester have always had this tremendous support and they are a very knowledgeable crowd. I love going to Kingsholm – I think it's magic – it's a great atmosphere.

In 1991, in celebration of the centenary of rugby at Kingsholm, both England and Ireland played warm-up games against Gloucester as preparation for their forthcoming participation in the Rugby World Cup. On 14th September 1991, Mike Teague was given the honour of leading the England side out, which meant that the Kingsholm crowd of 8,200 probably gave their warmest reception ever to a visiting team. Gloucester gave a good account of themselves, but they were outgunned to the tune of 4-34. Fred Howard, a distinguished referee, enjoyed one of his many good games in this match, but, like every referee before and after him, he sometimes failed to meet with the approval of the Kingsholm faithful. On one occasion he gave a stream of decisions against Gloucester, with which the inhabitants of the Shed failed to concur, and when he went over to the touchline for a line-out on that side of the ground, a voice boomed out "Fred Howard! – Pah! – More like xxxxxxx Frankie Howerd!" Fred loved it and dined out on this story for many a year thereafter.

A week later, a virtually full-strength Ireland side, with only two first-choice players left out, but labelled as the Irish President's XV, came to Kingsholm and were defeated 13-14. Gloucester produced one of their

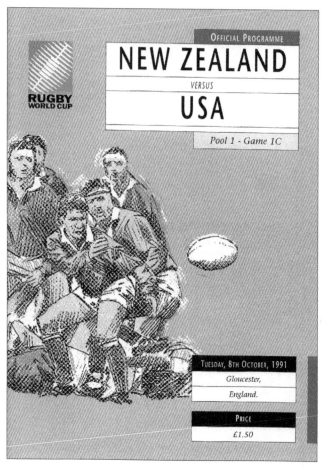

[John Theyers]

best ever performances to comprehensively outplay their distinguished opponents. They were confident and ferocious, whereas Ireland became increasingly desperate as their attacks broke down against Gloucester's mean defence. The only disappointment for Gloucester was that they squandered several clear scoring opportunities, which would have allowed the score to reflect their superiority more accurately.

When the Rugby World Cup proper got underway, Kingsholm was proud to host a pool game, especially since it involved the mighty All Blacks against the US Eagles. A capacity crowd of 12,000, with supporters from around the world, made for a festive occasion. Eagles centre, Mark Williams, claimed that this was 11, 995 more than they were used to. He had previously found Kingsholm an intimidating place to play when he lost there with both Middlesex and Wasps, but he was now delighted to find the Kingsholm crowd rooting for the underdogs. The All Blacks may have won 46-6, but it was the Eagles captain, Kevin Swords who was named as man of the match.

Chris White, international referee:

I think it's the dream of every referee in Britain to referee a Gloucester game at Kingsholm. All the top referees love coming there. And they think if they can have a good game at Kingsholm then they've made it.

In 1993 the Club was still running two senior XVs, as it had for most of its existence, but there was also now a Colts XV and an Under-21 XV. Additional space was needed for training and for pitches for these junior teams. A ground was leased at the local Oxstalls Community School, and £40,000 was spent on renovating it and installing floodlights.

Just before Christmas in December 1993, a storm hit Kingsholm and brought down one of the floodlight pylons. The other pylons which had been installed in 1967 were judged to be in a poor state of repair, so it was decided to replace them all as a matter of urgency. A contract was placed with Gloucestershire Building Consultancy, who had recently installed the floodlights at Oxstalls, and a new set was put in place at a cost of £65,000 within six weeks. They were first used for the match against Pontypool on 4th February 1994. The new lights were reputed to be the best at any rugby ground in Great Britain. They were designed to be operated at half power much of the time, this producing sufficient illumination for most matches, but they were turned up to full power when a match was being televised. There were also options for fewer lights to be turned on for training nights.

When the original sponsorship deal ran out in 1993, a new deal was agreed with Bass, consisting of a sponsorship package worth £40,000 per season, and an extension of the interest-free loan by a further £56,000. Although the game was not openly professional at this time, players were being paid, and a number left Gloucester when offered more money by other clubs. Despite these pressures, the Club committee remained

committed to trying to develop the Kingsholm ground, and indeed during 1992 an extension to the grandstand of 325 square metres, which included new metal walls and roof, was being planned by Guilor Petch for an estimated cost of £280,000. By 1993 the cost of this work, which would have increased the 1330 seated capacity of the grandstand by a further 700, had increased to £400,000 and this appears to have rendered it unaffordable.

New Zealand returned to Kingsholm in November 1993 to play against a side labelled as England Emerging Players, which was coached by Keith Richardson of Gloucester. As usual, the All Blacks came and saw and conquered to the tune of 30-19, watched by a crowd of 10,500.

Keith Richardson (281 appearances for Gloucester, 1968-78) said of his own playing experiences on the ground:

Kingsholm was just the greatest place to play rugby. It was far better than anywhere else. But then, there weren't big crowds everywhere, but Gloucester used to get them, and they were totally biased. They didn't want anything else in the way of entertainment but a Gloucester win. We ran the Cherry Pickers rugger golf charity day for blind golfers, and the first time, one of the blind golfers, the Chairman I think, is from Gloucester and he's a Cherry and White supporter. And he told this lovely story of how he started supporting rugby and he lost the sight in one eye. But he went in the Shed and he suddenly found that he was with three thousand others just the same.

In July 1994, an application was made to the Foundation for Sports and the Arts for a grant of £150,000 towards enhanced and new facilities estimated to cost a total of £895,000. It was proposed that this should take the form of a three storey extension to the main grandstand, including seating for an additional 2,400 spectators, improved changing rooms, a new medical treatment room, a fitness training room, a social/function room, improved catering and bar facilities, new meeting, committee and conference spaces and designated areas for press and TV. The bid was supported by Club accounts which showed assets valued at £637K and an annual profit of £83K. Designs were drawn up by Gloucestershire Building Consultancy and the aim was to complete the build in 1995-96.

By October 1994, the estimates had increased and funding was being sought from a number of sources including a grant from the Sports Council. However, these plans were overtaken by events, including growing expenditure on players as the game lurched from being an amateur to being a professional sport, and came to nothing.

During the early 1990s, the financial pressures had been growing as the Club committee tried to balance their traditional emphasis on using any available funding for ground development against the need to spend more money on players. Some help appeared when a contract was signed with Sky for games to be televised; £110,000 was allocated for distribution by the RFU to the senior clubs, but there were strings attached restricting

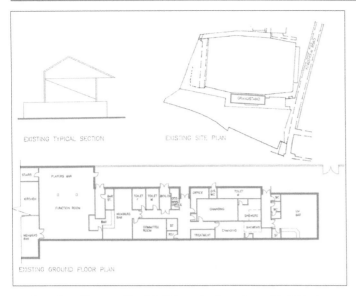

A floor plan of the ground level facilities under the main stand in 1994, above which it was planned to build another three storeys [Gloucester Rugby]

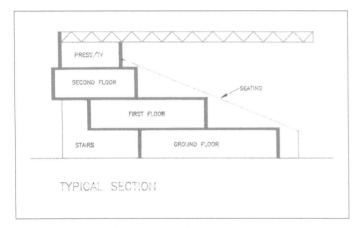

The side elevation of the build planned in 1994, which never came to fruition [Gloucester Rugby]

its use to ground improvements. Although it was evident that many clubs were paying their players, this was not done openly, and the Rugby Football Union insisted that it was not allowed whenever they were asked. However, it became increasingly apparent that the RFU was not being consulted, as many clubs quickly learned not to ask questions to which they knew they would not like the answers.

Gloucester held to the amateur line more determinedly than most. For example, they noted that some Clubs were giving sponsored cars to players, asked the RFU if this was permissible, and when told not, refused to do it. But they had to stomach players from visiting clubs driving into Kingsholm in cars emblazoned with their sponsorship. In one or two cases these were ex-Gloucester players, and the prospect of losing more players as a result was real. So, a sub-committee was set up under David Foyle to forge links with the local business community, and to look after the players by finding them jobs in the area. Dave Sims was the only player employed directly by the Club.

The committee realised that Gloucester was not ready for professional rugby, and asked the Club Secretary, Doug Wadley, to look into what they needed to do. He decided to use David Foyle's business sub-committee to undertake this task. Consultants from outside rugby, Lybrand Deloitte, were also engaged to advise on the way forward in 1993. They recommended that the Club should become a limited liability

company, which was dismissed as too radical a step at the time, although it would not be long before it became a necessity.

As late as 1995 the Gloucester committee was still uncomfortable about breaking the amateur laws and earmarked £150,000 for ground development. But this was at the risk of further diluting the playing strength and thereby threatening the first-class status of the Club. The pressure to pay players was mounting, or in the case of many other clubs to legalise the payments already being made, and the dam was about to burst.

Andy Deacon (253 appearances for Gloucester, 1987-2004) had a long career at Kingsholm straddling the amateur and professional eras. He reminisces:

I was certainly fortunate to have a long career at Gloucester Rugby with many great memories playing on Kingsholm. To choose one isolated match, incident, or try is extremely difficult. To play at Kingsholm is an experience which will be with me for the rest of my life. Waking up on the morning of the game, I had a feeling of excitement, nervousness, pride, and anticipation. I often walked to the ground, with many supporters stopping me on route to wish me luck, and have some banter. When I turned into Kingsholm Road I started to feel the atmosphere from the supporters in the bars, having a great time looking forward to the game ahead. Entering the changing rooms and meeting my fellow team mates, the camaraderie was special and I knew every player would go that little bit further for each other.
Running out on to the pitch for the warm up was the start, running along the touchline in front of the Shed was a truly amazing experience. Gloucester players have said this many times, as have the All Blacks and many capped internationals. End of warm up, going back to the changing room, was the moment I enjoyed most. A packed ground, the supporters in full voice and the kick off only moments away. Whilst playing the noise levels went up and down, supporters having banter with the opposing players and referees. Of course they can hear the banter, and some referees and players would react, which the crowd could not always see. This further encouraged the players to succeed.
Scrums down in the far corner, were great, the crowd so close, the try line even closer and the opposition trying to stop the tidal wave of power and emotion growing. Some games with 10 minutes to go and we were 20 points up, the crowd in full voice, you knew you were going to win the pressure was easing and as a player you could soak up all the atmosphere. End of the game with a win, walking around the ground taking the applause and seeing the joy of young and old, male and female was so satisfying and humbling. To be carried off shoulder high on my last game at Kingsholm was an experience that I will never forget, and remember forever. When I enter the ground now I still get excited and feel the history surrounding our ground. To be part of this, I will cherish forever.

Kingsholm gets to Grips with Professional Rugby

WHEN THE GAME went overtly professional, it happened very suddenly, and without any consultation or warning at club level. Peter Ford recalls that he first heard of the professionalisation of Rugby Union when listening to the radio on a Sunday evening. It was reported that a meeting in Paris had taken the momentous decision, with the International Rugby Football Board declaring on 27th August 1995 that "rugby would become an open game and there will be no prohibition on payment or the provision of other material benefit to any person involved in the game". The Gloucester Club committee spent the next week desperately trying to find out what it meant for the Club, but answers were hard to come by.

These were worrying times, and there were considerable differences of opinion within the Club, as elsewhere, as to how desirable a professional game would prove to be. There was much speculation, but little informed opinion, as to what changes would be necessary, and the RFU proved to be no help in clarifying the situation. Consultation with other clubs such as Leicester and Harlequins proved more fruitful, and Gloucester turned to their business committee chaired by David Foyle to recommend how to handle the new circumstances of the Club, as everyone tried to grope their way forward. Some breathing space was provided by the RFU imposing a one-year moratorium in England, before the first season of fully professional rugby in 1996-97.

The Club appointed a Chief Executive, Mike Coley, who proposed an ambitious development of Kingsholm. This would include a new grandstand, estimated to cost £2.5 million, thereby increasing the ground capacity to 18,500 all seated. In the event, priority was given to the retention and recruitment of players in order to enhance the Club's prospects of staying in the top tier of English rugby. The advent of player contracts soon ate into the Club's financial reserves, and with the accounts heading into the red, only relatively minor development projects at Kingsholm could be undertaken. In 1996, after generations of inconvenience for spectators, new toilets were installed behind the Shed at a cost of £20,933.

The advent of professional rugby demanded changes in the organisational structure of the Club, involving a transition from a members' club to a limited company. This caused the Gloucester Football and Athletic Ground Company Ltd to assume an importance which it had not had for very many years. Originally set up to buy the Kingsholm ground, it was responsible for the development and maintenance of the ground, and charged the Gloucester Rugby Football Club rent to play there. However, the intention of the founders and Board of the Company had always been for the Club to assume ownership of the ground. This was achieved by the Club buying up almost all of the shares in the Company during the first third of the twentieth century; these shares were held by Trustees on behalf of the Club. Thereafter, although still holding a very brief AGM each year, the Company had ceased to pay a dividend, and had effectively ceased to trade. The Club had assumed responsibility for development and maintenance of the ground, and was no longer required to pay rent. So, the position in 1996 was that the Company still owned the land at Kingsholm, but was itself almost entirely owned by the Club's Trustees, whilst the Club owned outright nearly all of the assets on the ground.

Legal advice was sought, and in March 1996 solicitors Rickerby Jessop recommended that all the assets and liabilities of the Club be transferred to the Ground Company as the simplest way in which the Club could transform into a limited liability company. Investors could then be attracted to put money into a company which owned the whole of Kingsholm. On 30th April 1996, the assets owned by the Club were valued at £635,880. By mid-May 1996 all the legal and financial arrangements were in place, and the remaining members of the Board of the Ground Company – Peter Ford, Alan Brinn, Kenneth Jackson and Canon Mervyn Hughes – resigned to make way for a new Board to head the restructured company. There was no role as Chief Executive in the new organisation and Mike Coley resigned and left the Club.

An Extraordinary General Meeting of the shareholders of the Ground Company was held on 15th May. This agreed to convert the structure to a trading company, which would handle the finances and commercial enterprises of the Club, including the players' contracts, and to re-name it as Gloucester Rugby Football Club Limited. The new Memorandum and Articles of Association of GRFC Ltd were issued on the same day, followed by the Certificate of Incorporation on 28th May. These documents are shown in Appendix P.

The new Board of Directors for GRFC Ltd first met on 20th May 1996. The Board members were selected for their business and legal acumen as well as for their commitment to the Club, much as the Directors of the Ground Company had been all those years earlier in 1891. Many had previously served on the Club's development sub-committee. Those who took up the reins were:

David Foyle – owner of an auction centre and formerly partner in a firm of chartered surveyors, who had previously been membership secretary of the Club for 11 years, and as a member of the general committee had overseen the organisational and business development of the Club; he now became Chairman of GRFC Ltd;

Tim Curtis – a solicitor, responsible for media, entertainment and sports issues;

John Hall – Managing Director of Gulliver's Travels, a sports travel agency, responsible for marketing operations;

John Milner — Managing Director of Huntsman Quarries, responsible for the development of the Kingsholm ground (who later earned the nickname "W C" because his brief included responsibility for development of the toilet facilities at Kingsholm);

Doug Wadley – Club stalwart and long-time official, a retired accountant and son of a former captain of the Club, who continued as Secretary;

Mike Warner – a local businessman with car dealership franchises.

David Foyle recalls that

I first went to Kingsholm with my grandfather at the age of 8 and I have enjoyed some of my happiest memories there. It will always be very close to my heart.

His words reflect the fact that the new Board was made up of committed Gloucester Rugby supporters, but were also people who knew what it took to run a successful business. The issues needing their immediate attention were marketing, sponsorship and players' contracts. It was estimated that turnover needed to be increased ten-fold to sustain the Club in the professional era.

On 25th July 1996, the Annual General Meeting of the Gloucester Club was held with about 500 members in attendance. A resolution was put to the meeting designed to streamline the organisation of the Club by transferring the assets and liabilities of the Club into GRFC Ltd. The six-man Board of the Company would then run the business, but there would continue to be a Club committee, slashed from 26 to a much more efficient 10 members, and the Club through its Trustees would still own almost all of the shares in the Company.

It was proposed that the new organisation should take effect from 31st July 1996. Although there were concerns about the Club passing out of the day-to-day control of those who in many cases had devoted their lives to it, the Company Board and the Club Committee were convinced that there was no realistic alternative, although it was hoped that GRFC Ltd would retain the feel of a members' club. The resolution was passed by an overwhelming majority, with only two votes registered against, and the transition of Club and ground into a limited company was thereby finalised. Of the 3,150 shares in GRFC Ltd, 3,088 were held by the Club's Trustees and 62 were in the hands of minor shareholders.

The Company's six-man Board was confirmed, and the new Club Committee was voted in, with Matt Bayliss, Alan Brinn, John Fidler, Mike Nicholls and Allan Townsend elected for two years, and John Beaman, Bob Clewes, Jim Jarrett, Andy Mitchell and Eric Stephens for one. Alan Brinn was appointed as Chairman of this Committee, which was now chiefly responsible for social matters and providing representation of the views of Club officials and supporters to the Board. Foyle and Brinn worked closely together to run the Club, but both Brinn and Richard Hill, as Club Coach, reported to the Board. The Club's Trustees, holding nearly all the shares in the Company, had the right to call the Board to account, but this sanction existed more in theory than in practice.

Richard Hill gave a stirring speech at the AGM, which was loudly applauded. He claimed that the Gloucester Club was handling the transition to the professional era better than other clubs:

What we have seen is summer madness with most clubs. They have been panicking. One or two people are worried that we haven't signed these so-called superstars, but will they really want to win for Saracens, Sale or whoever? Our team spirit counts for a lot. The future is bright as long as we develop quickly. Gloucester will have as their main advantage the best team spirit in the whole of Division One.

The price of season tickets at Kingsholm rose sharply for the 1996-97 season, but it was argued that these represented better value per match. Grandstand seats were £150 (£95 in the previous season), and ground tickets £80 (£45). Juniors were half-price and seniors £110 and £60. Gate prices varied according to the opposition, with derby matches and top-rated sides such as Bath, Bristol and Wasps commanding a premium.

At this stage the first priority of the Board of GRFC Ltd was stated to be the development of the Kingsholm ground, as it had been for the Ground Company. In particular, improvements were required in catering, the baths and other commercial activities. At this time the social club was still being run independently. John Horner was again engaged to plan a refurbishment and extension of the Social Club; he presented these plans in September 1996, but there was so much uncertainty about the finances of the Club that they were not put into effect immediately.

In reality the most pressing need was to secure contracts with existing players and to enhance the playing strength. This demanded the development of a commercially orientated infrastructure in order to finance the retention and recruitment of players. On 19th August 1996, GRFC Ltd paid the first professional transfer fee for a player in the Club's history. It was reported to be about £10,000 for Craig Emmerson, a centre who was already on a one-year contract with his previous club, Morley. Tim Curtis, with his experience in the entertainment business, took responsibility for drawing up the contracts for players.

Also in August 1996, the Peter Mann Partnership and Stephen Limbrick Associates were engaged to work on planning the future of the Club, and, in April 1997, they produced an outline proposal for the development and implementation of a long-term master plan for GRFC Ltd. This encompassed the executive management team (off the field), the playing team (on the field), the physical assets such as land, buildings and infrastructure, the financial plan (investment and commercial trading activities), and the problems (car parking, etc). It asked a lot questions and proposed a brainstorming session, with Mann to act as facilitator, assisted by experts on particular facets of sports clubs, all of which was designed to help GRFC Ltd to arrive at a coherent plan for the future. However, in the event, this process was swept aside by the pace at which things developed.

The Board of GRFC Ltd recognised that two problems needed to be addressed urgently. Firstly the corporate governance of the Club was inappropriate for the new professional game, and restructuring was required to turn GRFC Ltd into a professional business. Secondly something drastic was required to bolster the finances of the Club, since the existing income streams, in which season tickets and gate money were predominant, were not generating sufficient income to pay for the expenditure necessary on contracts to retain and recruit players. A think tank of twenty local professional people, including bankers, entrepreneurs, accountants and the like, was engaged to advise on how best to address this issue.

Meanwhile the leasing of hospitality boxes was contracted out to Gullivers Chilcott Marketing, and John Hall and Gareth Chilcott turned one of these boxes into their office. Their remit was to devise a new approach to marketing, which included letting hospitality boxes and selling advertising opportunities at the ground. The growth in the hospitality business led to a temporary expansion of such facilities with the erection of a marquee behind the existing hospitality boxes on the Tump at the Deans Walk end of the ground.

The payments now being made to players were rapidly eating into the Club's financial reserves, or "Doug Wadley's War Chest" as it was known around Kingsholm. It was estimated that the Club needed an injection of about £2million of additional capital. The Board of GRFC Ltd considered three options:

- to stay as they were;
- to float the Club with a public issue of shares or debentures;
- to find a sugar daddy to buy and invest in the Club.

The first of these options was rejected because Doug Wadley's War Chest was running out, the cost of maintaining a competitive squad of professional players would only be affordable for a limited time, and an inevitable consequence would be Gloucester dropping down the rugby pecking order. The second option, which had a parallel in the issue of shares to purchase Kingsholm back in 1891, was ruled out because soundings of members and supporters indicated that the necessary levels of investment would not be forthcoming a century later. Attention therefore focused on the third option as the only way in which Gloucester might keep its place in the top flight of English rugby. In December 1996, and in conditions of the utmost secrecy, feelers were put out to try to identify a suitable investor, and preliminary negotiations then took place, which increased confidence that this way forward might provide the necessary lifeline for the Club.

On 13th March 1997, the Directors were given permission by the Club committee and the Trustees to find a substantial investor. It was recognised that a Special General Meeting of the Club's members would be needed to approve this course of action, and arrangements were put in hand to hold this the following month. Alan Brinn, Club Chairman, summarised the situation: "The Board have looked at every avenue in connection with financing and, if it is the desire of Gloucester RFC to remain in the top flight of the game, there is no other alternative". The following day, David Foyle, Board Chairman, explained:

We have had various sub-groups looking at the way in which we should finance the Club and we have come up with the very firm view that this is what we need to do. If Gloucester are going to stay in the first division and get to the top of it, the financial structure as it is is not sufficient.

On 11th April 1997, about 800 Club members packed into the Birds Eye Wall's social club for a Special General Meeting of GRFC Ltd to discuss the Board's recommendation that a new owner should be sought for the Company. David Foyle explained that the Club was expected to make a loss of about £360,000 in the current year. He estimated that this would rise to more than £1 million in the following year if Richard Hill, the Director of Coaching, were given the £1.8 million budget which he believed necessary for Gloucester to challenge for honours. Alan Brinn confirmed that he saw no alternative to bringing in an outside investor, and read a statement from Richard Hill saying: "the First Division next season will be even stronger than the current one and the only way we can stay in the league is with financial backing".

It was revealed that Foyle and Brinn were now talking exclusively to one interested party, a rugby fan, who would only be named when the deal was signed and sealed. Given the meeting's approval this would probably happen before the end of the season. It was also confirmed that this investor would buy 73% of the shares in the Club, but that there would be a condition which meant that, despite his majority shareholding, he would not be able to sell the Kingsholm ground without the permission of the Club's trustees.

Some members expressed dissent, arguing that it meant selling the Club's birthright. Mike Nicholls, the former Club captain and seen by one and all as Gloucester through and through, was asked for his opinion, and responded:

Most of you, including myself, have reservations about the way

rugby has gone, but I have no doubt that this is the way we must go. I want our Club and players to be successful. If we don't support this I can assure you we will be in the second division and then the third division maybe.

This intervention appeared to weigh heavily with many of the doubters, who were prepared to follow "Nick" through thick and thin as enthusiastically as they had seen the team doing under his leadership in seasons past.

The overwhelming majority of Club members had taken note of developments at other clubs, and realised that the resources available from a rich owner were essential for Gloucester to compete at the highest levels. The alternative was either relegation or even worse liquidation. Of course the Club's supporters did not just want their club to survive in the professional era, rather they wanted it to remain amongst the best in the land. For many it was a case of feeling that they "had to", rather than that they "wanted to", sell the Club. When it came to a vote, only one put his hand up against the proposed sale. Anne Compton, a solicitor at Rickerby's, provided legal advice at the meeting and was then entrusted with ensuring the propriety of the new arrangements. Foyle and Brinn were delighted with this outcome; Foyle was quoted as declaring "we have got everything we as directors asked for", and Brinn said "the members are behind everything we want to do; they are realistic and I am very pleased so many of them turned out".

Within a short time it was announced publicly that GRFC Ltd had secured a major outside investor although his identity was not immediately revealed (at the insistence of the new owner). Indeed speculation ran rife, and red herrings became as common as sea gulls around Kingsholm. At one stage a story caught on that a part of the car park at Kingsholm had been roped off as a landing area for Richard Branson's helicopter. Initially only David Foyle and Alan Brinn within the Club knew the true identity of the buyer.

In fact there had by now been four months of negotiations with Tom Walkinshaw, and these resulted in him buying the Club. On 18th April 1997, an Extraordinary General Meeting of GRFC Ltd increased the authorised share capital of the company from 3,150 to 11,667 ordinary £1 shares. The 8,517 new shares were then transferred to Cherry White Ltd (later renamed Try Investments Ltd), a holding company set up for this purpose by Tom Walkinshaw. In order to make his investment tax efficient, Walkinshaw paid £50,000 for these shares, with the £2.5 million he promised to the Club over the next 3 years being paid through a sponsorship agreement. Walkinshaw expressly stated that his objective was not to make money out of the Club. In fact, he would subsequently put substantially more funding into the Club than this initial commitment. At a stroke, survival of the Club was no longer an issue.

At this point, Tom Walkinshaw owned 73% of GRFC Ltd, and the Club Trustees retained a 26.5% stake, which provided a safeguard against asset stripping. At around this time the Trustees were listed as S T Day, J Jarrett, C Pope and A Townsend. The minor shareholders were left with a combined holding of 0.5% and were listed as M H Booth, A Brinn, A V Clark, R C Clark, D T Foyle, A J Hudson, A C Pope, J Simpson, N Tandy, T G B Voyce, and A D Wadley. There were also four minor shareholders thought to be deceased – F D Dane, M Durkin, I Meredith and W Newth.

On 29th April 1997 a press conference was held at Kingsholm to make public Tom Walkinshaw's ownership of the Gloucester Club and the Kingsholm ground.

Tom Walkinshaw at the press conference called to announce his ownership of GRFC Ltd; he is flanked on the right by David Foyle, Chairman of GRFC Ltd, and on the left by Alan Brinn, Chairman of the Gloucester Club [Martine Walkinshaw]

The Walkinshaw Era

Tom Walkinshaw set out his stall with a statement to supporters in the programme for the first home match in September 1997:

I make no secret of my passion for the game of rugby, and, therefore, I hope my involvement with Gloucester Rugby Club means I can make a contribution to a club with a great history. This is a game I played as a school boy and have followed ever since, and even though my playing days are over my enthusiasm hasn't dwindled. I share the pride in the club and the people of Gloucester, who see it as an important part of the community, and my hopes are that the programme of changes we are now embarking on will see an all round improvement in the club's performance and standing in the game. We want to be the best and, while aiming to be in the top four in the league, my natural desire is for us to be number one. For several years I have sat and watched the Gloucester games as a fan and shared the highs and lows with all those involved. Although my role has now changed slightly due to my closer involvement, for me the sport is still the most important factor."

The social club in April 1997 [Tony Hickey]

It was initially presumed that Tom would want to bring in his own people to run the Club, but in fact he asked the existing Board of GRFC Ltd to continue, and the Chairman of the Board, David Foyle, to act as his spokesman. However, he did fill two important posts within the Club from his own company, the TWR Group, which comprised some thirty companies world-wide, including the Arrows Formula One motor racing team. Hamish Brown, a TWR executive who had previously managed the Silverstone racing circuit, became Chief Executive of GRFC Ltd, responsible for sorting out a new administrative structure and for maximising the revenue earned from the fixed assets at Kingsholm. Peter Darnborough also came in from TWR as Finance Director. They ensured that Tom Walkinshaw had close control of the purse strings.

Developments which took place in 1997 included the installation of a temporary building for use as offices and club shop, and the two entrances to the ground from Worcester Street were rebuilt. The plans which John Horner had drawn up the previous year for refurbishment and extension of the social club were put into effect.

His brief had been to design a totally new sports bar, which would not only meet the needs of the members, but also provide a focus for the

local community and become an accessible venue for anything from a quiet pint after work to a wedding reception. John Horner's wife, Sarah, was responsible for the interior design, which included new fabrics, displays of Club memorabilia, inspirational quotes and cherry and white ceiling tiles. The Club badge was set into the floor of the main entrance from the pitch.

The main contractors were A E Construction Ltd, the work was completed in 12 weeks during the summer months of 1997, and the cost was £25,300. The social club reopened in August 1997, with new stewards in Rob and Sandra Gough, who had moved across the road from the Kingsholm Inn. Tom Walkinshaw and the Mayor of Gloucester were served the first two pints of beer to celebrate the opening.

Pete Glanville (141 appearances for Gloucester, 1991-2000) was captain of Gloucester in 1997-98 and reminisces:

I used to think back as a kid selling programmes at Kingsholm thinking "God, I wonder what it would be like to play out there". And then, what seems very quickly after thinking that, you're actually running out there in a Gloucester shirt, playing in front of the Shed

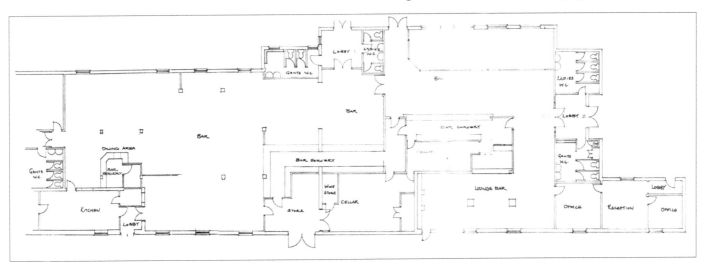

The plan for the 1997 refurbishment of the social club [John Horner]

The Club badge on the entrance floor [John Horner]

and the Kingsholm crowd. The hair stands up on the back of your neck – the atmosphere, it was so good and always so positive – electric really.

Kingsholm is a unique place where the fans are both passionate and honest. I don't have one moment that was special to me playing at Kingsholm – they were all great times! Every time I jogged in front of the famous Shed, it was always a spine-tingling experience, and if you weren't feeling quite ready for the game you would certainly be lifted after the vocal support of the Shedheads.

I remember the standing applause I used to get whenever I had to leave the field with an injury, which was quite often in my case! If the fans could see that you had given your all, they would passionately acknowledge and show their appreciation. Such memories stay with me to this day and are unforgettable."

The contractors who rebuilt the social club show where their loyalties lie [Citizen]

In the days of amateur rugby, the Gloucester Club had prided itself on being a tight-knit team drawn from the local community, Pete Glanville being a fine example. But this had to change with the advent of the professional game, and the Club was soon trawling the world for playing talent. One of the first such signings was Terry Fanolua, the Samoan centre, who would make 210 appearances for the Club, 1997-2006, and become a darling of the Shed for his whole-hearted commitment to the cause, which also led to him earning the nickname "Terry from Gloucester". The feeling was mutual, and, his playing days over, Terry has now returned to his beloved Kingsholm as a member of the Club's Community Department.

Terry Fanolua (210 appearances for Gloucester, 1997-2006) recalls:

My favourite moment was always the lap before the warm-up. Running past the Shed, hearing the roar of the Shedheads chanting "Gloucester! Gloucester!" Going absolutely crazy, the young and the old, sending chills down my spine, and the thought going through my mind was "do not let them down".

John Horner, on left, celebrates the reopening of the social club with Rob and Sandra Gough [Citizen]

The interior of the social club [John Horner]

Richard Tombs from New Zealand and Philippe Saint-Andre from France were other early signings, and in the first two seasons of the professional game, the operating costs of the Club rose from £600,000 to £3 million per annum, of which about £2.5 million financed the playing squad.

Hopes were still being nurtured for a grand design for the ground, but the immediate priority was for the provision of more hospitality boxes, since these had proved popular and offered the prospect of a better return on the investment, and more seating. Two different ideas emerged, John Horner again drew up the plans, and both were brought to fruition in 1997.

Firstly, a further set of eight hospitality suites with balconies were built under the existing fourteen boxes at the western Tump end of the ground to attract additional corporate sponsorship to the Club. This utilised some of the space used as terracing below the original boxes, which they were built to match. The catering facilities on the ground floor were extended and the police and commentary boxes were repositioned.

Secondly, at the western end of the main south stand, a permanent base was put in, on top of which a demountable stand was built providing 192 seats.

As a result of these changes the 1997-98 season kicked off with a total ground capacity of 10,800, with 1,770 seated (740 in the centre stand, 500 in the wings, 340 in hospitality boxes, and 190 in the temporary stand) and 9,030 standing places.

The temporary stand proved to be just that; it lasted for only one season. It was replaced in 1998 by an additional block of hospitality boxes three storeys high. These were rented for the season at an advantageous

rate from the Silverstone motor racing circuit, where they were only required for the summer months. At first they were indeed taken down at the end of each season and returned to Silverstone, but after a while this arrangement lapsed, and they remained in place permanently for some

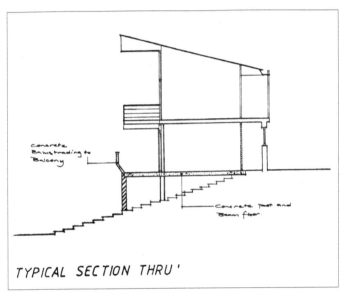

TYPICAL SECTION THRU'

The side elevation of the hospitality boxes added in 1997, showing how they fitted on top of the terracing and under the existing boxes [John Horner]

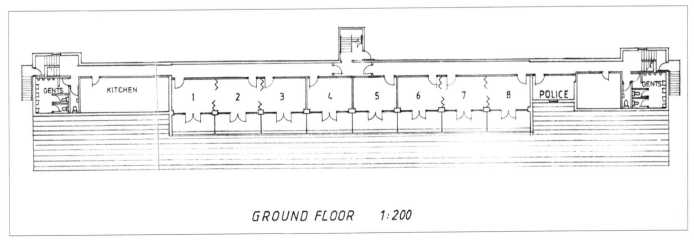

GROUND FLOOR 1:200

Image 620-9 – The plan for the layout of the additional boxes built in 1997 [John Horner]

A modern day view of the hospitality boxes on the old Tump, the top row built in 1990 and the lower storey added in 1997 [Malc King]

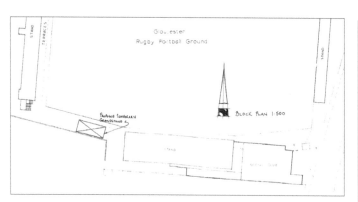

The position of the temporary stand [John Horner]

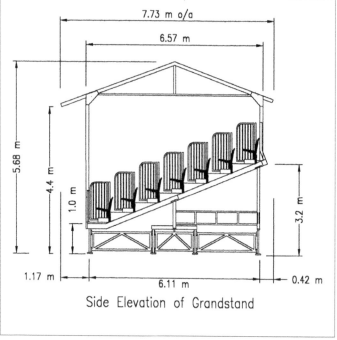

Side Elevation of Grandstand

The temporary stand installed in 1997 [John Horner]

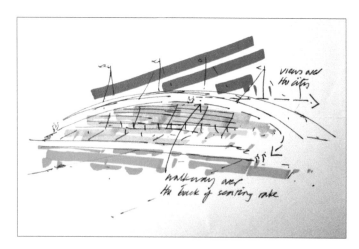

In October 1997, Arup Associates proposed this design for a new and futuristic stand at the western end of the ground, but it never got beyond the planning stage [Gloucester Rugby]

years before they were finally removed to make way for the new south stand in 2007.

Despite these short-term developments, there were concerns as to whether there was sufficient space at Kingsholm to allow a major expansion of facilities. It was assessed that the site would constrain stadium capacity to a maximum of 20,000. Therefore, in September 1998, discussions were held with the Gloucester Heritage Urban Regeneration Company about the Club moving away from Kingsholm to a purpose-built stadium on a larger site, known as the Railway Triangle, in the outskirts

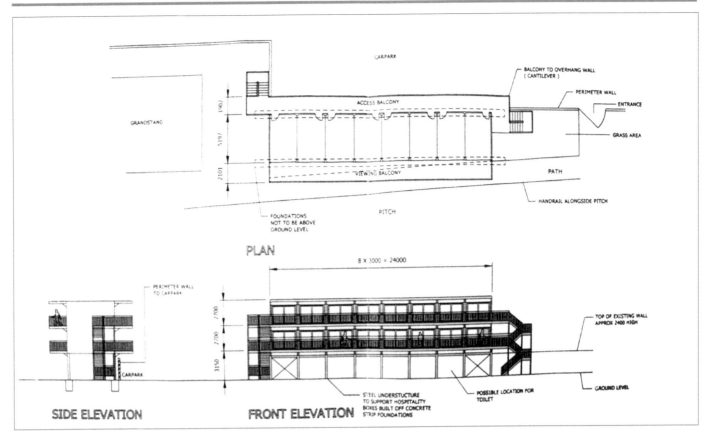

PLAN

SIDE ELEVATION FRONT ELEVATION

1998 plans for Silverstone boxes [Gloucester Rugby]

of the City. However, this would have involved ground sharing with Gloucester City FC and would have required joint funding. There were problems as regards potential flooding at the new site, and concerning the re-development of Kingsholm. Tom Walkinshaw was conscious of the heritage and atmosphere which would be cast aside in a move away from Kingsholm and he would no longer have had sole ownership of the stadium, so he killed the project before it had progressed beyond initial discussion.

One development which did go ahead in September 1998 was the installation of a big screen, 20 square metres in size, which was connected to a TV feed.

The stand which came from Silverstone to the right of the main stand [Gloucester Rugby]

Somewhat later, in June 1999, Walkinshaw brought in Ken Nottage as Chief Executive of the Club. For several years Board meetings at Kingsholm consisted of a chat between Tom and Ken, with no-one else present, an arrangement which allowed rapid and decisive decision making.

In December 1999 an agreement was forged between Tom Walkinshaw's Try Investments and the Trustees of GRFC Ltd to the effect that Try Investments would purchase the shares held by the Trustees in return for further investment in GRFC Ltd. A safeguard for the long term future of Kingsholm was included, whereby the Trustees were granted a right of first refusal in any future sale of the ground. The Trustees at this time were Sidney Thomas Day, James Spencer Jarrett and Arthur Cecil Pope, although Peter Ford was added to their number shortly afterwards. The authorised share capital of GRFC Ltd, which now consisted of 12,000 ordinary £1 shares, was increased to £812,000 by the creation of 800,000 new £1 preference shares at a meeting of the Company on 16th December 1999. The Kingsholm ground was registered at HM Land Registry as Title Number GR201673.

The six members of the Board who had been appointed on the formation of the Company in 1996 (David Foyle, Tim Curtis, John Hall, John Milner, Doug Wadley and Mike Warner) felt that this was an opportune time for a change of directors. Although Tom Walkinshaw asked them to continue, they decided to resign, and this was done quite amicably. They were able to step down in the knowledge that when they had been appointed more than three years previously the Club had been lurking near the bottom of the league, and when they left it was at the top. For a time the previous Board members continued to act as advisers to the new Managing Director, Ken Nottage, whilst he was still fairly new in the job

Thus by the start of 2000, Tom Walkinshaw was effectively the sole owner of Kingsholm, although a handful of GRFC Ltd shares remained in individual hands (as they continnue to be at the time of

The documentation referring to the 3088 shares which were being transferred from the Club Trustees and recording the new share capital of 812,000 shares [Gloucester Rugby]

writing in 2016). At the Annual General Meeting of GRFC Ltd on 6th January 2000, Hamish Brown and Ken Nottage were appointed as additional directors of the company. The following day, Tom Walkinshaw, Peter Darnborough, Hamish Brown and Alister Mitchell were named as the authorised nominees of Try Investments Ltd. The Board of GRFC Ltd now consisted of Tom Walkinshaw as Chairman, Ken Nottage as Managing Director, Hamish Brown as CEO and Peter Darnborough as Finance Director. Doug Wadley continued to act as Company Secretary. The Club Committee did not survive much longer, holding its last meeting on 4th May 2000.

The Club's training facilities at Oxstalls needed further development, and a sum of £2,930,000 was included in the 1999-2000 budget for this purpose. It would have provided a Rolls Royce training paddock plus a reserve playing pitch, and would have been part of a wider development of Oxstalls, funded jointly by Gloucester Rugby and the County Council. However, this plan foundered, and although Oxstalls continued to be used by the Club for some years, that gradually petered out as facilities were developed elsewhere. Other options included development of training facilities at Imjin Barracks, Innsworth, but this too bit the dust when the Ministry of Defence proved unwilling to commit as far into the future as the Club thought necessary.

In August 1999, a plan was put together for a Gloucester Rugby Academy at Hartpury College, which happened to have as its principal, Malcolm Wharton, a rugby man who had at one time played for Exeter. The plan was to recruit talented schoolboy and youth players at a national level onto courses at Hartpury. The College and GRFC Ltd agreed to

This photograph was taken of the Club Committee on their way into their last meeting — from left, rear: Mike Nicholls, Andy Mitchell, Allan Townsend, Alan Brinn, John Fidler, Jim Jarrett, John Beaman, Eric Stephens; front: Cecil Pope, Tom Day, Reg Collins, Doug Wadley, Bob Clewes [Tony Hickey]

work jointly to offer sponsored scholarships from local companies to cover residential fees. They also agreed to pursue RFU and Lottery funds for a regional centre of excellence, and Hartpury College committed to recruiting a top-flight coach. This was seen as an opportunity for GRFC Ltd to recruit high quality youngsters via a cost-effective route. The relationship has flourished in the years since, the Gloucester Academy based at Hartpury has become a centre of excellence, and the training facilities there for the first team squad now rank amongst the best in the country.

Phil Vickery (130 appearances for Gloucester, 1995-2006, England World Cup winner and British Lion) speaking of Kingsholm:

It's a special place; you realised you were part of a rugby club which meant something to the people of Gloucester. Having been part of that is a privilege, because it's meaningful. The big days – the really big ones and the magical evening kick-offs – the atmosphere – the tension. It's easy to keep a Gloucester crowd happy. If you go out there and you give everything you've got and you show people that you've left nothing behind. It doesn't matter that you might not be the best player in the world as long as they can see you're doing everything for the shirt.

Trevor Woodman (107 appearances for Gloucester, 1995-2004, and England World Cup Winner, who has now returned to the Club as a coach):

Just running out in front of the stadium – everyone goes on about the Shed, but you get just as much support from the other side when the old stand was here and everyone was on the terraces. You couldn't help but get excited. You still think now of when you used to do that lap before your warm-up and you go round in front of the Shed and you want to get as close as possible so you really feel that vibration

bouncing off the crowd. Gloucester is a great rugby town – I've made my home here now and I definitely see myself staying around this area - you wouldn't want to go anywhere else.

The Worcester Street stand built in 2005 [Malc King]

Whilst watching a Gloucester game at Bourgoin in France in January 2004, Tom Walkinshaw spotted a stand which he thought would be a suitably simple and cost-effective design to replace the covered terrace at the Worcester Street end of Kingsholm. It would be a substantial addition to the seating at the ground, but economical to build, being essentially scaffolding surrounded by metal cladding. As ever, he did not let the grass grow under his feet, and on the Monday morning he was out on the pitch with his Chief Executive, Ken Nottage, and groundsman, Dave Balmer, and a tape measure, working out whether it could be made to fit. The answer was yes, but it required the pitch to be moved eight metres towards the Deans Walk end, the in-goal areas to be shortened, and the groundsman's garage to be removed. All this was done and the new stand went up in 2005.

Adam Balding (45 appearances, 2004-08, captain 2005-06, who became Community Manager at Kingsholm in 2016):

Kingsholm was like a mirror with the crowd so passionate and quick to tell you when you had played well or badly. They would always back you if you had put your heart into it."

Nevertheless, demand continued to outstrip supply in terms of ground capacity, and by 2007 utilisation of the ground on match days had risen to 97%, with a whole lot of matches sold out. Tom Walkinshaw was originally keen to redevelop the whole ground up to a capacity of 20,000. His longer term ambition was for Kingsholm to become the biggest club rugby stadium in the country surpassing even Leicester. However, he was persuaded by the figures that there was not a sound business plan to

Demolition of the main stand [Douglas Gatfield]

Construction of the new grandstand underway in the summer of 2007 [Douglas Gatfield]

underpin this amount of expansion in 2007. But there was a good business case for a new grandstand incorporating a substantial increase in seating, a ticket office, staff offices, changing rooms, bars, hospitality boxes, a shop and a camera gantry.

Various plans for this to be constructed along the entire south side of the ground were drawn up. Initially these plans copied stands at many other grounds, with hospitality boxes placed at the back of the stand above and behind the main seating areas. However, Tom was not happy to fund a stand in which he and those customers paying the most for their

seats would be sitting at the back, furthest from the action on the pitch. Moving the hospitality boxes forward meant that they required support and rendered the use of a fully cantilevered roof too expensive. Pillars were required, which would obstruct the view from some seats. On the other hand the main seating could then be extended right to the back of the stand, thereby increasing overall capacity.

A compromise had to be reached between improving the position of the hospitality boxes, maximising the seating capacity and inserting

An open day was held before the start of the 2007-08 season to allow fans to see the new grandstand [Douglas Gatfield]

pillars. Initially four pillars were proposed, but the structural engineers later decided that eight were necessary, thereby doubling the number of obstructions to a clear view of the pitch from some seats. For a while this stopped the project whilst there was heated discussion about the competing priorities and cost. Tom Walkinshaw made the final decision and the result is that the hospitality boxes in the main stand are above the general seating, but placed well forward with a better view than similar facilities at many other grounds. The overall capacity was increased not only by extending the seating to the back of the stand but also by lowering the rake of the seating in the front half of the stand. This was another compromise in that it slightly worsened the view from those seats over the heads of the crowd in front, but increased the number of seats with a view unobstructed by pillars.

The architects used the half-way line on the day on which they came to measure up as the centre point for the new stand, not realising that the groundsman moves the half-way line a couple of feet either way during the season in order to spread the wear on the turf. Consequently the stand is not perfectly aligned with the pitch, but you have to look very hard to tell, and it is not far enough out to be a problem.

Whilst the new stand was being built, the opportunity was taken to instal new floodlights. The timing made sense because a new sub-station was installed to power the new stand. A set of lights, 30 metres high, in each corner of the ground replaced the previous four down each side, the new lights shedding three times more light than their predecessors.

James "Sinbad" Simpson-Daniel (250 appearances and 120 tries for Gloucester, 2000-14, and England international):

When I first looked around Kingsholm I didn't understand what the hype was all about as I had no idea of the history of Kingsholm. That didn't last long, as soon as there was a game there I immediately appreciated the noise and the atmosphere that you get with Kingsholm. Any one who has been privileged to have worn the Gloucester jersey will agree that the pre game warm up where you run as a group of players in front of the Shed is something that you will never forget, the hairs go up on the back of my neck every time I think about it. Another of the incredible Kingsholm memories I have was scoring my first try for the club against Rotherham at home. It was a forty yard run in and I remember dotting the ball down and jogging back to my position welcomed by the biggest roar I can remember. Kingsholm truly is a magical place with an incredible history.

Tom Walkinshaw

Tom was born in Scotland, the son of a farmer. He developed an interest in rugby at an early age, and attended international matches at Murrayfield. Although never losing his interest in rugby, motor racing then became his passion, and he spent many years driving competitively around the world. Whilst this was great fun, it was his talent for the design and manufacture of racing cars, and his penchant for running racing teams, which would make him a rich man. He set up his own company, Tom Walkinshaw Racing, and engineered the revival in the fortunes of Jaguar sports cars, which won the European Touring Car Championship and Le Mans. He became engineering director of the Benetton F1 team which won the 1995 championship, and set Michael Schumacher on the way to his first driver's title. He then bought his own Arrows F1 team, but this proved a huge drain on his resources, to the point where it also brought down his TWR business in 2002. Although he maintained motor racing interests around the world, this enabled him to devote much more of his time to his new love, Gloucester Rugby.

With the advent of professional rugby, Tom decided that he could again indulge his interest in the game by acquiring a club, and set Don

Tom Walkinshaw at Kingsholm with his wife, Martine, and his two sons, Sean and Ryan, who would later succeed him as Chairman of Gloucester Rugby [Martine Walkinshaw]

Macpherson, his Formula One agent, the task of finding him one. At first it seemed that Bath might be suitable, but advice from Stuart Barnes amongst others, pointed towards Gloucester, which was in danger of sinking fast for lack of money. Tom's involvement was cloaked in secrecy until the deal was done, but as soon as he was installed as the owner of the Gloucester Club in April 1997, poverty and decline were no longer in prospect at Kingsholm.

Tom surprised many people by asking the existing GRFC committee to continue, but he recognised the need to tap into their experience and knowledge of the Club. This also enabled him to stay out of the limelight, which he preferred. He was more comfortable operating behind the scenes, preferring to avoid personal publicity.

Tom, already a rugby fan, was soon infected by the heritage of the Gloucester Club and the Kingsholm ground, and developed a genuine passion for it. He liked to describe Gloucester as "a very special Club", and himself as the custodian of the Club rather than as the owner. He spoke of his role as "this is my time", recognising that the Club had a long history, and would continue long after his involvement. But he also liked to tell people that his motor racing interests were where he earned his money, and his rugby interests were where he spent his money. And indeed he eventually invested some £8 million in the Club. He proved to be a breath of fresh air at Kingsholm, bringing not only a huge injection of money, but also drive, determination and commitment.

Tom was the making of Gloucester in the professional rugby era. His deep pockets and rampant enthusiasm for the Club initially provided the means to purchase a host of rugby super-stars, even though this meant losses of £2.5 million a year. This could not last, and Tom focussed on the need to build a sustainable business model for Gloucester. He brought in Hamish Brown from Silverstone to help him achieve this objective, and then Ken Nottage from Newcastle to be his Chief Executive. He came to rely heavily upon Ken to both run the Club on a daily basis and to act as his confidant on the strategic issues. He recognised that he and other benefactors were essential to keep the Premiership clubs afloat until much larger sponsorship and television revenues could be generated, and saw the need to pull the various club owners together to negotiate a workable way forward with the RFU at Twickenham.

This came at a time when Tom had more time on his hands to devote to rugby, and he became a strong and effective chairman of Premiership Rugby, 1998-2002. This put him at the heart of the revolution then taking place in Rugby Union. It was a difficult time balancing the desire of the clubs for independence and the desire of the RFU for control. Tom's determination, love of the game and of the traditions in which he so believed at Gloucester, enabled him to drive through changes which brought order from chaos, and more substantial funding of professional rugby from the centre. These arrangements allowed professional rugby to prosper, which was a factor in the winning of the Rugby World Cup in 2003.

Tom was a visionary and a risk-taker, a racing car driver whose knee-jerk reaction was to seize the chance to win rather than be held back by worries. He was continually throwing up ideas, which had to be sifted to eliminate the impractical and to concentrate on the winners. He could be difficult to work with, since he was a hard task master, who might ring at any time of the day or night, who liked a stirring argument, and who was impatient for action to be taken as soon as a decision had been made. But he also excited, enthused and empowered those who worked for him, and believed in pushing the limits. He made things happen at Kingsholm.

Tom Walkinshaw poses with his dual interests – an Arrows car and the
Gloucester Rugby team [Gloucester Rugby]

He declared his objectives for the Club as being to win trophies
and to be financially viable. These objectives were somewhat incompatible,
given that the best teams tend to cost the most money, and that some clubs
continued to be owned by benefactors prepared to sustain huge losses,
as Tom himself did in his early years at Gloucester. He was keen to see
Kingsholm develop as a ground, but demanded that it be achieved on
the back of a sound business plan which would persuade others to lend
money, which he would then underwrite. He recognised the importance of
engaging and working with sponsors, but was not prepared to disturb the
heritage by having the ground or the team renamed after a sponsor.

Under Tom's stewardship, there were many improvements around
the ground. Initially the expansion of hospitality boxes took priority in
order to generate more revenue. Tom's first choice was to build them above
the Shed, but there was a problem about denying light to the houses in St
Marks Street, the business case was weak, and the design looked poor, so
he dropped the idea and put boxes into other parts of the ground. Then
the Worcester Street stand was built, based on a design which Tom had
seen in France, but the crowning glory was the magnificent new south
stand built in 2007. This included not only more spectator seating, but
also hospitality boxes and corporate entertaining areas, which could be
used for conferences and events during the week and the summer months.
This generated a new revenue stream which has made an important
contribution to the financial well being of the Club.

Indeed Tom's strategy as a whole met with a good deal of success,
with Kingsholm transformed into one of the very best stadia in English
rugby, a smattering of trophies in the cabinet, and an increasingly healthy
balance sheet. However, the level of expenditure on the ground and on
the team had now reached the point at which Tom felt the need to bring a
partner on board to provide a fresh impetus of capital, so in 2008 he sold a
25% stake in the Club to Martin St Quinton, and later an additional 15%
tranche.

Alastair Hignell interviewed Tom a couple of times, and
remembers that:

He had a quiet level of humour but he was fanatical about what he
wanted. I felt that he was passionate about Gloucester and he was
passionate about getting a good deal for the clubs and a good deal for
carving their way into this completely new territory that rugby had
never been into before. And I think that rugby was very well blessed
to have someone like Tom, who's come from a different sporting
environment – who knows what professionalism is about from the
money side of things if you like.

Tom's life was cut short by cancer at the age of 64 in December
2010, by which time he had earned a prominent place in the history
of Gloucester Rugby. His legacy was a Kingsholm which had been
transformed by his vision and drive, and a team which was competing
at the highest level in English rugby. A memorial service was held in
Gloucester Cathedral in February 2011.

During Prime Minister's Question time, Richard Graham, MP
for Gloucester, asked:

Last week there was a memorial service in Gloucester Cathedral for
Tom Walkinshaw, a constituent of the Prime Minister and a legend
in my city for all he did to revive Gloucester Rugby. Does the Prime
Minister agree that Tom, and many others like him who have invested
so much of their own money in our great sports, have done a lot to
increase self-belief and pride in our cities?

The picture of Tom Walkinshaw which hangs in the Kingsholm stadium
[Martine Walkinshaw]

The Prime Minister, David Cameron, MP for Witney, replied:

My Hon Friend speaks very well of someone who lived in my
constituency and invested not only in rugby, but in Formula 1, which
has been an absolutely world-beating industry for our country. We
should celebrate that, particularly in my region, where so many
people are employed in this incredibly high-tech endeavour.

Martyn Thomas, Chairman of the RFU Board, said:

Tom was always forthright and passionate and earned huge respect
because there was no doubting his commitment to his beloved club
and the game. I think the fact that we were able to reach an agreement
that delivered professionalism but which also protected the fabric of
the game we both held dear and which will safeguard its future is
to his huge credit. When the history of Rugby Union in England is
written then Tom's name will be to the fore.

In 2014, Tom was posthumously inducted into the Premiership
Rugby Hall of Fame for the exceptional contribution which he had made
to the professional game.

Ken Nottage

BORN IN CANADA, but growing up in London, Ken excelled at basketball from an early age, whilst his one game of rugby at school put him off playing the game for life. Trained as an engineer, he signed up to do an engineering degree in Newcastle, and to play basketball for Sunderland. The basketball went well, and he won the championship with Sunderland, set a record for the number of appearances in the league over the course of 19 seasons, played in Europe, and made 57 appearances for England.

The opportunity to take the first degree course offered in sports science and management seduced him away from engineering, and into a career in sport. His career flourished within the north-east sports empire which Sir John Hall set up around Newcastle United. Initially hired to run the basketball part of Newcastle Sporting Club, he soon became the Chief Executive of the whole company. Although Rob Andrew was in charge of the rugby element, Ken's wider responsibilities brought him into contact with Tom Walkinshaw.

In 1999, Tom asked Ken to meet him at Twickenham, landed his helicopter in the car park, and spent three minutes inviting him to be the Managing Director of GRFC Ltd. Tom pulled a document out of his pocket, tore off the corner and wrote some numbers on it by way of a salary offer. Tom flew off, and Ken went home with his scrap of paper to consider his future, but he was hooked, and accepted the job that evening. Tom set him the tricky objectives of both building a trophy-winning team and making the Club financially viable. Ken recognised that the winning of trophies would be the more memorable part of his job, but the financial side was the key to long term success. His early years involved a lot of frustrating negotiations with the RFU, helped only by the fact that having this common enemy served to pull together a disparate group of Premiership clubs and their owners.

As a very competitive sportsman in his own right, he brought to Kingsholm a hatred of losing which drove his desire to succeed. When Gloucester experienced their famous loss in Munster, he was determined that the Club should never again go into a match with that degree of complacency. He built a good team spirit amongst the staff at Kingsholm, developed an effective commercial model, laid the foundations for an affordable but successful team, and oversaw an extensive redevelopment of the ground.

Ken thought he would be doing the job for 5 years, and his success at Gloucester meant that he was head hunted by a variety of organisations, including other Premiership clubs. But he loved the job at Kingsholm, and working with Tom Walkinshaw. When he decided the time had finally come to move on, Tom's other businesses were in difficulty, and then Tom was struck down by his terminal illness. Ken stayed on as a result of a strong sense of loyalty to Tom and to the Club, so the expected 5 eventually stretched out to 13 years at Kingsholm.

In Ken's early years at Kingsholm the facilities were not deemed sufficient to attract representative matches, but when minimum standards for Premiership grounds were introduced, so investment had to follow and Kingsholm started to become a more attractive venue. Ken mounted a concerted campaign for the allocation of matches to Gloucester, but this was often hard going. He could not count on a warm welcome at Twickenham, where his two rugby bosses, John Hall and Tom Walkinshaw, had so often been at loggerheads with the RFU over the organisation and funding of professional rugby.

Ken Nottage [Lesley Nottage]

However, the Barbarians, with Mike Burton as their agent, came to play, as did the Combined Services and the Army, and a match in the Rugby League World Cup between New Zealand and Lebanon was also staged. The England Under-21s played both of their home matches at Gloucester in 2004, which represented another step forward in re-establishing Kingsholm as a venue for representative games.

With the construction of the two new stands in 2005 and 2007, Ken had the basis on which to lobby the RFU for Kingsholm to be allocated more international matches. It eventually paid off in terms of the rugby to be seen at Kingsholm with England Saxons and Under-20 matches coming to Gloucester. The financial returns from these matches were often paltry and the board needed to be persuaded that they were worthwhile. Indeed, when the All Blacks offered to play at Kingsholm for £250,000 plus a share of the ticket sales, a substantial loss was predicted, so the offer was declined. This decision was regretted in retrospect, and maybe the lessons of 1900 should have been relearned, when Kingsholm staged the England v Wales match and the Club made a huge loss financially, but the reputation of the ground was greatly enhanced and other big matches followed.

A major breakthrough came when Australia agreed to come to Kingsholm ahead of their autumn internationals in the northern hemisphere in November 2009. They charged a more reasonable but hardly insubstantial £190,000. Every effort was made to ensure the match was a success, including extensive hospitality for the RFU representatives who attended. Unfortunately Gloucester were put to the sword to the tune of 5-36 on the field of play, but off the pitch all went very well and the groundwork had been laid for a bid to host matches in the 2015 Rugby World Cup.

In August 2012, Ken left to become Chief Executive Officer of the Three Counties Agricultural Society, but he remained as a Board member of Gloucester Rugby for a further year in order to ensure a smooth transition to the new regime.

Ryan Walkinshaw

Following Tom Walkinshaw's death, his son, Ryan, took his place on the Board of Gloucester Rugby, representing the controlling interest of the Walkinshaw Family Trust. David McKnight, a friend of the family, was appointed Chairman for a year, before Ryan took up those reins.

comments on the terraces. Places like Ravenhill, Thomond Park, Welford Road and Kingsholm. I still remember arriving at Kingsholm with Ulster for a European game, failing to impress the Shed with my kicking warm up and then being intercepted twice during the game to concede two tries! Wearing a Gloucester shirt, Kingsholm has always inspired players but it is also somewhere opposition players want to perform, to earn respect and to silence the crowd. During my first two seasons with Gloucester there have been many highs and many disappointments but a sold out, passionate Kingsholm will always be the foundations of a successful Gloucester team.

The Board of Directors of Gloucester Rugby at the end of the 2014-15 season was:

Ryan Walkinshaw, Chairman, representing the Walkinshaw Family Trust which owned a 60% shareholding in Gloucester Rugby.

Martin St Quinton, Vice-Chairman, who owned a 40% shareholding in Gloucester Rugby.

Stephen Vaughan, Chief Executive Officer, responsible for the day-to-day running of the Club.

Ryan Walkinshaw [Martin Bennett]

In November 2014, Gloucester Rugby announced a pre-tax profit of £512,000 on a turnover of £12 million, the fourth successive year for which their accounts had been in the black. The level of support, with attendance figures second only to Leicester in the Premiership, contributed to this, but TV revenues, advertising, hospitality boxes and shirt sponsors were also important elements in this commercial success. Whilst investment in the players and coaches remained the top priority, development of the Kingsholm ground could also continue on the back of this sound financial position.

David Humphreys, appointed by Ryan Walkinshaw as Director of Rugby in 2014:

Throughout my playing career I was fortunate to play in some of the finest modern stadia throughout the world. And yet many of my clearest playing memories are from games played in smaller, traditional rugby grounds where there was no hiding place from the

David McKnight [Martin Bennett]

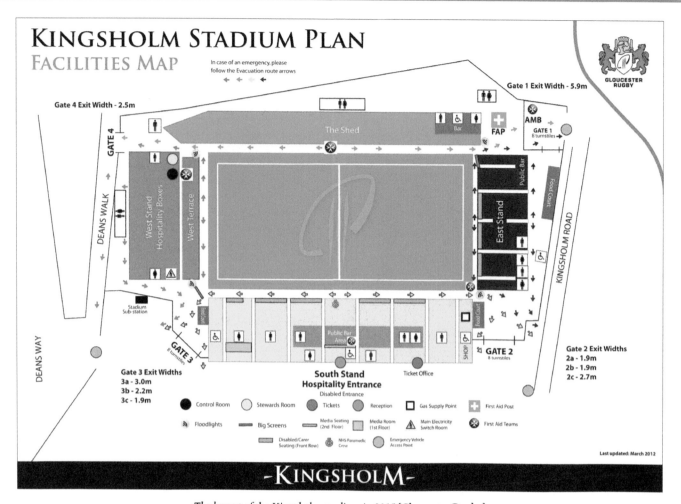

The layout of the Kingsholm stadium in 2015 [Gloucester Rugby]

The Board of Directors of Gloucester Rugby in November 2014. From left: Stephen Vaughan, John Parker, Ryan Walkinshaw, David Grainger, Martin St Quinton, Huw Morgan; inserts: Andy Hunt and Mark Fairbrother [Malc King]

| THE OPPORTUNITY

"FORTRESS" KINGSHOLM.
SITUATED IN THE CITY CENTRE OF GLOUCESTER WITH OVER 16,000 CAPACITY AND OWNED BY THE CLUB. THE GROUND HAS A TOP THREE ATTENDANCE RATE IN ENGLAND.

| PASSIONATE SUPPORT:
GLOUCESTER IS SUPPORTED BY THE RUGBY MAD AREA OF GLOUCESTERSHIRE IN THE WEST OF ENGLAND AND THE CLUB IS A MAJOR PART OF GLOUCESTER LIFE.

6. "FORTRESS" KINGSHOLM

6.1 OWNERS OF KINGSHOLM STADIUM

GLOUCESTER RUGBY OWNS ITS OWN STADIUM AND SOME SURROUNDING LAND.

This allows the club to benefit from driving non-rugby revenue, and the ability to control its own stadium development options in future. Kingsholm stadium is centrally located in the city of Gloucester and is a busy venue for conferences, meetings and other non-rugby events. Management has worked to ensure Kingsholm is a highly utilised stadium and focal point for the community.

Kingsholm's facilities include 38 Hospitality Boxes and two restaurants (55 seats and 230 seats). There are also two director's lounges that seat 24 each. In addition, Gloucester Rugby has a large business club bar and restaurant for the 1873 club. 1873 club memberships are long term deals up to 20 years in length which provide special access to member bars and entertainment facilities

on match day. 1873 memberships provide £800k in income per season. In the summer time, the Club hosts concerts for acts such as Tom Jones and Elton John.

6.2 RUGBY WORLD CUP LEGACY

During the 2015 Rugby World Cup Kingsholm stadium will host four games, more than any other club stadium in England. These games will drive continued support for Rugby in the region and will offer the opportunity to grow local audience numbers through exposure to non-traditional supporters. Further, as part of the Rugby World Cup hosting requirements Kingsholm has received RWC improvement money to fund upgrade projects across the stadium including new floodlights and other key infrastructure projects.

KINGSHOLM'S FACILITIES INCLUDE 38 HOSPITALITY BOXES AND TWO RESTAURANTS.

The front cover and sample pages from the brochure produced in 2015 to advertise the sale of Gloucester Rugby

[Martin St Quinton]

John Parker, Chief Finance Officer, a qualified accountant (since replaced by Mark Fairbrother)

David Grainger, Non-Executive Director, a farmer from West Wales and family friend of the Walkinshaws.

Huw Morgan, Non-Executive Director, formerly Marketing Director of European Rugby, CEO of Harlequins Rugby Club and CEO of British Basketball.

Andy Hunt, Non-Executive Director, formerly CEO of the British Olympic Association.

In April 2015 the Walkinshaw family decided that the time had come for them to sell their holding in Gloucester Rugby and the Club was put up for sale at an asking price of £25 million. The sale was put in the hands of Cavendish Corporate Finance, who specialise in selling companies.

Despite interest from a number of potential buyers, months went by without a sale being agreed, and in October 2015 this caused the Walkinshaw family to sound out Martin St Quinton as to whether he was still interested in taking over the Club. He was, but this triggered further negotiations for several months to sort out the details and prepare the paperwork. A deal was finally concluded in January 2016, which ended the Walkinshaw family involvement in Gloucester Rugby.

Martin St Quinton :

The Club is indebted to the Walkinshaw family for what they have done. We've all seen what happened to the big, old rugby clubs as the professional era came in. If Tom hadn't stepped in when he did to guide the Club through the early stages of the professional era, then Gloucester Rugby would not be in the position it is today. Myself included, the whole Club is indebted to the Walkinshaw family. They have done a tremendous amount and their contribution cannot be underestimated. Tom's intervention secured the foundations for a very successful professional rugby club. The fans and the City will always be grateful to Tom for guiding the Club through that period.

Stephen Vaughan

SPORT IS AN important part of Stephen Vaughan's life, and he has been active in football, rugby, and golf, as well as running half marathons and competing in tough guy competitions for charity. However, it was football which dominated in his younger days, and he became a professional player, securing a contact with Walsall FC and playing non-league football for a number of teams including Bromsgrove Rovers and Stourbridge Town.

Stephen Vaughan playing for Gloucester Rugby during the Cheltenham Cricket Festival in 2015 [Malc King]

He then joined the travel industry, working as an overseas representative and regional manager. A variety of jobs in tour operating and retail expanded his travel expertise and landed him his first appointment with Thomas Cook, where he was Managing Director of several of their specialist businesses, including Club 18-30 and the Big Events Group, before becoming Head of Sales and Commercial for part of the company.

In 2007 he had graduated in Business Studies from Loughborough University, and by 2009 he had made sufficient mark in his second career to be voted Young Business Man of the Year by the travel industry's Hall of Fame committee.

He was involved in securing the commercial and marketing rights for the London 2012 Olympic and Paralympic games for Thomas Cook, which became the largest project in the company's history. Stephen was responsible for an operation which sold tailor-made packages including 400,000 tickets, negotiated sponsorship deals with international companies, brought 15,000 children to the Games and generated £120million in revenue.

But once the Games were over, Stephen was looking for fresh employment and was appointed as CEO of Gloucester Rugby in December 2012. In this capacity he is a Gloucester Rugby board member. He also sits on the Premiership Rugby board and its finance and audit committees, and is a trustee for the Pied Piper children's charity, which has close associations with the Club. His time as CEO has seen the Club accounts stay in the black for three successive years.

Stephen Vaughan [Malc King]

Stephen Vaughan (CEO, Gloucester Rugby):

I have visited all the grounds in England and many around Europe and as yet I haven't experienced anywhere that generates the atmosphere that makes the hairs stand up like Kingsholm under the floodlights. A really special place.

Rugby World Cup 2015

Kingsholm in RWC 2015 colours [Martin Bennett]

THE POSSIBILITY OF Kingsholm being used to stage matches in the 2015 Rugby World Cup first arose in 2009 and the management of Gloucester Rugby were keen to make it happen. This led to a lot of investigatory visits to the ground by ER 2015, the body set up to organise the tournament, and negotiations soon got under way with both Gloucester Rugby and Gloucester City Council. Ken Nottage took the lead for Gloucester Rugby in the early stages, and Paul James led throughout for Gloucester City Council. Phil Vickery and Andy Deacon, amongst others, played a part in supporting the bid for Host City status. There was endless canvassing at Twickenham, which contrasted with many other Premiership clubs who were more complacent in assuming that they would stage matches and were ultimately disappointed.

There were several factors seen to be in favour of Kingsholm as a venue. It had a recent track record of hosting big matches successfully. It had a long and distinguished rugby heritage. Gloucester was a rugby city with passionate support for the game. The Club and City organising teams were judged to be capable and cooperative, and willing to contribute financially. Gloucester was in an attractive part of the country and readily accessible, and the proximity of the railway station to both the City centre and the Kingsholm stadium was convenient for visiting fans. Just before Ken Nottage left the Club in August 2012, he put on a show involving 15 of the staff at Gloucester Rugby aimed at convincing the RFU that Kingsholm would be a splendid choice. At the end of this the RFU team

assured him that things were looking good for the RWC to come to Kingsholm, but it was not yet a done deal.

Steve Vaughan took over as CEO of Gloucester Rugby towards the end of 2012 and, fresh from his involvement in the London Olympics, found that he was dealing with many of the same people. They had moved across from London 2012 to ER 2015, including Debbie Jeavons as the CEO. The negotiations now centred on commercial rights and how to meet the standards being set down by ER 2015 for participating grounds. A priority for Gloucester Rugby was to ensure that the Kingsholm experience would be as positive as possible, especially for children, in the hope that the RWC matches would encourage supporters to return for Club matches. Another key objective was to showcase Kingsholm as an impressive venue not only for big rugby matches, which would impress players, coaches and sponsors, but also for other events as a place with which performers and organisers would want to be associated.

It was announced at a press conference in May 2013 that Kingsholm had been selected as one of only two club grounds, the other being Exeter, to host matches in RWC 2015. Four matches were allocated to Kingsholm. Detailed planning got underway immediately and ER 2015 representatives were frequent visitors to Kingsholm for a couple of years before the tournament took place. Rachel Facer, a New Zealander, was appointed by ER 2015 to mastermind their arrangements at Kingsholm; she was also responsible for Manchester.

Gloucester City Council understood the economic benefits to the City of the RWC, estimated as £48M, and saw it as a once-in-a-generation chance to promote the City on a world stage. They allocated a budget of £350,000 to ensuring that locals enjoyed the tournament being in the City and that visiting fans went away with a positive impression. Adam Balding, the former Gloucester player, was appointed as RWC Event Coordinator, responsible for masterminding the detailed arrangements within the City.

There were weekly meetings, which gave rise to 54 projects covering a wide assortment of changes required at Kingsholm for the tournament. These ranged from altering the pitch size to installing new WiFi communications technology and medical facilities to putting bulbs with twice the illumination into the floodlights.

The draw for the group stages of the tournament was made three years before the event and, since it was based on world rankings at the time, resulted in Australia, Wales, England and Fiji being drawn in the same group, with disastrous results for the home nation when it was played out. However, the early draw meant that Japan knew well in advance that they were likely to play at Kingsholm. So, they decided to familiarise themselves with the ground at the earliest opportunity, and, fresh from playing Scotland at Murrayfield, they came to play Gloucester in November 2013. About 7,000 turned out to watch the match under floodlights. Against a Japanese team which was a mix of experienced internationals and up-and-coming players, Gloucester prevailed 40-5. In the event, Japan were to play two RWC matches at Kingsholm.

One of the changes required by ER 2015 to meet the standards required at all the RWC grounds was implemented early. The cherry and white posts which had graced Kingsholm for the previous 50 years were taken down before the start of the 2014-15 season. They were superseded by plain white posts, which were seen to bend much more in a stiff breeze than their spun steel predecessors, but they were not about to fall down, each being encased in a metre of concrete below ground.

When the Rugby World Cup qualifications were confirmed, two sides due to perform at Kingsholm, Tonga and USA, took the opportunity to become accustomed with the ground, and played one another at Kingsholm in November 2014. Both had the confidence of victories the previous week and they attracted a crowd of 8,949. Tonga, ranked 13th in the world were marginal favourites against the USA with a ranking of 16th, and this was borne out by Tonga's victory, 40-12.

Different policing and stewarding arrangements were implemented for the RWC games, but Gloucester's usual stewards were included in these arrangements. A host of people, known as "The Pack", were recruited to act as helpers during the tournament. There was a competitive interviewing process to select these volunteers. Although they were able to state a preference for the area in which they would prefer to work, it was not possible to allocate all of them to their first choice. On match days, many were scattered around both inside the ground and in the surrounding streets, and provided a very cheerful and helpful interaction with the visiting supporters.

A first tranche of tickets for the RWC games went on sale in the spring of 2015, and a second tranche was made available in the summer. It was quickly announced that all the matches at Kingsholm were sold out.

Just before the tournament started in September 2015, Japan and Georgia came to Kingsholm to play a final warm-up match. It was a closely fought affair and Georgia led for much of the match, but with two minutes left Japan scored a late try to secure a narrow win, 13-10.

Eddie Jones, Head Coach of Japan (but soon to be Head Coach of England):

We played at Kingsholm a few years ago and we are excited to get to play here again. It's a fantastic opportunity to walk out there again.

Kingsholm is a unique ground, a truly special place. You have the Shed on one side; people pile in there hours before kick-off, full of cider and beer, and they generate a great noise and a great atmosphere. The ground is a little bit different to what you might often be used to. The Gloucester team wear is the same as ours, so hopefully the good folk of Gloucester will be Japanese supporters. We've had a great welcome, Gloucester is always welcoming until you get on the field against them; thankfully we are not playing against them this time.

The outside of the stadium in RWC colours [Malc King]

ER2015 hired the Kingsholm stadium in its entirety for 37 days from early September to mid October 2015. The whole ground was decorated in vibrant RWC colours. Gloucester Rugby staff moved into temporary offices at Hartpury, Gloucester Quays and on the University of Gloucestershire campus. This caused considerable disruption to normal Gloucester Rugby business and cash flow, but compensation was paid for expenses and lost income, in addition to the compensation paid to all Premiership clubs for the delay to the start of their season.

However, Dave Balmer, the Stadium Manager, and his staff remained in place, although supplemented by additional manpower at times. As usual the old playing surface was removed during the summer – in 2015 this was done in mid-June before plastic ground covers were put in place for the Elton John and Madness concerts. Perennial rye grass seed was then sown across the 8,500 square metres of the playing surface, and 120 tons of a 70-30 mix of sand-soil was added as a top dressing. Slow-release fertiliser was added and the grass could almost be seen springing up – it required a first mow after only 12 days, and was then mown every day if the weather was suitable. Regular spiking and irrigation to air and water the grass roots kept them in prime condition, and additional fertiliser was applied every six weeks. The playing surface was in superb condition for the start of the tournament.

There were further changes on the ground before the tournament started. Although Gloucester Rugby funded some improvements, most were paid for by ER 2015. It was agreed that these would remain in place after the tournament if Gloucester Rugby so chose; if not, then ER 2015 would pay for restoration to the previous state; many have been retained. The Club shop was turned over to RWC merchandise with Gloucester Rugby merchandise being sold behind the Worcester Street stand.

Outside the ground, the City was polished and painted. A trail of Scrumpty mascots was put in place around the City, lamp posts were festooned with RWC banners, the streets leading to the ground were given a thorough clean, and rubbish bins were redecorated to celebrate the teams playing at Kingsholm. For supporters who had not been able to obtain tickets for the matches at Kingsholm, a fan zone was built in the Gloucester docks complete with stands and a big screen. Thousands of people took

The car park was largely filled with temporary buildings, marquees and vans. A tent accessible from Worcester Street was used as the venue accreditation centre. A two-storey tented media area was positioned in the corner of the car park; the upper area was used as a work room for the media and the lower level was used as a media lounge and for press conferences. Another tented area was used as a kitchen staffed by members of the Jockey Club and provided catering for guests, players and match officials.

Two temporary buildings were stacked on top of one another in the car park to save space, the upper one occupied by Match Management and Sports Presentation, who provided the match entertainment, and the lower one was divided into three rooms for anti-doping staff, players' medical facilities and ball boys. Two other temporary buildings in the car park were used by ITV as the host broadcaster and other rights-holding broadcasters from around the world. From here the TV coverage went all over the globe and facilities were also provided for the TMO (Television Match Official) who provided advice to the referee when an incident called for review.

Changes inside the ground included the usual local advertisements being replaced with fancy electronic panels promoting national and international companies. The size of the pitch was slightly reduced to conform with the standard adopted for RWC. Additional floodlights were installed under the roof of the main stand. The media facility at the back of the seating in the main stand was considerably expanded by taking over about a dozen rows of seats, removing the seats on alternate rows and installing white wooden desks with power and internet cabling. Two boxes were built either side of this area to allow a panoramic view of the pitch for the coaching staff of each team; these also had access to broadcast and internet feeds. A new area was built in the top corner of the main stand with access and match viewing for 11 wheelchair occupants and their carers.

The main entrance to the stadium transformed for RWC with a banner depicting the Webb Ellis trophy [Malc King]

advantage of this facility, creating their own big match atmosphere. A Wow! Rugby exhibition was put on at Gloucester City Museum, featuring rugby memorabilia and portraits of Gloucester players painted by Russell Haines, and a commemorative bench was installed in Kings Square. There was also a cultural programme with a variety of street art and musical events. These included performers associated with the teams playing at Kingsholm. So, there were Japanese drummers, Scottish pipers and a Georgian choir, which held a concert in Gloucester Cathedral.

The Shed in RWC colours [Malc King]

A TV studio was erected at the corner of the pitch by ITV. The existing gantry above the Shed was used for TV cameras, but when it was discovered that cameras in this position picked up a lot of reflection from the glass on the new coaching boxes on the opposite side of the ground, a second TV gantry was constructed above the Shed to look across at an angle which gave a clear view. A new TV gantry was also installed on top of the hospitality boxes at the Tump end.

Following the opening ceremony and the England match at Twickenham the previous evening, the second game in RWC 2015 was Tonga v Georgia at Kingsholm, played at noon on 19th September on a lovely sunny day. There was a very festive atmosphere around the ground with bands playing and "The Pack" volunteers in blue uniforms rendering cheery greetings and advice.

RWC rubbish bins [Malc King]

Tonga and Georgia parade out for the match [Malc King]

There may have been relatively few nationals present from either of the participants, but some of the Kingsholm faithful in the crowd of 14,200 had nailed their colours to one mast or the other, and even more were there just to enjoy the occasion and cheer on both teams. Certainly neither team lacked for vociferous support. Kingsholm was rocking.

It was a hard fought encounter in which Tonga started as clear favourites. They numbered in their ranks several present or former Gloucester players, including Sione Kalamafoni, player of the season at Kingsholm in 2013, Sila Puafisi and Tukulua Lokotui. However, Georgia, with superior organisation and discipline, eventually prevailed, their smothering defence making four times as many tackles as Tonga. Almost every Georgian player looked the right build to play in the front row, and those who actually did established a dominance in the scrum which the Tongans were unable to break. When Georgia substituted their entire front row after an hour, if anything they exerted even more control up front. Their commitment and determination were just what the Kingsholm crowd value most highly and they showed their appreciation. Georgia scored a try in each half, through Gorgodze, who was man of the match, and Tkhilaishvili. Vainikolo replied late on with a try for Tonga, but the Georgian defence held out for a famous victory, 17-10.

After the match, Milton Haig, head coach of Georgia said:

It was like playing in Tbilisi today. We've had a great time in Gloucester. We know what the ground's like, the atmosphere and we really enjoy playing here. We appreciate that the Gloucester people have supported us.

Next up at Kingsholm, four days later, were Scotland and Japan. Before the start of the tournament Scotland had received their official welcome to the City in Gloucester Cathedral, and Kingsholm was packed out for their first appearance in the tournament. Japan had played four days previously at Brighton, where they had scored a fantastic victory over South Africa. There were plenty of Gloucester jerseys in the crowd, which matched nicely those of the Cherry Blossoms, and many neutrals supported Japan both as the under-dogs and for their attractive and attacking style of play. However, Scotland also enjoyed vociferous support from a hefty turnout of travelling Scottish supporters, many sporting kilts. There was also plenty of local support for the Scottish captain, Greig Laidlaw, a Gloucester player, and the two Alasdairs, Dickinson and Strokosch, both former Gloucester players. The television audience for this match was 25 million; Kingsholm had been propelled onto the world stage.

The first half was a tightly contested affair, Greig Laidlaw punishing Japanese indiscretions with four penalty goals, but Japan took a brave decision to kick for touch rather than goal. The Kingsholm crowd roared their approval and loved the resulting rolling maul, which rumbled over the line with most of the Japanese team throwing themselves into the fray; 12-7 at half-time. Early in the second half, Japan narrowed the gap with a penalty, but that was as close as they got. Mafi was brought down just short of scoring a second Japanese try, but had to be carried from

Scotland and Japan line up for the national anthems [Malc King]

the field on a stretcher. The resulting penalty hit the post and stayed out, and Japan started to show the effects of their heroics against South Africa. As they tired, their ability to turn pressure into points declined, whilst Scotland became ruthlessly clinical in seizing their opportunities. Five tries ensured a 45-10 victory which seemed more comprehensive on the score board than it had on the run of play, but it meant that the latter stages of the match were accompanied by the Flower of Scotland reverberating around the ground.

On 25th September, there were 14,256 packed into Kingsholm to enjoy the clash between Argentina and Georgia, the Pumas and the Lelos, who shared a belief in the strength of their forwards, much to the delight of the Kingsholm crowd. Argentine fans seemed to be in the majority, but the many neutrals contributed to noisy support for both teams.

The match was far more of a contest than the final score of 54-9 in favour of Argentina suggests, with a fairly even first half resulting in a narrow14-9 advantage. The only try was scored by Levanini; Georgia

The Webb Ellis Trophy makes an appearance at Kingsholm [Martin Bennett]

Argentinian supporters before they got really excited [Martin Bennett]

The Cathedral View lounge area [Malc King]

The box under the roof of the main stand from which announcements are made [Malc King]

The home changing room [Malc King]

The plunge baths in the home changing room [Malc King]

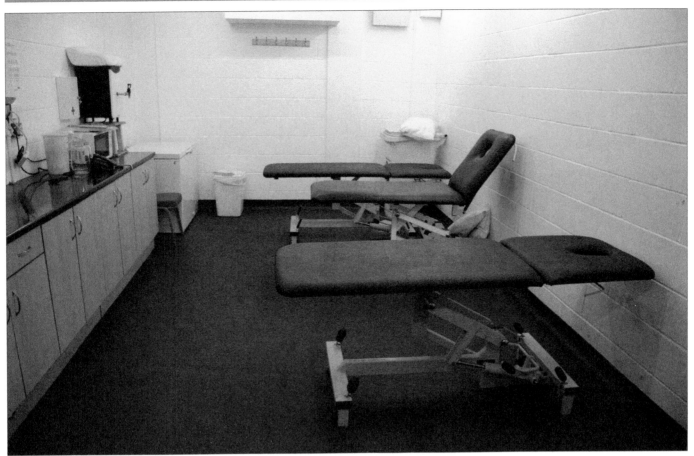

The treatment room next to the home changing room [Malc King]

The away changing room [Malc King]

The Lions' Den, built as the gymnasium in 1905 [Malc King]

The Glo'ster Boys' Bar, home of the Gloucester Players' Association [Malc King]

The honours boards and team photographs which hang in the Lions' Den [Malc King]

More memorabilia in the Lions' Den [Malc King]

𝕸𝖊𝖒𝖔𝖗𝖆𝖓𝖉𝖚𝖒 𝖔𝖋 𝕬𝖘𝖘𝖔𝖈𝖎𝖆𝖙𝖎𝖔𝖓

OF

THE GLOUCESTER FOOTBALL AND ATHLETIC GROUND COMPANY, LIMITED.

1. The name of the Company is THE GLOUCESTER FOOTBALL AND ATHLETIC GROUND COMPANY, LIMITED.

2. The Registered Office of the Company will be situate in England.

3. The objects for which the Company is established are :—

(*a*) To purchase a certain Freehold Estate of seven acres, or thereabouts, with the buildings thereon, known as Castle Grim, situate at Kingsholm, in the City of Gloucester, with a view thereto to adopt and carry into effect, with or without modification, the agreements referred to in Clause 3 of the Company's Articles of Association, and, if considered advisable, to purchase additional lands in Gloucester or the neighbourhood thereof.

(*b*) To let on lease, or otherwise, and generally render available, a portion of the said Estate to or for the use of the Gloucester Rugby Union Football Club for the purposes of Football.

(*c*) To let portions of such ground to or for the benefit of any other clubs or associations, whether for cricket, football, or other athletic sports.

(*d*) Generally to let or utilize the ground aforesaid, or any part thereof, for the purpose of athletic sports of all kinds, including cricket, football, lawn tennis, polo, bowls, curling, and cycling, and for matches and exhibitions, and for any other kind of amusement, recreation, sport or entertainment, and, if considered advisable, to promote such sports, matches, exhibitions, amusements, recreations, and entertainments, and to give and contribute towards prizes, cups, stakes, and other rewards.

(*e*) To erect and construct any grand or other stands, stables, refreshment rooms, all lavatories and other buildings and conveniences, and to make all proper and necessary approaches and roads for the purpose of so utilizing the said ground.

(*f*) To apply for and obtain licenses for the sale of refreshments and spirituous liquors to be consumed on the ground, and to supply refreshments of all kinds, whether liquid or solid ; or, if thought desirable, to let the right of selling such refreshments and liquors to such persons, for such periods and on such terms as may be thought desirable.

(*g*) As regards any of the Company's landed property for the time being to develop the same as a building estate, and to sell or lease the whole or any portions thereof in fee or for years, and either absolutely or on ground rents, or otherwise to dispose of or turn the same to account.

(*h*) To construct, erect, carry out and maintain, either by the Company or other parties, sewers, drains, roads, streets and buildings, houses, and all other works and things of any and every description whatsoever upon the lands acquired by the Company. To lend or advance money to builders or other persons upon such terms as may seem expedient. To win, work, convert and dispose of, in any manner they may think fit, any mineral properties of the Company.

(*i*) To enter into partnership or into any arrangement for sharing profits, union of interest, reciprocal concession or co-operation with any person or company carrying on or about to carry on any business which this Company is authorized to carry on, or any business or transaction capable of being conducted so as directly or indirectly to benefit this Company, and to take or otherwise acquire and hold Shares or Stock in, or securities of, and to subsidize or otherwise assist any such Company, and to sell, hold, re-issue, with or without guarantee, or otherwise deal with such Shares or securities.

(*j*) Generally to purchase, take on lease or in exchange, hire or otherwise acquire, any real or personal property, and any rights or privileges which the Company may think necessary or convenient with reference to any of these objects, and capable of being profitably dealt with in connection with any of the Company's property or rights for the time being, and in particular any land, buildings, easements, licenses, patents, machinery, ships, barges, rolling stock, plant, and stock-in-trade.

(*k*) To sell the undertaking of the Company or any part thereof for such consideration as the Company may think fit, and in particular for Shares, Debentures, or securities of any other Company having objects altogether or in part similar to those of this Company. To promote any other Company for the purpose of acquiring all or any of the property, rights and liabilities of this Company, or for any other purpose which may seem directly or indirectly calculated to benefit this Company.

(*l*) To invest and deal with the moneys of the Company not immediately required upon such securities and in such manner as may from time to time be determined.

(*m*) To obtain any Provisional Order of the Board of Trade or Act of Parliament for enabling the Company to carry any of its objects into effect or for effecting any modification of the Company's constitution.

(*n*) To raise or borrow money in such manner and on such terms as may seem expedient and in particular by the issue of Debentures or Debenture Stock, whether perpetual or otherwise, and charged or not charged upon the whole or any part of the property of the company, both present and future, including its uncalled Capital.

(*o*) To remunerate any parties for services rendered or to be rendered in placing or assisting to place, or guaranteeing the placing of any Shares in the Company's Capital, or any Debentures, Debenture Stock or other securities of the Company, or in or about the formation or promotion of the Company.

(*p*) To sell, improve, manage, develop, lease, mortgage, dispose of, turn to account or otherwise deal with all or any part of the property and rights of the Company.

(*q*) To do all such other things as are incidental or conducive to the attainment of the above objects, and so that the word "Company" in this clause shall be deemed to include any partnership or other body of persons, whether incorporated or not incorporated, and whether domiciled in the United Kingdom or elsewhere.

4. The liability of the Members is limited.

5. The Capital of the Company is £4000, divided into Shares of One Pound each. Any Shares in the original or any increased Capital may be issued with any preferential, qualified or special rights, privileges or conditions attached thereto, with full power to increase or decrease such Capital at such times, in such manner, and on such terms as the Company shall determine.

We the undersigned, whose Names and Addresses are subscribed, are desirous of being formed into a Company, in pursuance of this Memorandum of Association, and we respectively agree to take the number of Shares in the Capital of the Company set opposite to our respective names.

Names, Address and description of Subscriber	Number of Shares taken by each Subscriber.
GEORGE CUMMINGS, Spa Road, Gloucester, Maltster	Fifty.
CHARLES HENRY DANCEY, 6, Midland Road, Gloucester, Plumber	Twenty-five.
WILLIAM HENRY PHILLIPS, 81, Worcester Street, Gloucester, Painter	Nine.
ALFRED JOHN BARNES, 24, St. Aldate Street, Gloucester, Decorator	Five.
HENRY WILLIAM BENNETT, 70, London Road, Gloucester, Compositor	Five.
JAMES PHILIP MOORE, 9, Berkeley Street, Gloucester, Architect	Twenty.
HERBERT SUMNER SIMPSON, 60, Wellington Street, Gloucester, Bank Cashier ...	Ten.

Dated the 11th day of August, 1891

Witness to the above Signatures,

ARTHUR E. SHORTLAND,

Clerk to Messrs. Bretherton, Son, and Boughton,

Solicitors, Gloucester.

Articles of Association

OF

THE GLOUCESTER FOOTBALL AND ATHLETIC GROUND COMPANY, LIMITED.

PRELIMINARY.

1. In these Articles, unless there be something in the subject matter or context inconsistent therewith—

> "The Company" means THE GLOUCESTER FOOTBALL AND ATHLETIC GROUND COMPANY, LIMITED.

> "The Office" means the Registered Office for the time being of the Company.

> "The Register" means the Register of Members to be kept pursuant to Section 25 of "The Companies Act, 1862."

> "Month" means Calendar Month.

> "In Writing" means written or printed, or partly written and partly printed.

> "The Seal" means the Common Seal of the Company.

> "The Directors" means the Directors for the time being.

> "Special Resolution" and "Extraordinary Resolution" have the meaning assigned thereto respectively by "The Companies Act, 1862."

> Words importing the singular only include the plural number, and *vice versâ*.

> Words importing the masculine gender only include the feminine gender.

> Words importing persons include Corporations.

2. The regulations contained in Table A in the First Schedule to "The Companies Act, 1862," shall not apply to the Company.

3. The Company shall forthwith adopt an Agreement dated the 7th day of August, 1891, and made between Arthur Vincent Hatton of the one part and Hubert James Boughton and Arthur Williams Vears of the other part, whereby the said Arthur Vincent Hatton agrees to sell to the said Hubert James Boughton and Arthur Williams Vears about seven acres of Land, with Buildings thereon, situate at Kingsholm in the City of Gloucester. And the Company shall also adopt an Agreement, dated the 10th day of August, 1891, and made between the said Hubert James Boughton and Arthur Williams Vears of the one part and Tom Graves Smith and Sidney Stephen Starr of the other part, for letting portions of the said land to the Gloucester Rugby Union Football Club. The Directors shall carry the said Agreements into effect, with full power nevertheless from time to time to agree to any alteration or modification of the terms thereof.

4. The Directors shall not employ the funds of the Company, or any part thereof, in the purchase of Shares of the Company.

5. The business of the Company may be commenced as soon after the incorporation of the Company as the Directors in their absolute discretion shall think fit, and notwithstanding that part only of the Shares may have been taken.

6. The Shares shall be under the control of the Directors, who may allot or otherwise dispose of the same to such persons, on such terms and conditions, and either at a discount, premium or otherwise, and at such times as the Directors think fit.

7. If by the condition of allotment of any Share the whole or part of the amount thereof shall be payable by instalments, every such instalment shall when due be paid to the Company by the holder of the Share.

8. The joint holders of a Share shall be severally as well as jointly liable for the payment of all instalments and Calls due in respect of such Share.

9. In case of the death of any one or more of the joint registered holders of any Share or Stock, the survivors shall be the only persons recognised by the Company as having any title to, or interest in, such Shares or Stock.

6

CERTIFICATES.

10. Every Member shall be entitled to a Certificate under the Seal of the Company, and signed by two Directors specifying the share or shares held by him, and the amount paid up thereon.

11. If any Certificate is proved to the satisfaction of the Directors to have been worn out or defaced, or lost, or destroyed, it may be renewed on payment of one shilling, and giving such indemnity (if any) as the Directors deem adequate.

12. The Certificate of Shares registered in the names of two or more persons shall be delivered to the person first named on the register.

CALLS.

13. The Directors may from time to time make such Calls as they may think fit upon the Members in respect of all moneys unpaid on the Shares held by them, and not by the conditions of allotment thereof made payable at fixed times, and each Member shall pay the amount of every call so made on him to the person, and at the time, and at the place, appointed by the Directors. A Call may be made payable either in one sum or by two or more instalments.

14. A Call shall be deemed to have been made at the time when the resolution of the Directors authorizing such call was passed. Fourteen days notice at the least of any Call shall be given, specifying the time and place of payment, and to whom such Call shall be paid.

15. If the sum payable in respect of any Call or instalment is not paid on or before the day appointed for payment thereof, the holder for the time being of the Share in respect of which the Call shall have been made, or the instalments shall be due, shall pay interest for the same at the rate of ten per cent. per annum from the day appointed for the payment thereof to the time of the actual payment. But the Directors may, where they think fit, remit altogether or in part any sum becoming payable for interest under this clause.

16. The Directors may receive from any Member willing to advance the same, and upon such terms and conditions as they think fit, all or any parts of the moneys due upon the Shares held by such Member beyond the sums paid up or payable thereon, and, in particular, such money may be received upon the terms that interest shall be paid thereon, or on so much thereof as for the time being exceeds the amount called up.

TRANSFER AND TRANSMISSION OF SHARES OR STOCK.

17. Shares and Stock shall be transferable subject to the following provisions:—The instrument of transfer shall be signed both by the transferror and the transferee, and the transferror shall be deemed to remain a holder of the Shares or Stock until the name of the transferee is entered in the Register in respect thereof.

18. The instrument of transfer of any Shares shall be in the usual common form, or in the following form, or as near thereto as circumstances will admit:—

"I   of   in consideration
"of the sum of £   paid to me by
"of   hereinafter called the transferee, do hereby transfer
"to the transferee the Share (or Shares) numbered   standing in my name
"in the books of The Gloucester Football and Athletic Ground Company, Limited,
"to hold unto the transferee, his executors, administrators, and assigns, subject to
"the several conditions on which I held the same immediately before the execution
"hereof. And I, the transferee, do hereby agree to take the said Share (or Shares)
"subject to the same condition.
"As witness our hands the   day of   ."

19. The Directors may decline to register any transfer of Shares or Stock on which the Company has a lien, and in the case of Shares not fully paid up may refuse to register a transfer to a transferee of whom they do not approve.

20. Every instrument of transfer shall be delivered to the Company for registration accompanied by the Certificate of the Share or Stock to be transferred, and such other evidence as the Directors may require to prove the title of the transferror or his right to transfer the Shares or Stock.

21. All instruments of transfer which shall be registered shall be retained by the Company, but any instrument of transfer which the Directors may decline to register shall, on demand, be returned to the person depositing the same.

22. A fee of one shilling, or such smaller sum as the Directors may determine, may be charged for each transfer, and shall, if required by the Directors, be paid before the registration thereof. The transfer book may be closed during such time as the Directors think fit, not exceeding in the whole thirty days in each year.

23. The executors or administrators of a deceased Member (not being one of several joint holders) shall be the only persons recognized by the Company as having any title to the Shares or Stock registered in the name of such Member.

24. Any guardian of any infant Member, and any Committee of a lunatic Member, and any person becoming entitled to Shares or Stock in consequence of the death, bankruptcy or liquidation of any Member, upon producing such evidence that sustains the character in respect of which he proposes to act under this clause, or of his title, as the Directors think sufficient, may, with the consent of the Directors, which they shall be under no obligation to give, be registered himself as a Member in respect of such Shares or Stock, or, subject to the regulations as to transfer hereinbefore contained, may transfer the same to some other person. This clause is hereinafter referred to as "the transmission clause."

FORFEITURE AND LIEN.

25. If any Member fail to pay any Call or instalment on or before the day appointed for the payment of the same, the Directors may at any time thereafter during such time as the Call or instalment remains unpaid serve a notice on such Member requiring him to pay the same, together with any interest that may have accrued, and all expenses that may have been incurred by the Company by reason of such non-payment.

26. The notice shall name a day (not being less than fourteen days from the date of the notice) and a place or places on and at which such Call or instalment and such interest and expenses as aforesaid are to be paid. The notice shall also state that in the event of non-payment at or before the time and at the place appointed, the Shares in respect of which the Call was made or instalment is payable will be liable to be forfeited.

27. If the requisitions of any such notice as aforesaid are not complied with, any Shares in respect of which such notice has been given may at any time thereafter, before payment of Calls or instalments, interest and expenses due in respect thereof, be forfeited by a resolution of the Directors to that effect.

28. Any Shares so forfeited shall be deemed to be the property of the Company, and the Directors may sell, re-allot or otherwise dispose of the same in such manner as they think fit,

29. Any Member whose Shares have been forfeited shall notwithstanding be liable to pay and shall forthwith pay to the Company all Calls, instalments, interest and expenses owing upon or in respect of such Shares at the time of forfeiture, together with interest thereon from the time of forfeiture until payment at the rate of ten per cent. per annum, and the Directors shall enforce the payment of such moneys or any part thereof if they think fit, but shall not be under any obligation so to do.

30. The Directors may at any time before any Share so forfeited shall have been sold, re-allotted or otherwise disposed of, annul the forfeiture thereof upon such conditions as they think fit.

31. The Company shall have a first and paramount lien upon all the Shares and Stock registered in the name of each Member (whether solely or jointly with others) for his debts, liabilities and engagements, solely or jointly with any other person to or with the Company, whether the period for the payment, fulfilment or discharge thereof shall have actually arrived or not, and such lien shall extend to all dividends declared on such Shares or Stock.

32. For the purpose of enforcing such lien the Directors may sell the Shares or Stock subject thereto in such manner as they think fit, but no sale shall be made until such period as aforesaid shall have arrived, and until notice in writing of intention to sell shall have been served on such Member, his executors and administrators, and default shall have been made by him or them in the payment, fulfilment or discharge of such debts, liabilities or engagements, for seven days after such notice.

33. The net proceeds of any such sale shall be applied in or towards satisfaction of the debts, liabilities or engagements, and the residue (if any) paid to such Member or his executors, administrators or assigns.

34. Upon any sale in purported exercise of the powers given by clauses 28 and 32 hereof respectively, the Directors may cause the purchaser's name to be entered in the Register in respect of the Shares or Stock sold, and the purchaser shall not be bound to see to the regularity of the proceedings or the application of the purchase money, and after his name has been entered in the Register in respect of such Shares or Stock the sale shall not as against him be impeached by the former holder of the Shares or Stock or any other person, and the remedy of any Member or person aggrieved by such sale shall be in damages only against the Company exclusively.

CONVERSION OF SHARES INTO STOCK.

35. The Company (in General Meeting) may convert any paid-up Shares into Stock. When any Shares have been converted into Stock, the several holders of such Stock may thenceforth transfer their respective interests therein, or any part of such interests, in the manner and subject to the regulations hereinbefore provided. Provided always that the Directors may from time to time, if they think fit, fix the minimum amount of Stock transferable, and direct that fractions of a pound shall not be dealt with, but with power at their discretion to waive such rules in any particular case.

36. The Stock shall confer on the holders thereof respectively the same privileges and advantages for the purpose of voting at Meetings of the Company, and as regards participation in profits and for other purposes, as would have been conferred by Shares of equal amount in the Capital of the Company, but so that none of such privileges or advantages, except the participation in the dividends and profits of the Company, shall be conferred by any such aliquot part of Stock as would not if existing in Shares have conferred such privileges or advantages, but no preference or other special privileges shall be effected by any such conversion.

8

INCREASE AND REDUCTION OF CAPITAL.

37. The Company in General Meeting may from time to time increase the capital by the creation of new Shares of such amount as may be deemed expedient.

38. The new Shares shall be issued upon such terms and conditions, and with such rights and privileges annexed thereto as the General Meeting resolving upon the creation thereof shall direct, and if no direction be given as the Directors shall determine, and in particular such Shares may be issued with a preferential or a qualified right to dividends, and in the distribution of the assets of the Company, and with a special or without any right of voting.

39. The Company in General Meeting may, before the issue of any new Shares, determine that the same or any of them shall be offered in the first instance to all the then Members in proportion to the amount of capital held by them, or make any other provision as to the issue and allotments of the new Shares which they may think fit, but in default of any such determination or so far as the same shall not extend the new Shares shall be issued on the same terms as the original Shares.

40. Except so far as otherwise provided by the conditions of issue, or by these presents, any capital raised by the creation of new Shares shall be considered part of the original capital, and shall be subject to the provisions herein contained with reference to the payment of sums, calls, and instalments, transfer and transmission, forfeiture, lien, surrender, and otherwise.

41. The Company may from time to time reduce its capital in any manner permitted by law, and may consolidate or sub-divide any of its Shares, and paid-up capital may be paid off upon the footing that the amount may be called up again or otherwise.

BORROWING POWERS.

42. The Directors may from time to time at their discretion borrow from the Directors or other persons, or otherwise raise any sum or sums of money for the purposes of the Company.

43. The Directors may raise or secure the repayment of such moneys in such manner, and upon such terms and conditions in all respects, as they think fit, and in particular by the issue of Debentures of the Company charged upon the property and rights of the Company (both present and future), including the uncalled capital, or by accepting or endorsing on behalf of the Company any promissory notes or bills of exchange.

44. Every Debenture or other instrument for securing the payment of the money issued by the Company may be so framed that the moneys thereby secured shall be assignable free from any equities between the Company and the person to whom the same may be issued. Any Debenture Bonds or other instruments or securities may be issued at a discount, premium or otherwise, and with any special privileges as to redemption, surrender, drawings, allotment of Shares or otherwise.

45. The Directors shall cause a proper Register to be kept, in accordance with Section 43 of "The Companies' Act, 1862," of all mortgages and charges specifically affecting the property of the Company.

46. If any uncalled Capital of the Company is included in or charged by any mortgage or other security, the Directors may by deed under the seal authorize the person in whose favour such mortgage or security is executed, or any trustee for him, to make calls on the members in respect of such uncalled capital, and such authority may be made exercisable, either presently or contingently, and either conditionally or unconditionally, and either in exclusion of the Directors' power or otherwise, and the provisions in regard to calls hereinbefore contained shall, *mutatis mutandis*, apply to calls made or to be made on such authority, and such authority shall be assignable if expressed so to be.

GENERAL MEETINGS.

47. The first General Meeting shall be held at such time, not being more than four months after the registration of the Memorandum of the Association of the Company, and at such place as the Directors may determine.

48. Subsequent General Meetings shall be held at such time and place as may be prescribed by the Company in General Meeting, and if no other time or place is prescribed, a General Meeting shall be held in the month of May in every year at such time and place as may be determined by the Directors.

49. The General Meetings mentioned in the last preceding clause shall be called Ordinary General Meetings, all other Meetings of the Company shall be called Extraordinary General Meetings.

50. The Directors may, whenever they think fit, and they shall, upon a requisition made in writing by members holding not less than one-tenth of the nominal amount of the issued Capital, convene an Extraordinary Meeting.

51. Any such requisition shall specify the object of the Meeting required, and shall be signed by the Members making the same, and shall be deposited at the Office. It may consist of several documents in like form, each signed by one or more of the requisitionists. The Meeting, whether convened by the Directors or the requisitionists, must be convened for the purposes specified in the requisitions.

52. In case the Directors for fourteen days after such deposit shall fail to convene an Extraordinary Meeting, to be held within twenty-one days after such deposit, the requisitionists, or any other Members holding the like proportion of the Capital, may themselves convene a meeting, to be held within six weeks after such deposit.

53. Seven clear days' notice at the least, specifying the place, day, and hour of meeting, and, in case of special business, the general nature of such business, shall be given, either by advertisement or notice sent by post or otherwise served as hereinafter provided. Whenever any meeting is adjourned for fourteen days or more, at least five days' notice of the place and hour of meeting of such adjourned meeting shall be given in like manner.

54. The accidental omission to give any such notice to any of the Members shall not invalidate any resolution passed at any such Meeting.

PROCEEDINGS AT GENERAL MEETINGS.

55. The business at an Ordinary Meeting shall be to receive and consider the statement of income and expenditure, the balance sheet, the ordinary reports of the Directors and Auditors, to elect Directors and other officers in the place of those retiring by rotation or otherwise, to declare dividends, and to transact any other business which under these presents ought to be transacted at any Ordinary Meeting. All other business transacted at an Ordinary Meeting, and all business transacted at an Extraordinary Meeting, shall be deemed special.

56. Three Members personally present shall be a quorum for a General Meeting for the choice of a Chairman, the declaration of a dividend, and the adjournment of the meeting. For all other purposes the quorum for a General Meeting shall be three Members personally present, holding or representing by proxy not less than one-tenth of the nominal amount of the issued Capital of the Company. No business shall be transacted at any General Meeting unless the requisite quorum be present at the commencement of the business.

57. The Chairman of the Directors, if any, (and in his absence the Deputy-Chairman, if any) shall be entitled to take the chair at every General Meeting. If such officers have not been appointed, or if neither of them be present at a Meeting within fifteen minutes after the time appointed for holding such meeting, the Directors present, or in default the Members present, shall choose a Director as Chairman, and if no Director be present, or if all the Directors present decline to preside, then the Members present shall choose one of their number to be Chairman.

58. If within half-an-hour from the time appointed for the meeting a quorum is not present, the Meeting, if convened upon such requisition as aforesaid, shall be dissolved, but in any other case it shall stand adjourned to the same day in the next week at the same time and place, and if at such adjourned Meeting a quorum is not present, those Members who are present shall be a quorum, and may transact the business for which the meeting was called.

59. Every question submitted to a meeting shall, unless unanimously decided, be decided in the first instance by a show of hands, and in the case of an equality of votes the Chairman shall, both on show of hands and at the poll, have a casting vote in addition to the vote or votes to which he may be entitled as a Member.

60. At any General Meeting (unless a poll is demanded by at least three Members, or by a Member or Members holding or representing by proxy, or entitled to vote in respect of at least one-tenth of the nominal amount of the Capital represented at the Meeting) a declaration by the Chairman that a resolution has been carried, or carried by a particular majority, or lost, or not carried by a particular majority, and an entry to that effect in the book of the proceedings of the Company, shall be conclusive evidence of the fact without proof of the number or proportion of the votes recorded in favour of or against such resolutions.

61. If a poll is demanded as aforesaid, it shall be taken in such manner and at such time and place, and either immediately or after an interval or adjournment not exceeding seven days, as the Chairman of the Meeting directs, and the result of the poll shall be deemed to be the resolution of the Meeting at which the poll was demanded.

62. The Chairman of a General Meeting may, with the consent of the Meeting, adjourn the same from time to time and from place to place, but no business shall be transacted at any adjourned Meeting other than the business left unfinished at the Meeting from which the adjournment took place.

63. The demand of a poll shall not prevent the continuance of a Meeting for the transaction of any business other than the question on which a poll has been demanded.

64. Any poll demanded upon any question of adjournment, or as to the election of a Chairman, shall be taken at the Meeting without adjournment.

65. Every Member shall have one vote for every Share held by him.

66. Any guardian or other person entitled under the transmission clause to transfer any Shares or Stock may vote at any General Meeting in respect thereof in the same manner as if he were the registered holder of such Shares or Stock, provided that forty-eight hours at least before the time of holding the Meeting at which he proposes to vote he shall satisfy the Directors of his right to transfer such Shares or Stock, or that the Directors shall, previously to such Meeting, have admitted his right to vote thereat in respect of such Shares or Stock.

67. Where there are any joint registered holders of any Share or Stock, any one of such persons may vote at any Meeting, either personally or by proxy, in respect of such Shares or Stock as if he were solely entitled thereto : and if more than one of such joint holders be present at any Meeting personally or by proxy, that one of the said persons so present whose name stands first in the Register in respect of such Shares or Stock shall alone be entitled to vote in respect thereof.

68. Votes may be given personally or by proxy. The instrument appointing a proxy shall be in writing under the hand of the appointor, or if such appointor is a Corporation, under its common seal. No person shall be appointed a proxy who is not a Member of the Company and qualified to vote.

69. The instrument appointing a proxy shall be deposited at the Registered Office of the Company not less than twenty-four hours before the time for holding the Meeting at which the person named in such instrument proposes to vote, but no instrument appointing a Proxy shall be valid after the expiration of six months from the date of its execution.

70. A vote given in accordance with the terms of an instrument of proxy shall be valid, notwithstanding the previous death of the principal or revocation of the appointment, unless notice in writing of the death or revocation shall have been received at the office of the Company twenty-four hours at the least before the Meeting.

71. The instrument of proxy, whether for a specified Meeting or otherwise, shall, as far as the circumstances will admit, be in the form or to the effect following :—

THE GLOUCESTER FOOTBALL AND ATHLETIC GROUND COMPANY, LIMITED.

I   of   in the
  of   being a Member of the above-named Company, hereby
appoint   of
or failing him   of
failing him   of
as my proxy, to vote for me and on my behalf at the Ordinary [or Extraordinary, as the case may be] General Meeting of the Company to be held on the
day of   and at any adjournment thereof.
As witness my hand this   day of

72. No Member shall be entitled to be present or to vote on any question, either personally or by proxy, or as proxy for another Member, at any General Meeting, or upon a poll, or be reckoned in a quorum whilst any Call or other sum shall be due and payable to the Company in respect of any of the Shares of such Member.

DIRECTORS.

73. The number of Directors shall not be less than three or more than ten, but the continuing Directors may act notwithstanding any vacancies.

74. The City of Gloucester Rugby Union Football Club shall from time to time by writing, signed by the Chairman of their Committee and the majority of members of that Committee, be at liberty to nominate and appoint one Director, and at any time to remove such Director so appointed.

75. The following persons shall be the first Directors :—

1. GEORGE CUMMINGS, of Wotton, Gloucester.
2. CHARLES HENRY DANCEY, of Midland Road, Gloucester.
3. SAMUEL DAVIS, of Westgate Street, Gloucester.
4. THOMAS GURNEY, of Widden Street, Gloucester.
5. ARTHUR VINCENT HATTON, of the Northgate Brewery, Gloucester.
6. LEWIS HENRY PRIDAY, of Longford Court, near Gloucester.
7. ARTHUR WILLIAMS VEARS, of 25, Brunswick Square, Gloucester.
8. ALFRED WOODWARD, of Spa Road, Gloucester.
9. SIDNEY STEPHEN STARR, of Northgate Street. Gloucester, (Nominated on behalf of the Gloucester Football Club.)

76. The Directors shall from time to time, and at any time have power to appoint any other persons to be Directors, but so that the total number of Directors shall not at any time exceed the maximum number fixed as above.

77. As remuneration for their services the Directors shall be paid out of the funds of the Company such sum as the Company in General Meeting shall from time to time determine.

78. The qualification of a Director shall be the holding of Shares or Stock of the Company of the nominal value of £20 at the least, except that the Director from time to time holding office as the nominee of the Gloucester Football Club shall not require such qualification, provided he is a Shareholder or Stockholder in the Company to some extent.

79. The office of Director shall be vacated—

(a) If he become bankrupt, or suspend payment, or compound with his creditors.

(b) If he be found lunatic or become of unsound mind.

(c) If he absent himself from the meetings of the Directors during a period of three calendar months without special leave of absence from the Directors.

(d) If he cease to hold his qualification Shares, or do not acquire the same within three months after election or appointment.

(e) If by notice in writing to the Company he resign his office.

80. No Director or intended Director shall be disqualified by his office from contracting with the Company, either as Vendor or otherwise, nor shall any such contract, or any contract or arrangement entered into by or on behalf of the Company with any Company or partnership of, or in which any Director shall be a member or otherwise interested be avoided, nor shall any Director so contracting, or being such member or so interested, be liable to account to the Company for any profit realized by any such contract or arrangement by reason only of such Director holding that office, or of the fiduciary relation thereby established ; nevertheless, it is declared that no Director shall vote in respect of any such contract or arrangement in which he is interested, and the nature of his interest must be disclosed at the Meeting at which the contract is determined on if it then exists, and in any other case at the first Meeting of the Directors after the acquisition of his interest ; but this direction shall not apply to the agreements referred to in Clause 3 hereof, or any matters arising thereout.

ROTATION OF DIRECTORS.

81. At the Ordinary General Meeting to be held in the year 1892, and at the Ordinary General Meeting in each succeeding year, one-third of the Directors, or if their number is not a multiple of three, then the number nearest to but not exceeding one-third of the Directors, shall retire from office.

82. The Director nominated by the Gloucester Football Club shall not retire by rotation, but is removable by the Committee of the Gloucester Football Club at any time, in accordance with Clause 74.

83. The Directors to retire on each occasion shall be those who have been longest in office. As between two or more who have been in office for a like period, the Director to retire shall in default of agreement between them be selected by ballot. For the purposes of this clause the length of time a Director has been in office shall be computed from his last election or appointment. A retiring Director shall be eligible for re-election.

84. The Company at any General Meeting at which any Directors retire in manner aforesaid, or otherwise, shall fill up the vacated offices by electing a like number of persons to be Directors, unless at such Meeting it is determined to reduce the number.

85. If at any General Meeting at which an election of Directors ought to take place the places of the retiring Directors are not filled up, the retiring Directors or such of them as have not had their places filled up, shall continue in office until the Ordinary Meeting in the next year, and so on from year to year until their places are filled up, unless it shall be determined at such General Meeting to reduce the number of Directors.

86. The Company in General Meeting may from time to time increase or reduce the number of Directors and alter their qualifications, and may also determine in what manner or rotation such increased or reduced number is to go out of office.

87. The Company may by Extraordinary Resolution remove any Director before the expiration of his period of office, and if thought fit may by Ordinary Resolution appoint another person in his stead, and the person so appointed shall hold office during such time only as the Director in whose place he is appointed would have held the same if he had not been removed.

88. No person not being a Director shall, unless recommended by the Directors for election, be eligible as a Director at any general Meeting unless he, or some other member intending to propose him has, at least seven clear days before the Meeting, left at the office of the Company a notice in writing under his hand signifying his candidature for the office, or the intention of such Member to propose him.

MANAGING DIRECTOR.

89. The Directors may from time to time appoint one of their body to be Managing Director of the Company, either for a fixed term, or without any limitation as to the period for which he is to hold such office, and may, subject to any contract between him and the Company, from time to time remove or dismiss him from office, and appoint another in his place.

90. A Managing Director shall not, while he continues to hold that office, be subject to retire by rotation as hereinbefore provided, but (subject to the provisions of any contract between him and the Company and to the foregoing provisions) he shall be subject to the same provisions as to resignation and removal as the other Directors of the Company, and if he cease to hold the office of Director from any cause he shall, *ipso facto* and immediately, cease to be a Managing Director.

91. The remuneration of a Managing Director shall from time to time be fixed by the Directors, and may be by way of salary or commission or participation in profits, or by any or all of those modes, and either in addition to his share of the remuneration assigned to the Directors or otherwise.

92. The Directors may from time to time entrust to and confer upon a Managing Director for the time being such of the powers exercisable under these presents by the Directors as they may think fit, and may confer such powers for such time, and to be exercised for such objects and purposes, and upon such terms and conditions, and with such restrictions as they think expedient, and may from time to time revoke, withdraw, alter, or vary all or any of such powers.

PROCEEDINGS OF DIRECTORS.

93. The Directors may meet together for the despatch of business, adjourn and otherwise regulate their business as they think fit (but so that there shall be a Board Meeting at least twice a year), and may determine the quorum necessary for the transaction of business, and until otherwise determined, three Directors shall be a quorum. A Director may, and the Secretary at the request of any Director shall, at any time summon a Meeting of the Directors.

94. Questions arising at any Meeting of Directors shall be decided by a majority of votes, and in case of equality of votes, the Chairman shall have a second or casting vote.

95. The Directors may elect a Chairman and Deputy Chairman of their Meetings, and may determine the period for which such officers shall respectively hold office. In the absence of the Chairman (if any) the Deputy Chairman (if any) shall preside. If such officers have not been appointed, or if neither be present at the time appointed for a Meeting, the Directors present shall choose some one of their number to be Chairman of such Meeting.

96. A Meeting of Directors at which a quorum is present shall be competent to exercise all or any of the authorities, powers, and discretions by or under these presents vested in or exercisable by the Directors generally.

97. The Directors may delegate any of their powers to Committees consisting of such Member or Members of their body as they think fit. Any Committee so formed shall, in the exercise of the powers so delegated, conform to any regulations that may from time to time be imposed on it by the Directors.

98. The Meetings and proceedings of any such Committee consisting of two or more Members, shall be governed by the provisions herein contained for regulating the Meetings and proceedings of Directors, so far as the same are applicable thereto, and are not superseded by the express terms of the appointment of the Committee, or by any such regulations as aforesaid.

99. All acts done at any Meeting of the Directors, or of a Committee of Directors, or by any person acting as a Director shall, notwithstanding that it shall afterwards be discovered that there was some defect in the appointment of such Directors or persons acting as aforesaid, or that they or any of them were disqualified, be as valid as if every such person had been duly appointed and was qualified to be a Director.

100. A resolution in writing signed by all the Directors shall be as valid and effectual as if it had been passed at the Meeting of the Directors duly called and constituted.

101. If any of the Directors shall be called upon to perform extra services, or to make any special exertions in going or residing abroad for any of the purposes of the Company or the business thereof, the Company shall remunerate the Director or Directors so doing, either by a fixed sum or by a percentage of profits, or otherwise as may be determined, and such remuneration may be either in addition to or in substitution for his or their share in the remuneration hereinbefore provided for the Directors.

102. A Director may hold any other office under the Company in conjunction with his office of Director.

POWERS OF DIRECTORS.

103. The management of the business and the control of the Company shall be vested in the Directors, who in addition to the powers and authorities by these presents expressly conferred upon them, may exercise all such powers and do all such acts and things as may be exercised or done by the Company, and are not hereby or by statute expressly directed or required to be exercised or done by the Company in General Meeting, but subject nevertheless to such regulations not being inconsistent with these presents as may from time to time be made by Extraordinary Resolution ; but no regulation shall invalidate any prior act of the Directors which would have been valid if such regulation had not been made.

104. Without prejudice to the general powers conferred by the last preceding clause, and to the other powers and authorities conferred as aforesaid, it is hereby expressly declared that the Directors shall be entrusted with the following powers, namely :—

(1) To pay the costs, charges and expenses, preliminary and incidental to the formation and establishment of the Company.

(2) To purchase or otherwise acquire for the Company any property, rights or privileges which the Company is authorized to acquire at such price and generally on such terms and conditions as they may think fit.

(3) To sell any property belonging to them, and either absolutely or reserving fee farm rents thereout, or let any portions thereof on lease or otherwise on such terms and conditions as they may think fit.

(4) At their discretion to pay for any property or rights acquired by or services rendered to the Company either wholly or partially in cash or Shares, Bonds, Debentures, or other Securities of the Company, and any such Shares may be either issued as fully paid up, or with such amount credited as paid up thereon as may be agreed upon, and any such Bonds, Debentures, or other Securities may be either specially charged upon all or any part of the property and rights of the Company (including its uncalled Capital) or not so charged.

(5) To secure the fulfilment of any contracts or engagements entered into by the Company by mortgage or charge of all or any of the property and rights of the Company, including its uncalled Capital for the time being, or in such other manner as they may think fit.

(6) To appoint, and at their discretion remove or suspend such Managers, Secretaries, Officers, Clerks, Agents, and Servants for permanent, temporary, or special services as they may from time to time think fit, and to invest them with such powers as they may think expedient, and to determine their duties and to fix their salaries or emoluments, and to require security in such instances and to such amount as they think fit.

(7) To attach to any Shares to be issued as the consideration or part of the consideration for any contract with or property acquired by the Company such conditions as to transfer thereof as they think fit.

(8) To appoint any person or persons to accept and hold in trust for the Company any property belonging to the Company, or in which it is interested, and to execute and do all such deeds and things as may be requisite to vest the same in such person or persons.

(9) To execute in the name and on behalf of the Company such mortgages, charges, and other securities on the Company's property (present and future), including its uncalled Capital, as they think fit in favour of any Director or Directors of the Company who may incur, or be about to incur, any personal liability for the benefit of the Company, and any such instrument may contain a power of sale and such other powers, covenants, and provisions as may be agreed on.

(10) To institute, conduct, defend, compound, or abandon any legal proceedings by and against the Company or its officers, or otherwise concerning the affairs of the Company, and also to compound and allow time for payment or satisfaction of any debts due and of any claims or demands by or against the Company.

(11) To refer any claims or demands by or against the Company to arbitration, and observe and perform the awards.

(12) To make and give receipts, releases, and other discharges for money payable to the Company, and for the claims and demands of the Company.

(13) To act on behalf of the Company in any matters relating to bankrupts and insolvents.

(14) To accept, on such terms as may seem expedient, the surrender of the whole or any part of the Shares or Stock of any Member.

(15) To give any officer or other person employed by the Company a commission on the profits of any particular business or transaction, or a share in the general profits of the Company, and such interest, commission, or share of profits shall be treated as part of the working expenses of the Company, and to pay commissions and make allowances to any persons introducing business to the Company or otherwise promoting the business thereof.

(16) From time to time to set aside such of the assets of the Company as they think proper as a reserve fund, to meet contingencies or for equalizing dividends, or for repairing, improving, and maintaining any of the property of the Company, and for such other purposes as the Directors shall in their absolute discretion think conducive to the interests of the Company, and to invest the several sums so set aside upon such investments as they think fit, and from time to time to deal with and vary such investments and dispose of all or any part thereof for the benefit of the Company, and to divide the reserve fund into such special funds as they think fit, with full power to employ the whole or any of the assets constituting the reserve fund in the business of the Company, and that without being bound to keep the same separate from the other assets. But so much only of the reserve fund as represents profits shall be applicable to the payment of dividends.

DIVIDENDS.

105. Subject to the rights of Members entitled to Shares issued upon special conditions, the profits of the Company shall be divisible among the Members in proportion to the amount paid up on the Shares held by them respectively, provided, nevertheless, that where money is paid up in advance of Calls upon the footing that the same shall carry interest, such money shall carry interest accordingly, and not (whilst carrying interest) confer a right to participate in profits.

106. The Company in General Meeting may declare a dividend to be paid to the Members according to their rights and interest in the profits, and may fix the time for payment.

107. No larger dividend shall be declared than is recommended by the Directors, but the Company in General Meeting may declare a smaller dividend.

108. No dividend shall be payable except out of the profits arising from the business of the Company.

109. The Directors may from time to time pay to the Members such interim dividends as in their judgment the position of the Company justifies.

110. Any General Meeting declaring a dividend may make a Call on the Members whose Shares are not fully paid up of such amount as the meeting fixes, but so that the Call on each Member shall not exceed the dividend payable to him, and so that the Call be made payable at the same time as the dividend, and the dividend may, if so arranged between the Company and the Member, be set off against the Call. The making of a Call under this Clause shall be deemed ordinary business of an Ordinary General Meeting which declares a dividend.

111. The Directors may retain dividends payable on any Shares upon which the Company has a lien, and may apply the same in or towards satisfaction of the debts, liabilities and engagements in respect of which the lien exists.

112. The Directors may retain the dividends payable upon registered Shares or Stock in respect of which any person is, under the transmission clause, entitled to become a Member, or which any person under that clause is entitled to transfer until such person shall become a Member in respect of such Share or Stock, or shall duly transfer the same.

113. In case several persons are registered as the joint holders of any Shares or Stock, any one of such persons may give effectual receipts for all dividends and payments on account of dividends in respect of such Shares or Stock.

114. Notice of declaration of any dividend, whether interim or otherwise, shall be given to the registered Members in manner hereinafter provided.

115. The Company shall not be responsible for the loss of any cheque, dividend warrant, or post office order which shall be sent by post to any Member in respect of dividends.

ACCOUNTS.

116. The Directors shall cause true accounts to be kept of the sums of money received and expended by the Company, and all matters in respect of which such receipt and expenditure takes place, and of the assets, credits and liabilities of the Company.

117. The Directors shall from time to time determine whether, and to what extent, and at what times and places, and under what conditions or regulations, the accounts and books of the Company, or any of them, shall be open to the inspection of the Members, and no Member shall have any right of inspecting any account or book or document of the Company except as conferred by statute or authorized by the Directors or by a resolution of the Company in General Meeting.

118. At the Ordinary Meeting in every year the Directors shall lay before the Company a statement of the income and expenditure and a balance sheet containing a summary of the property and liabilities of the Company made up to the date not more than three months before the Meeting from the time when the last preceding statement and balance sheet were made, or, in the case of the first statement and balance sheet, from the incorporation of the Company.

119. Every such statement shall be accompanied by a report of the Directors as to the state and condition of the Company, and as to the amount which they recommend to be paid out of the profits by way of dividends or bonus to the Members, and the amount (if any) which they propose to carry to the reserve fund according to the provisions in that behalf hereinbefore contained, and the statement, report and balance sheet shall be signed by two Directors and countersigned by the Secretary.

120. A printed copy of such balance sheet and report shall three days at least before the Meeting be served on the registered holders of Shares and Stock in the manner in which notices are hereinafter directed to be served.

AUDIT.

121. Once at least in every year the Accounts of the Company shall be examined and the correctness of the statement and balance sheet ascertained by one or more Auditor or Auditors.

122. The first Auditor or Auditors shall be appointed by the Directors: subsequent Auditors shall be appointed by the Company at the Ordinary Meeting in each year. The remuneration of the Auditor or Auditors shall be fixed by the Company in General Meeting. Any Auditor quitting office shall be eligible for re-election. If one Auditor only is appointed all the provisions herein contained relating to Auditors shall apply to him.

123. The Auditors may be Members of the Company, but no person shall be eligible as an Auditor who is interested otherwise than as a Member of the Company in any transaction thereof, and no Director or other officer shall be eligible as Auditor during his continuation in office.

124. If any casual vacancy occurs in the office of Auditor the Directors shall forthwith fill up the same.

125. The Auditors shall be supplied with copies of the statement of accounts and balance sheet intended to be laid before the Company in General Meeting seven days at least before the Meeting to which the same are to be submitted, and it shall be their duty to examine the same with the accounts and vouchers relating thereto, and to report to the Company in General Meeting thereon.

126. The Auditors shall at all reasonable times have access to the books and accounts of the Company, and they may, in relation thereto, examine the Directors or other officers of the Company.

127. Every account of the Directors when audited and approved by a General Meeting shall be conclusive, except as regards any error discovered therein within three months next after the approval thereof. Whenever any such error is discovered within that period the account shall forthwith be corrected and thenceforth shall be conclusive.

NOTICES.

128. A notice may be served by the Company upon any Member either personally or by sending it through the post in a prepaid letter addressed to such Member at his registered place of address.

129. A Member whose registered place of address is not in the United Kingdom may from time to time notify in writing to the Company some place for service in the United Kingdom, and such place shall be regarded as his registered place of address for the purpose of the last preceding clause hereof.

130. As regards Members (if any) who have no registered address or no registered address in England, a notice posted up in the office shall be deemed to be duly served on them at the expiration of twenty-four hours after it is so posted.

131. Any notice required to be given by the Company to the Members, or any of them, and not expressly provided for by these presents, shall be sufficiently given by advertisement, and any notice required to be or which may be given by advertisement, shall be advertised once in two London daily newspapers.

132. All notices with respect to Shares or Stock standing in the names of joint holders shall be given to whichever of such persons is named first in the Register, and notice so given shall be sufficient notice to all the holders of such Shares or Stock.

133. Any notice sent by post shall be deemed to have been served on the day following that on which the letter or wrapper containing the same is posted, and in proving such service it shall be sufficient to prove that the letter or wrapper containing the notice was properly addressed and put into the Post Office.

134. Any person who by operation of law, transfer, or other means whatsoever, shall become entitled to any Share or Stock, shall be bound by every notice in respect of such Share or Stock which, previously to his name and address being entered in the Register, shall be duly given to the person from whom he derives title to such Share or Stock.

135. Where a given number of days' notice, or notice extending over any other period, is required to be given, the day of service shall be counted in such number of days or other period.

WINDING UP.

136. If the Company shall be wound up and the surplus assets shall be insufficient to repay the whole of the paid-up Capital, such surplus assets shall be distributed so that as nearly as may be the losses shall be borne by contributories in proportion to the Capital paid up, or which ought to have been paid up, on the Shares in respect of which they are contributories at the commencement of the winding-up. But this clause is to be without prejudice to the rights of the holders of Shares issued upon special conditions.

137. If the Company shall be wound up, the Liquidators, whether voluntary or official, may with the sanction of an Extraordinary Resolution divide among the contributories in specie any part of the assets of the Company, and may with the like sanction vest any part of the assets of the Company in Trustees upon such trusts for the benefit of the contributories as the Liquidators with the like sanction shall think fit.

138. If at any time the Liquidators of the Company shall make any sale or enter into any agreement pursuant to Section 161 of "The Companies Act, 1862," a dissentient Member within the meaning of that section shall not have the rights thereby given to him, but instead thereof he may by notice in writing (addressed to the Liquidators and left at the office not later than fourteen days after the Meeting at which the Special Resolution authorizing such sale or arrangement was passed) require the Liquidators to sell the Share, Stock or other benefits to which under the said sale or arrangement he would otherwise have become entitled, and to pay the net proceeds over to him, and such sale and payments shall be made accordingly. Such last mentioned sale may be made in such manner as the Liquidators think fit.

139. Any such sale or arrangement, or the Special Resolution confirming the same, may provide for the distribution or appropriation of the Shares, cash or other benefits to be received in compensation otherwise than in accordance with the legal rights of the contributories of the Company, and in particular any class may be given preferential or special rights, or may be excluded altogether or in part; but in case any such provision shall be made, the last preceding clause shall not apply to the intent that a dissentient Member in such case may have the rights conferred on him by Section 161 of "The Companies Act, 1862."

INDEMNITY.

140. Every Director, Manager, Secretary and other officer or servant of the Company shall be indemnified by the Company against, and it shall be the duty of the Directors out of the funds of the Company to pay, all costs, losses and expenses which any such officer or servant may incur or become liable to by reason of any contract entered into, or act or deed done by him as such officer or servant, or in any way in the discharge of his duties. And no Director or other officer of the Company shall be liable for the acts, receipts, neglects or defaults of any other Director or officer, or for joining in any receipt or other act for conformity, or for any loss or expense happening to the Company through the insufficiency or deficiency of title to any property acquired by order of the Directors for or on behalf of the Company, or for the insufficiency or deficiency of any security in or upon which any of the moneys of the Company shall be invested, or for any loss or damage arising from the bankruptcy, insolvency or tortious act of any person with whom any moneys, securities or effects shall be deposited, or for any other loss, damage or misfortune whatever which shall happen in the execution of the duties of his respective office or in relation thereto, unless the same happen through his own wilful act or default.

Names, Addresses, and Descriptions of Subscribers.

CHARLES HENRY DANCEY, 6, Midland Road, Gloucester, Plumber.

GEORGE CUMMINGS, Spa Road, Gloucester, Maltster.

WILLIAM HENRY PHILLIPS, 81, Worcester Street, Gloucester, Painter.

ALFRED JOHN BARNES, 24, St. Aldate Street, Gloucester, Decorator.

HENRY WILLIAM BENNETT, 70, London Road, Gloucester, Compositor.

JAMES PHILIP MOORE, 9, Berkeley Street, Gloucester, Architect.

HERBERT SUMNER SIMPSON, 60, Wellington, Street, Gloucester, Bank Cashier.

Dated this 11th day of August, 1891.

Witness to the above Signatures,

ARTHUR E. SHORTLAND,

Clerk to Messrs. Bretherton, Son, and Boughton,

Solicitors, Gloucester.

No. 34603C.

N.L. 2673

Certificate of Incorporation

OF THE

Gloucester Football and Athletic Ground Company, Limited.

I hereby Certify, That the

Gloucester Football and Athletic Ground Company, Limited,

is this day Incorporated under the Companies' Acts, 1862 to 1890, and that the Company is **Limited**.

Given under my hand at London this *Twelfth* day of *August* One Thousand Eight Hundred and Ninety *One*.

Fees and Deed Stamps £ 5 5/-

Stamp Duty on Capital £ 4

Registrar of Joint Stock Companies.

Appendix E
The Original Shareholders in the Gloucester Football & Athletic Ground Company, Ltd.

Registered Number	Certificate of	Share Numbers	Issued To	Occupation	Address	Date of Issue
1	50 Shares	1 to 50	Chas. George Clark	Wine Merchant	Blackfriars, Gloucester.	15th Sept. 1891
2	10 Shares	51 to 60	Ernest Wright	Tobacconist	Southgate Street, Gloucester.	15th Sept. 1891
3	5 Shares	61 to 65	Walter Thomas Herring	Clerk	124 Oxford Road, Gloucester.	15th Sept. 1891
4	5 Shares	66 to 70	Evan Grismond Hughes	Chemist	Northgate Street, Gloucester.	15th Sept. 1891
5	2 Shares	71 to 72	Chas. Edwin Turner	Plumber	75 Barton Street, Gloucester.	15th Sept. 1891
6	2 Shares	73 to 74	Chas. Pritchard	Plumber	1 Clarence Terrace, Gloucester.	15th Sept. 1891
7	5 Shares	75 to 79	William Brendon Selley	Commercial Traveller	Glenmore, London Road, Gloucester.	15th Sept. 1891
8	5 Shares	80 to 84	George Onley	Pawnbroker	Southgate Street, Gloucester.	15th Sept. 1891
9	5 Shares	85 to 89	Henry Smith Crump	Iron Merchant	Worcester Street, Gloucester.	15th Sept. 1891
10	2 Shares	90 to 91	Edward Clark	Foreman	Bristol Road, Gloucester.	15th Sept. 1891
11	5 Shares	92 to 96	William Roberts	Fruiterer	Northgate Street, Gloucester.	15th Sept. 1891
12	20 Shares	97 to 116	Annie Jebb	Wife of D. G. Jebb	Oaklands, Brockwith, Nr. Gloucester.	15th Sept. 1891
13	10 Shares	117 to 126	James Herbert Seabrook	Clerk in Holy Orders	Brockworth Vicarage, Gloucester.	15th Sept. 1891
14	20 Shares	127 to 146	William George Ayliff	Gentleman	125 Oxford Road, Gloucester.	15th Sept. 1891
15	5 Shares	147 to 151	Ernest Moase Newcombe	Corn Merchant	18 Brunswick Road, Gloucester.	15th Sept. 1891
16	2 Shares	152 to 153	Thomas Smith	Merchant's Clerk	79 Oxford Road, Gloucester.	15th Sept. 1891
17	5 Shares	154 to 158	John William Coren	Solicitor	Belgrave Road, Gloucester.	15th Sept. 1891
18	20 Shares	159 to 178	Mary Baker	Widow	The Cottage, Hardwicke, Nr. Gloucester.	15th Sept. 1891
19	10 Shares	179 to 188	Frank Tandy	Brickmaker	Sandhurst Road, Gloucester.	15th Sept. 1891
20	5 Shares	189 to 193	Edwin Richings	No Occupation	38 Oxford Street, Gloucester.	15th Sept. 1891
21	10 Shares	194 to 203	Harry Godwin Chance	Journalist	6 Palace Yard, Gloucester.	15th Sept. 1891
22	10 Shares	204 to 213	William Edwin Berry	Gentleman	Hucclecote, Nr. Gloucester.	15th Sept. 1891
23	20 Shares	214 to 233	George Berry	Jeweller	70 Northgate Street, Gloucester.	15th Sept. 1891
24	6 Shares	234 to 239	Thomas Henry Simmons	Printer	c/o John Bellows, Eastgate, Gloucester.	15th Sept. 1891
25	1 Share	240	John Lewis	Unknown (blank)	20 St. Catherine Street, Gloucester.	15th Sept. 1891
26	1 Share	241	John Frederick Lewis	Unknown (blank)	20 St. Catherine Street, Gloucester.	15th Sept. 1891
27	1 Share	242	Charles Davis	Unknown (blank)	26 St. Catherine Street, Gloucester.	15th Sept. 1891
28	2 Shares	243 to 244	Eliza Messenger	Inn Keeper	Horse & Groom Inn, London Road, Gloucester.	15th Sept. 1891
29	25 Shares	245 to 269	Conway Jones	Decorator, House	Blenheim Villa, Hucclecote, Nr. Gloucester.	15th Sept. 1891
30	4 Shares	270 to 273	Rosa Annie Williams	Spinster	29 Clement Street, Gloucester.	15th Sept. 1891
31	10 Shares	274 to 283	David Jones	Clothier	The Golden Anchor, Gloucester.	15th Sept. 1891
32	2 Shares	284 to 285	Ralph John Browning	Farmer	Quedgeley, Nr. Gloucester.	15th Sept. 1891
33	5 Shares	286 to 290	William Young	Inn Keeper	15 St. Mary's Square, Gloucester.	15th Sept. 1891
34	3 Shares	291 to 293	Edwin Gunnell	Labourer	10 Clarence Street, Gloucester.	15th Sept. 1891
35	20 Shares	294 to 313	John Edward Dorington	Baronet; M. P.	Lypiatt Park, Stroud, Glos.	15th Sept. 1891
36	5 Shares	314 to 318	Henry William Bennett	Printer's Manager	70 London Road, Gloucester.	15th Sept. 1891
37	5 Shares	319 to 323	Frederick Joseph Bennett	Newspaper Reporter	122 Oxford Road, Gloucester.	15th Sept. 1891
38	1 Share	324	George Walter Coates	Boiler Maker	34 Wellesley Street, Gloucester.	15th Sept. 1891
39	5 Shares	325 to 329	John Gwilliam Critchley	Farmer	Longford, Gloucester.	15th Sept. 1891
40	5 Shares	330 to 334	Ernest John Critchley	Postal Clerk	Longford, Gloucester.	15th Sept. 1891
41	5 Shares	335 to 339	Susan Dainton	Widow	46 Northgate Street, Gloucester.	15th Sept. 1891
42	1 Share	340	William Chas. Watkins	Clerk	4 Park Road, Gloucester.	15th Sept. 1891
43	1 Share	341	William Caswell Hardman	Auctioneer	Brunswick Road, Gloucester.	15th Sept. 1891
44	5 Shares	342 to 346	John Vaughan Payne	Clerk in Holy Orders	Kempsford House, Gloucester.	15th Sept. 1891
45	10 Shares	347 to 356	Harry Warner Grimes	Solicitor	Queen Street, Gloucester.	15th Sept. 1891
46	10 Shares	357 to 366	Charles Blagden Hale	Esquire	Claremont House, Gloucester.	15th Sept. 1891
47	5 Shares	367 to 371	Harry Fletcher Minchin	Solicitor's Clerk	5 Jersey Road, Gloucester.	15th Sept. 1891
48	12 Shares	372 to 383	Daniel Thomas Mitchell	Gentleman	Foley House, Hucclecote, Nr. Gloucester.	15th Sept. 1891
49	5 Shares	384 to 388	Charles Isaacs	Hatter & Hosier	17 Northgate Street, Gloucester.	15th Sept. 1891
50	5 Shares	389 to 393	Thomas Wright	Clerk	Pembroke Street, Gloucester.	15th Sept. 1891
51	2 Shares	394 to 395	John James Romans	Telegraphist	13 Parliament Street, Gloucester.	15th Sept. 1891
52	10 Shares	396 to 405	Harry Alfred Dancey	Architect	Woodlands, Midland Road, Gloucester.	15th Sept. 1891
53	2 Shares	406 to 407	John Mills	Post Office Clerk	27 Archibald Street, Gloucester.	15th Sept. 1891
54	5 Shares	408 to 412	Charles Roberts & Sidney Stephen Starr	Seedsmen	both of, 92 Northgate Street, Gloucester.	15th Sept. 1891
55	10 Shares	413 to 422	John Ward	Gentleman	Bohanan House, Wotton, Gloucester.	15th Sept. 1891
56	2 Shares	423 to 424	Charles Granville Clutterbuck	Clerk	Weston Road, Gloucester.	15th Sept. 1891
57	5 Shares	425 to 429	Harry Frederick Blizard	Maltster	Fernlea, Belgrave Road, Gloucester.	15th Sept. 1891
58	2 Shares	430 to 431	Ralph Jenkins	Postman	New Street, Newent, Glos.	15th Sept. 1891
59	5 Shares	432 to 436	Walter Henry Fox	Dentist	Clarence Street, Gloucester.	15th Sept. 1891
60	2 Shares	437 to 438	John Howard Clinch	Gentleman	Wotton, Gloucester.	15th Sept. 1891
61	2 Shares	439 to 440	Hugh Douglas Clinch	Gentleman	Wotton, Gloucester.	15th Sept. 1891
62	1 Share	441	Arthur Howard Clinch	Corn Merchant	Wotton, Gloucester.	15th Sept. 1891
63	5 Shares	442 to 446	Samuel Henry Fox	Corn Merchant	Hillfield, Gloucester.	15th Sept. 1891
64	5 Shares	447 to 451	George Keeling	Hairdresser	13 London Road, Gloucester.	15th Sept. 1891
65	5 Shares	452 to 456	George Lewis	Inn Keeper	The Dolphin Inn, Northgate Street, Gloucester.	15th Sept. 1891
66	25 Shares	457 to 481	Charles Henry Dancey	No Occupation	6 Midland Road, Gloucester.	15th Sept. 1891
67	25 Shares	482 to 506	Thomas Nelson Foster	Merchant	Gloucester.	15th Sept. 1891
68	25 Shares	507 to 531	Richard Gibbs Foster	Merchant	2 Spa Villas, Gloucester.	15th Sept. 1891
69	3 Shares	531 to 534	Joseph Edward Dutton	Clerk	Ryecroft Street, Gloucester.	15th Sept. 1891
70	3 Shares	535 to 537	John Edward Hullett	Solicitor's Clerk	39 Regent Street, Gloucester.	15th Sept. 1891
71	10 Shares	538 to 547	William Turk	Furniture Dealer	9 Southgate Street, Gloucester.	15th Sept. 1891
72	5 Shares	548 to 552	Samuel Septimus Higgs	Traveller, Salesman	Vyner House, Park End Road, Gloucester.	15th Sept. 1891
73	5 Shares	553 to 557	William Charles Poulton	Upholsterer	121 Southgate Street, Gloucester.	15th Sept. 1891
74	2 Shares	558 to 559	Charles Donington Smith	No Occupation	c/o Samuel Smith, Brunswick Sq., Gloucester.	15th Sept. 1891
75	1 Share	560	George Perris	Shoeingsmith	3 Commercial Road, Gloucester.	15th Sept. 1891

76	1 Share	561	John William Hawker	Coachman	59 Southgate Street, Gloucester.	15th Sept. 1891
77	5 Shares	562 to 566	John Gurney	Builder	Albert Villa, Derby Road, Gloucester.	15th Sept. 1891
78	5 Shares	567 to 571	Joseph Gurney	Builder	Charles Street, Gloucester.	15th Sept. 1891
79	20 Shares	572 to 591	Thomas Gurney	Builder	1 Widden Street, Gloucester.	15th Sept. 1891
80	10 Shares	592 to 601	Edward Plant	Gentleman	Clarence Street, Gloucester.	15th Sept. 1891
81	1 Share	602	Percival John Orchard	No Occupation	King Street, Gloucester.	15th Sept. 1891
82	5 Shares	603 to 607	Robert William Orchard	Clothes Dealer	6 King Street, Gloucester.	15th Sept. 1891
83	10 Shares	608 to 617	John Minahan	Engine Driver	6 Clarence Terrace, Barton Street, Gloucester.	15th Sept. 1891
84	1 Share	618	George Francillon	Clerk, Telegraph	5 Stroud Road, Gloucester.	15th Sept. 1891
85	5 Shares	619 to 623	Hubert Gopsill Brown	Clerk	Saintbridge House, Nr. Gloucester.	15th Sept. 1891
86	2 Shares	624 to 625	Frank Edward Jones	Builder	Cromwell Street, Gloucester.	15th Sept. 1891
87	5 Shares	626 to 630	Alfred John Barnes	Decorator	St. Aldate Street, Gloucester.	15th Sept. 1891
88	2 Shares	631 to 632	William Curtis	Clerk	118 Westgate Street, Gloucester.	15th Sept. 1891
89	5 Shares	633 to 637	George Frank Merrett	Commercial Clerk	13 Goodyere Street, Gloucester.	15th Sept. 1891
90	5 Shares	638 to 642	George James Dewey	Corn Merchant	Heathville Road, Gloucester.	15th Sept. 1891
91	1 Share	643	Frank Jones	Collector for Gas Co.	25 Eastgate Street, Gloucester.	15th Sept. 1891
92	1 Share	644	Thomas Bailey	Bricklayer	5 Victoria Street, Gloucester.	15th Sept. 1891
93	10 Shares	645 to 654	James Crofts	Schoolmaster	Sir Thomas Rich's School, Gloucester.	15th Sept. 1891
94	5 Shares	655 to 659	George James Witcomb	Farmer	The Knapp, Pixley, Ledbury.	15th Sept. 1891
95	10 Shares	660 to 669	William Clark	Grocer	Southgate Street, Gloucester.	15th Sept. 1891
96	1 Share	670	Edward Dairs	Wagon Fitter	9 Lidney Street, Gloucester.	15th Sept. 1891
97	5 Shares	671 to 675	Raymond Phillip Lewis	Bricklayer	56 Blenheim Road, Gloucester.	15th Sept. 1891
98	5 Shares	676 to 680	Arthur Henry Lewis	Toll Collector; Market	Prospect House, Gloucester.	15th Sept. 1891
99	2 Shares	681 to 682	Thomas Little	Draper	Worcester Street, Gloucester.	15th Sept. 1891
100	1 Share	683	Walter Baxendale	Journalist	Echo Office, Gloucester.	15th Sept. 1891
101	10 Shares	684 to 693	John Bellows	Printer	Eastgate, Gloucester.	15th Sept. 1891
102	10 Shares	694 to 703	Thomas Henry Washburn	Solicitor	1 Newland Villas, London Road, Gloucester.	15th Sept. 1891
103	5 Shares	704 to 708	William Williams	Haulier	18 Llanthony Road, Gloucester.	21st Sept. 1891
104	1 Share	709	William Burnell	Printer	30 Worrall Street, Gloucester.	21st Sept. 1891
105	1 Share	710	Charles Fox	Elocutionist	Kingsholm Square, Gloucester.	21st Sept. 1891
106	9 Shares	711 to 719	William Henry Phillips	Painter & Decorator	81 Worcester Street, Gloucester.	21st Sept. 1891
107	1 Share	720	William Henry Phillips Jr.	House Decorator	81 Worcester Street, Gloucester.	21st Sept. 1891
108	20 Shares	721 to 740	Thomas Amphlett	Labourer	77 St. Catherine Street, Gloucester.	21st Sept. 1891
109	1 Share	741	Hubert James Amphlett	Labourer	90 St. Catherine Street, Gloucester.	21st Sept. 1891
110	10 Shares	742 to 751	Frederick Haine	Farmer	Over Farm, Nr. Gloucester.	21st Sept. 1891
111	25 Shares	752 to 776	Francis Treleaven Vibert	Timber Merchant	1 Western Terrace, Gloucester.	21st Sept. 1891
112	10 Shares	777 to 786	Thomas Addison Washbourn	Wine Merchant	Hucclecote, Nr. Gloucester.	21st Sept. 1891
113	5 Shares	787 to 791	Lewis Peake	Timber Merchant	9 College Green, Gloucester.	21st Sept. 1891
114	1 Share	792	Edwin Thomas Phillips	Turner	81 Worcester Street, Gloucester.	21st Sept. 1891
115	5 Shares	793 to 797	Charles Edward Brown	Clerk	Saintbridge House, Nr. Gloucester.	21st Sept. 1891
116	5 Shares	798 to 802	Walter Madge	Timber Dealer & Joiner	Brunswick Road, Gloucester.	21st Sept. 1891
117	2 Shares	803 to 804	Frederick White	Auctioneer	77 Barton Street, Gloucester.	21st Sept. 1891
118	5 Shares	805 to 809	James Godwin Vicker	Provision Dealer	Westgate Street, Gloucester.	21st Sept. 1891
119	50 Shares	810 to 859	Dennis Reardon	Commission Agent	26 London Road, Gloucester.	21st Sept. 1891
120	10 Shares	860 to 869	Charles Hopkins	Inn Keeper	Deans Walk, Gloucester.	21st Sept. 1891
121	10 Shares	870 to 879	Herbert Sumner Simpson	Bank Cashier	4 Birchwood Terrace, Gloucester.	21st Sept. 1891
122	5 Shares	880 to 884	Edwin Lea	Furnishing Contractor	St. Aldate House, Gloucester.	21st Sept. 1891
123	10 Shares	885 to 894	William Washbourn	Surgeon	Blackfriars.	21st Sept. 1891
124	15 Shares	895 to 909	Charles Thorne	Insurance Manager	6 Lower Barton Street, Gloucester.	21st Sept. 1891
125	5 Shares	910 to 914	Edwin Calton	Gentleman	Kingsholm, Gloucester.	21st Sept. 1891
126	10 Shares	915 to 924	Frederick William Wood	Commercial Traveller	19 Park End Road, Gloucester.	21st Sept. 1891
127	5 Shares	925 to 929	William George Roberts	Turner; Iron	65 Blenheim Road, Gloucester.	21st Sept. 1891
128	1 Share	930	David Gurney	Tailor	3 Queen Street, Gloucester.	21st Sept. 1891
129	10 Shares	931 to 940	George Symonds	Job Master	College Mews, Gloucester.	21st Sept. 1891
130	5 Shares	941 to 945	Trevor Barrett Powell	Clerk	Beaufort Buildings, Spa, Gloucester.	21st Sept. 1891
131	5 Shares	946 to 950	William Maitland	Commercial Traveller	Western Road, Gloucester.	21st Sept. 1891
132	100 Shares	951 to 1050	Richard Vassar Vassar Smith	Esquire, J.P.	Charlton Park, Charlton Kings, Cheltenham, Glos.	21st Sept. 1891
133	10 Shares	1051 to 1060	William Dancey	Land Agent's Clerk	Cobden House, Park Road, Gloucester.	21st Sept. 1891
134	2 Shares	1061 to 1062	Alfred Curtis Townsend	Merchant's Clerk	Copia Villas, Stroud Road, Gloucester.	21st Sept. 1891
135	1 Share	1063	James Lafford	Dentist	14 Hethersett Road, Gloucester.	21st Sept. 1891
136	20 Shares	1064 to 1083	William Edwin Phelps	Dairyman	5 Lower Westgate Street, Gloucester.	21st Sept. 1891
137	10 Shares	1084 to 1093	Charles Priday	Steamship Owner	Westgate Bridge, Gloucester.	21st Sept. 1891
138	1 Share	1094	Richard James	Grocer's Assistant	5 Kings Barton Street, Gloucester.	21st Sept. 1891
139	50 Shares	1095 to 1144	George Cummings	Maltster	Spa, Gloucester.	21st Sept. 1891
140	1 Share	1145	Raymond John Wilkins	Dentist	c/o Mrs. Trigg, Bearland, Gloucester.	21st Sept. 1891
141	20 Shares	1146 to 1165	James Philip Moore	Architect	9 Berkeley Street, Gloucester.	21st Sept. 1891
142	2 Shares	1166 to 1167	William Charles Bailey	Clerk	14 Upton Street, Gloucester.	21st Sept. 1891
143	5 Shares	1168 to 1172	Demetrius Bevan Pegler	Gentleman	1 Brook Street, Gloucester.	21st Sept. 1891
144	3 Shares	1173 to 1175	William Alfred Thomas	Commercial Traveller	19 St. Michael's Square, Gloucester.	21st Sept. 1891
145	2 Shares	1176 to 1177	Henry Woolley	House Decorator	Southgate Street, Gloucester.	21st Sept. 1891
146	5 Shares	1178 to 1182	Edwin Richards	Gentleman	Park Road, Gloucester.	21st Sept. 1891
147	5 Shares	1183 to 1187	Alfred James Mills	Baker & Grocer	78 Lower Barton Street, Gloucester.	21st Sept. 1891
148	5 Shares	1188 to 1192	Ernest David Tandy	Licensed Victualler	Northgate Street, Gloucester.	21st Sept. 1891
149	5 Shares	1193 to 1197	Charles Apperley	Clerk	Laburnum Brewery, Ryecroft Street, Gloucester.	21st Sept. 1891
150	5 Shares	1198 to 1202	Walter John Apperley	Clerk	Laburnum Brewery, Ryecroft Street, Gloucester.	21st Sept. 1891
151	20 Shares	1203 to 1222	Herbert James Berry	Licensed Victualler	The New Inn, Gloucester.	21st Sept. 1891
152	20 Shares	1223 to 1242	Robert Wood	Commercial Traveller	6 Birchwood Terrace, Gloucester.	21st Sept. 1891
153	10 Shares	1243 to 1252	Henry Cosens	Bank Accountant	26 Cromwell Street, Gloucester.	21st Sept. 1891
154	5 Shares	1253 to 1257	William James Bartlett	Hairdresser	Brunswick Road, Gloucester.	21st Sept. 1891
155	2 Shares	1258 to 1259	Albert Cole Seymour	Cabinet Maker	54 Westgate Street, Gloucester.	21st Sept. 1891

156	5 Shares	1260 to 1264	William Thomas Clutterbuck	Maltster	4 Brunswick Square, Gloucester.	21st Sept. 1891
157	3 Shares	1265 to 1267	Fred Whithorn Lovesy	Grocer	24 St. Mary Street, Gloucester.	21st Sept. 1891
158	50 Shares	1268 to 1317	Thomas Robinson	Esquire; M.P.	Maisemore Park, Nr. Gloucester.	21st Sept. 1891
159	1 Share	1318	Frederick Mansfield	Cabinet Maker	Oxford Terrace, Gloucester.	21st Sept. 1891
160	5 Shares	1319 to 1323	Tom Graves Smith	Engineer	13 Clarence Street, Gloucester.	21st Sept. 1891
161	5 Shares	1324 to 1328	John James Fisher	Grocer's Assistant	Canute Villas, Kingsholm Square, Gloucester.	21st Sept. 1891
162	2 Shares	1329 to 1330	Joseph Henry Brown	Coachman	Upton St. Leonards, Nr. Gloucester.	21st Sept. 1891
163	5 Shares	1331 to 1335	Richard Probyn	Shipwright; Master	22 Parliament Street, Gloucester.	21st Sept. 1891
164	2 Shares	1336 to 1337	Henry Roberts	Baker & Grocer	65 Millbrook Street, Gloucester.	21st Sept. 1891
165	2 Shares	1338 to 1339	Walker Brabent	House Agent	Kingsholm, Gloucester.	21st Sept. 1891
166	3 Shares	1340 to 1342	Caleb Stephens	Decorator	9 Worcester Street, Gloucester.	21st Sept. 1891
167	1 Share	1343	Dennis Stephens	Bricklayer	43 Worcester Street, Gloucester.	21st Sept. 1891
168	5 Shares	1344 to 1348	David Beale	Baker	Westgate Street, Gloucester.	21st Sept. 1891
169	100 Shares	1349 to 1448	Hubert James Boughton	Solicitor	Linden Grove, Spa, Gloucester.	21st Sept. 1891
170	5 Shares	1449 to 1453	John Charles Richards	Solicitor	Queen Street, Gloucester.	21st Sept. 1891
171	20 Shares	1454 to 1473	John Williams (Sergt. Major)	Instructor; Sergt.	Artillery Grounds, Clifton, Bristol.	21st Sept. 1891
172	10 Shares	1474 to 1483	James Clarke	Builder	9 Kingsholm Road, Gloucester.	21st Sept. 1891
173	25 Shares	1484 to 1508	Samuel Davis	Haberdasher	24 Westgate Street, Gloucester.	21st Sept. 1891
174	100 Shares	1509 to 1608	Arthur Williams Vears	Timber Merchant	25 Brunswick Square, Gloucester.	21st Sept. 1891
175	5 Shares	1609 to 1613	Henry Thomas Compton	Corn Dealer	Kingsholm, Gloucester.	21st Sept. 1891
176	3 Shares	1614 to 1616	Job Edward Mayo	Confectioner	94 Northgate Street, Gloucester.	21st Sept. 1891
177	20 Shares	1617 to 1636	Henry Mansell	Carrier	Quedgeley Court, Nr. Gloucester.	21st Sept. 1891
178	10 Shares	1637 to 1646	Charles Frank Green	Gunsmith	16 Northgate Street, Gloucester.	21st Sept. 1891
179	1 Share	1647	Frederick Benjamin Lewis	Printer	134 Lower Barton Street, Gloucester.	21st Sept. 1891
180	1 Share	1648	Joseph Nugent Lewis	Undertaker & Builder	134 Lower Barton Street, Gloucester.	21st Sept. 1891
181	20 Shares	1649 to 1668	Alfred Gyde	Builder	St. Mary's Street, Gloucester.	21st Sept. 1891
182	5 Shares	1669 to 1673	Herbert Collier	House Salesman	35 Brunswick Square, Gloucester.	21st Sept. 1891
183	5 Shares	1674 to 1678	William Charles Ferris	Hatter & Hosier	90 Northgate Street, Gloucester.	21st Sept. 1891
184	5 Shares	1679 to 1683	Geo. Pike	Banker	Eastgate Street, Gloucester.	21st Sept. 1891
185	100 Shares	1684 to 1783	Lewis Henry Priday	Land Agent	Longford Court, Nr. Gloucester.	21st Sept. 1891
186	5 Shares	1784 to 1788	Charles Bramham	Eating House Keeper	Eastgate Street, Gloucester.	21st Sept. 1891
187	5 Shares	1789 to 1793	William Piff	Inspector of Police	Police Station, Gloucester.	21st Sept. 1891
188	5 Shares	1794 to 1798	John William Goddard	Commercial Traveller	5 Russell Street, Gloucester.	21st Sept. 1891
189	2 Shares	1799 to 1800	Charles Firmin Cuthbert	Surgeon	Barton Street, Gloucester.	21st Sept. 1891
190	5 Shares	1801 to 1805	William Charles Mann	Watchmaker	The Cross, Gloucester.	21st Sept. 1891
191	1 Share	1806	Alick Rigby	Fish Salesman	5 Columbia Street, Gloucester.	21st Sept. 1891
192	5 Shares	1807 to 1811	George Holford	Fish Salesman	31 Columbia Street, Gloucester.	21st Sept. 1891
193	5 Shares	1812 to 1816	John William Bayley	Wine Merchant	Geyfriars, Gloucester.	21st Sept. 1891
194	2 Shares	1817 to 1818	Henry Wells	Foreman	Albert Villa, Southgate Street, Gloucester.	21st Sept. 1891
195	10 Shares	1819 to 1828	William Albert Boughton	Corn Merchant	Severn House, Kings Road, Cardiff.	21st Sept. 1891
196	5 Shares	1829 to 1833	William Sadler Hall	Gentleman	Cranham, Nr. Painswick.	21st Sept. 1891
197	50 Shares	1834 to 1883	Arnold Perrett & Co., Ltd.	Brewers	Wickwar, Gloucestershire.	21st Sept. 1891
198	5 Shares	1884 to 1888	Charles Morris	Grocer	Romsdal House, Brunswick Road, Gloucester.	21st Sept. 1891
199	10 Shares	1889 to 1898	Alfred William Bott	Gentleman	Barnwood, Nr. Gloucester.	21st Sept. 1891
200	5 Shares	1899 to 1903	Charles Bossom	Glass & China Dealer	95 Northgate Street, Gloucester.	21st Sept. 1891
201	50 Shares	1904 to 1953	Albert James Lane	Gentleman	Fairview House, St. Mary's Square, Gloucester.	21st Sept. 1891
202	2 Shares	1954 to 1955	William James Robinson	Pattern Maker	14 Clifton Road, Gloucester.	21st Sept. 1891
203	5 Shares	1956 to 1960	George Merrylees	Manager	Lothian House, Stroud Road, Gloucester.	21st Sept. 1891
204	5 Shares	1961 to 1965	Edmund Joseph Cullis	Civil Engineer	8 Midlands Road, Gloucester.	21st Sept. 1891
205	3 Shares	1966 to 1968	Daniel Bretherton	Stationer & Printer	4 King Street, Gloucester.	24th Sept. 1891
206	25 Shares	1969 to 1993	Sidney Lane	Warehouseman	Brunswick Square, Gloucester.	24th Sept. 1891
207	5 Shares	1994 to 1998	Oliver Henry Brendon	Provision Dealer	Northgate Street, Gloucester.	24th Sept. 1891
208	3 Shares	1999 to 2001	George Phillip Jones	Engineer	139 Oxford Road, Gloucester.	24th Sept. 1891
209	5 Shares	2002 to 2006	Thomas Allard	Builder	Stroud Road, Gloucester.	24th Sept. 1891
210	5 Shares	2007 to 2011	Harold Cadle	Commercial Traveller	Cuthill House. Stroud Road, Gloucester.	24th Sept. 1891
211	10 Shares	2012 to 2021	Thomas Enstone	Haulier	Coach & Horses Inn, St. Catherine St., Gloucester.	24th Sept. 1891
212	1 Share	2022	William Gray	Curator of Oddfellows H.	81 Barton Street, Gloucester.	24th Sept. 1891
213	1 Share	2023	Thomas Jabez	Tobacconist	47 Northgate Street, Gloucester.	24th Sept. 1891
214	50 Shares	2024 to 2073	Alfred Woodward	Gentleman	Egerton Villa, Spa, Gloucester.	24th Sept. 1891
215	2 Shares	2074 to 2075	William Clutterbuck	Draper	Northgate Street, Gloucester.	24th Sept. 1891
216	10 Shares	2076 to 2085	John Barnard	Corn Merchant	Granville House, Spa, Gloucester.	24th Sept. 1891
217	5 Shares	2086 to 2090	Alfred Ernest Healing	Miller	The Crescent, Tewkesbury.	24th Sept. 1891
218	5 Shares	2091 to 2095	James Holmes	Grocer	65 Worcester Street, Gloucester.	24th Sept. 1891
219	5 Shares	2096 to 2100	George Aaron Baker	Watchmaker	95 Northgate Street, Gloucester.	24th Sept. 1891
220	15 Shares	2101 to 2115	Ellen Gertrude Brendon	Spinster	Clarefield, London Road, Gloucester.	24th Sept. 1891
221	10 Shares	2116 to 2125	Henry Albert Ryland	Licensed Victualler	Fountain Inn, Westgate Street, Gloucester.	24th Sept. 1891
222	10 Shares	2126 to 2135	Charles Morgan	Tailor	Westgate Street, Gloucester.	24th Sept. 1891
223	5 Shares	2136 to 2140	Charles Niblett	Clerk	3 Cambridge Street, Gloucester.	24th Sept. 1891
224	5 Shares	2141 to 2145	Henry Lukes	Miller	The Island, Gloucester.	24th Sept. 1891
225	5 Shares	2146 to 2150	Samuel Bland	Journalist	Wells Green, Park Road, Gloucester.	24th Sept. 1891
226	1 Share	2151	Joseph Owner Jr.	Clerk	Market Parade, Gloucester.	24th Sept. 1891
227	2 Shares	2152 to 2153	Robert Jones Vallender	Printer	16 Oxford Street, Gloucester.	24th Sept. 1891
228	5 Shares	2154 to 2158	Henry William Bruton	Land Agent	Wotton, Gloucester.	24th Sept. 1891
229	10 Shares	2159 to 2168	George Peters	Contractor	Brunswick Square, Gloucester.	24th Sept. 1891
230	10 Shares	2169 to 2178	Sidney Goldwin Simpson	Accountant	60 Wellington Street, Gloucester.	24th Sept. 1891
231	5 Shares	2179 to 2183	Thomas Southern	Grocer	Northgate Street, Gloucester.	24th Sept. 1891
232	50 Shares	2184 to 2233	James Buchanan	Newspaper Proprietor	The "Standard" Office, Gloucester.	24th Sept. 1891
233	2 Shares	2234 to 2235	Tom Blinkhorn	Draper	Denmark Road, Gloucester.	24th Sept. 1891
234	5 Shares	2236 to 2240	Benjamin Coombs	Accountant	The Manor House, Kinsholm Square, Gloucester.	24th Sept. 1891
235	5 Shares	2241 to 2245	Thomas Organ	Licensed Victualler	The Black Dog Hotel, Gloucester.	24th Sept. 1891

236	10 Shares	2246 to 2255	Julia Agnes Teague Phelps	Spinster	105 Falkner Street, Gloucester.	24th Sept. 1891
237	10 Shares	2256 to 2265	John Henry Kilminster	Inn Keeper	The Nelson Inn, Gloucester.	24th Sept. 1891
238	20 Shares	2266 to 2285	James Bruton	Gentleman	Wotton Hill, Gloucester.	24th Sept. 1891
239	5 Shares	2286 to 2290	Alfred Berry	Builder	London Road, Gloucester.	24th Sept. 1891
240	10 Shares	2291 to 2300	John Hanman	Grocer	Southgate Street, Gloucester.	24th Sept. 1891
241	6 Shares	2301 to 2306	Rosa Annie Williams	Spinster	29 Clement Street, Gloucester.	2nd Nov. 1891
242	5 Shares	2307 to 2311	Edward Chessall Scobell	Clerk in Holy Orders	Upton St. Leonards, Nr. Gloucester.	2nd Nov. 1891
243	100 Shares	2312 to 2411	Arthur Vincent Hatton	Brewer	Worcester Street, Gloucester.	2nd Nov. 1891
244	2 Shares	2412 to 2413	Ralph Houldey	Wine & Spirit Merchant	Southgate Street, Gloucester.	2nd Nov. 1891
245	2 Shares	2414 to 2415	Thomas Godwin Briggs	Traveller	Albion House, Falkner Street, Gloucester.	2nd Nov. 1891
246	5 Shares	2416 to 2420	John Ambrose Fisher	Confectioner	Westgate Street, Gloucester.	2nd Nov. 1891
247	1 Share	2421	Thomas George Beak Goddard	No Occupation	5 Russell Street, Gloucester.	2nd Nov. 1891
248	5 Shares	2422 to 2426	Elizabeth Frances Moffatt	Wife of H. Moffatt	Kingsholm, Gloucester.	2nd Nov. 1891
249	5 Shares	2427 to 2431	George Philip Gilson	Corn Merchant	2 Birchwood Terrace, Alexandra Row, Gloucester.	2nd Nov. 1891
250	10 Shares	2432 to 2441	Samuel John Moreland	Match Manufacturer	Brunswick Square, Gloucester.	2nd Nov. 1891
251	5 Shares	2442 to 2446	Thomas Wright	Clerk	Pembroke Street, Gloucester.	2nd Nov. 1891
252	10 Shares	2447 to 2456	William John Newth	Wine Merchant	St. Aubius, Heathville Road, Gloucester.	2nd Nov. 1891
253	10 Shares	2457 to 2466	Joseph Clissold	Brewer	Nailsworth, Nr. Stroud.	2nd Nov. 1891
254	5 Shares	2467 to 2471	William Thomas Taylor	Grocer	Station Road, Gloucester.	2nd Nov. 1891
255	15 Shares	2472 to 2486	Leonard Stanley Pinnegar	Clerk	Sharpness, Nr. Berkeley, Glos.	2nd Nov. 1891
256	5 Shares	2487 to 2491	Ephraim Pickford	Decorator	Brunswick Square, Gloucester.	2nd Nov. 1891
257	5 Shares	2492 to 2496	Daniel Lane	Builder	Worcester Street, Gloucester.	2nd Nov. 1891
258	5 Shares	2497 to 2501	David Lane	Gentleman	Hardwicke, Nr. Gloucester.	2nd Nov. 1891
259	10 Shares	2502 to 2511	Henry Robert Hooper	Cloth Manufacturer	Eastington Lodge, Nr. Stonehouse, Glos.	2nd Nov. 1891
260	20 Shares	2512 to 2531	Charles Frampton	Commercial Traveller	15 Falkner Street, Gloucester.	2nd Nov. 1891
261	25 Shares	2532 to 2556	Arthur Williams Vears and Charles Robbins	Gentlemen	Gloucester.	2nd Nov. 1891
262	10 Shares	2557 to 2566	John Jennings	Printer	Caxton House, Brunswick Road, Gloucester.	2nd Nov. 1891
263	5 Shares	2567 to 2571	Charles Holbrook, Jnr.	Draper	Elvanhurst, Barnwood, Nr. Gloucester.	2nd Nov. 1891
264	5 Shares	2572 to 2576	William Woodward	Gas Fitter	Lower Barton Street, Gloucester.	2nd Nov. 1891
265	5 Shares	2577 to 2581	James Herbert	Commercial Traveller	35 Brunswick Square, Gloucester.	2nd Nov. 1891
266	10 Shares	2582 to 2591	Frederick May	Stockbroker	Eldon Chambers, Gloucester.	30th Nov. 1891
267	10 Shares	2592 to 2601	Walter James Ruegg	Stockbroker	6 Rowcroft, Stroud, Glos.	30th Nov. 1891
268	5 Shares	2602 to 2606	Daniel Crump	Commercial Traveller	Brunswick Square, Gloucester.	30th Nov. 1891
269	5 Shares	2607 to 2611	William James Johnston Vaughan	Gentleman	The Old Rectory, Wotton, Gloucester.	30th Nov. 1891
270	5 Shares	2612 to 2616	Daniel Cripps Jones	Contractor	Cromwell Street, Gloucester.	30th Nov. 1891
271	50 Shares	2617 to 2666	James Bretherton	Solicitor	Bell Lane, Gloucester.	30th Nov. 1891
272	100 Shares	2667 to 2766	Hawkins Bretherton	Solicitor	Belgrave Road, Gloucester.	30th Nov. 1891
273	2 Shares	2767 to 2768	Edward Oliver Murray	Brewer's Traveller	100 Oxford Road, Gloucester.	30th Nov. 1891
274	5 Shares	2769 to 2773	Peter Grant	Foreman	Edwy Parade, Kingsholm, Gloucester.	9th Dec. 1891
275	5 Shares	2774 to 2778	Henry Charles Frith	Sculptor	Lower Barton Street, Gloucester.	9th Dec. 1891
276	10 Shares	2779 to 2788	James Wareing	Tailor	The Cross, Gloucester.	9th Dec. 1891
277	5 Shares	2789 to 2793	Henry Burton Berry	Chemist	The Cross, Gloucester.	9th Dec. 1891
278	5 Shares	2794 to 2798	Edward Dallimore	No Occupation	Conduit Street, Gloucester.	9th Dec. 1891
279	2 Shares	2799 to 2800	Cyrus Maule	Fish Salesman	Southgate Street, Gloucester.	15th Dec. 1891
280	5 Shares	2801 to 2805	Edward Arthur Twinney	Clerk	1 Spring Villas, Wotton, Gloucester.	19th Dec. 1891
281	2 Shares	2806 to 2807	Henry Hale	Goods Guard	9 Millbrook Street, Gloucester.	16th Jan. 1892
282	20 Shares	2808 to 2827	John Martin Collett	Gentleman	Brunswick Square, Gloucester.	25th Feb. 1892
283	20 Shares	2828 to 2847	John Fielding	Gentleman	Somerset Lawn, Gloucester.	25th Feb. 1892
284	20 Shares	2848 to 2867	Henry Moffatt	Butcher	Kingsholm, Gloucester.	16th Mar. 1892
285	5 Shares	2868 to 2872	Ernest Godfrey Moffatt	Butcher	Kingsholm, Gloucester.	16th Mar. 1892
286	1 Share	2873	Hugh Moreton Goddard	No Occupation	5 Russell Street, Gloucester.	16th Mar. 1892
287	5 Shares	2874 to 2878	William Symons	Gentleman	17 Weston Road, Gloucester.	13th Apr. 1892
293	50 Shares	2879 to 2928	Mary Hemingway	Widow	Longford House, Gloucester.	26th Apr. 1892
294	50 Shares	2929 to 2978	T. G. Smith; H. W. Bennett; S. S. Starr;	Gentlemen	Gloucester Football Club.	8th Jun. 1892
295	10 Shares	2979 to 2988	Sarah Jane Cooke	Wife of Herbert Cooke	Filely House, St. Michael Square, Gloucester.	8th Jun. 1892
296	7 Shares	2989 to 2995	Charles Henry Dancey	No Occupation	6 Midland Road, Gloucester.	8th Jun. 1892
297	5 Shares	2996 to 3000	Theophilus Chivers	Gentleman	Wellington Parade, Gloucester.	17th Jun. 1892

Appendix F
The Conveyance of Castle Grim, 1891

T H I S I N D E N T U R E made the 11th day of November A.D. 1891

BETWEEN THE DEAN & CHAPTER of the Cathedral Church of the Holy & Indivisible

Trinity in Gloucester (hereinafter called the said Dean & Chapter) of the

1st part THE ECCLESIASTICAL COMMISSIONERS FOR ENGLAND (hereinafter called

the said Commissioners) of the 2nd part ARTHUR VINCENT HATTON of the City

of Gloucester Brewer of the 3rd part and THE GLOUCESTER FOOTBALL & ATHLETIC

GROUND CO. LTD. (hereinafter called the said Company) of the 4th part

WHEREAS the said Dean & Chapter as such are lawfully seised of or otherwise

well and sufficiently entitled to the hereditaments hereinafter described

subject as hereinafter mentioned and it has been made to appear to the

satisfaction of the said Commissioners that the said hereditaments may

to the permanent advantage of the estate or endowments belonging to the said

Dean and Chapter be sold for the sum and in manner hereinafter mentioned

AND WHEREAS the said Dean & Chapter in exercise and in pursuance of the

powers given to or vested in them by the Ecclesiastical Leasing Acts and all

other powers enabling them in this behalf have with the approval of the said

Commissioners testified as hereinafter mentioned contracted to sell to

the said A. V. Hatton for the sum of £3600 the said hereditaments hereinafter

described subject as hereinafter mentioned AND WHEREAS since the date of the

said Contract the said A. V. Hatton hath agreed to resell the said here-

ditaments to the said Company for the sum of £4400 NOW THIS INDENTURE

WITNESSETH that in pursuance of the said Contract and Agreement and in

consideration of the sum of £3600 paid by the said Co. before the execution

of these presents into the Bank of England to the account of the said

Commissioners as directed by them in that behalf the payment whereof is

intended to be acknowledged by the memoranda endorsed on these presents

AND also in consideration of the sum of £800 sterling (making with the said sum of £3600 the said sum of £4400) now paid by the said Co. to the said

A. V. Hatton the receipt whereof he doth hereby acknowledge The said Dean &

Chapter in exercise and pursuance of the powers and authorities given to or

vested in them by the Ecclesiastical Leasing Acts and of every other power

enabling them in this behalf and with the approval of the said Commissioners

testified by this deed under their Common Seal and at the request and by

the direction of the said A. V. Hatton testified by his executing these

presents do hereby convey and the said A. V. Hatton doth hereby confirm

unto the said Co.   ALL THAT messuage or dwellinghouse known as "Castle Grim"

with the 2 cottages (formerly one cottage) builders yard pieces or parcels

of pasture land and garden ground thereunto adjoining and belonging containing

altogether 7a. 0r. 4p. or thereabouts situate at Kingsholm in the City of

Gloucester and more particularly delineated and shewn in the map or plan

thereof drawn in the margin of these presents being thereon coloured pink

together with (if and so far as the said Dean & Chapter have power to convey

and the said A. V. Hatton hath power to confirm the same but not further

or otherwise) one half of the bed of the River Twyver on the Southern side

of the said premises TO HAVE and to hold the said hereditaments subject

to Tithe Commutation Rent Charge or Rent Charges and all other duties and

payments Ecclesiastical or Civil charged upon or payable out of the same

hereditaments and to all rights of way and water and other easements (if any)

affecting the same unto and to the use of the said Co. in fee simple subject

to the existing tenancies AND the said Dean & Chapter do hereby covenant

with the said Co. that they have not at any time heretofore done committed

or executed or knowingly suffered any act deed matter or thing whereby or

by reason or on account whereof the said hereditaments or any part thereof

have or hath been charged incumbered or prejudicially affected in title estate or otherwise howsoever IN WITNESS whereof the said Dean & Chapter

the said Ecclesiastical Commissioners and the said Co. have caused their

respective Common Seals to be hereunto affixed and the said A. V. Hatton

hath hereunto set his hand and seal the day and year first above written.

THE COMMON SEAL of the within named Company)
was hereunto affixed in the presence of   )

    A. W. Vears   )
) Directors
    L. H. Priday)

    H. S. Simpson, Secretary.

SIGNED SEALED AND DELIVERED by the within)
named Arthur Vincent Hatton in the   )
presence of   A. V. Hatton   L.S.

    R. S. Smith,
        Clerk to Messrs. Whitcombe & Gardom,
            Solicitors, Gloucester.

Appendix M
The Advice given to the Ground Company by their Solicitors in 1923 on the Procedure by which the Club might take Ownership of the Kingsholm Ground

PCL/VHL.

GRIMES, MADGE & LLOYD,
Solicitors.
PARTNERS.
W. H. MADGE, LL.B., NOTARY PUBLIC.
PERCY C. LLOYD.

TELEGRAMS: GRIMES, GLOUCESTER.
TELEPHONE: 224.

20, Bell Lane,
Gloucester.

29th January, 1923.

Dear Sir,

We enclose herewith some Notes on the procedure if the Football Club acquire the Assets of the Football Company.

We should add here that these Notes should first come before the Chairman of the Directors of the Football Company, before they are shown to any other Director or to any other interested person.

When the Chairman is free to deal with the matter, please pass the enclosed on to him and he and you may like to see us on the matter, before calling a special Meeting of the Directors to discuss the procedure.

Yours faithfully,

Grimes Madge & Lloyd

Mr. Sidney Starr,
    Secretary,
        The Gloucester Football &c. Co. Ltd.
            Gloucester.

THE GLOUCESTER FOOTBALL & ATHLETIC GROUND COMPANY LIMITED.

and

THE GLOUCESTER RUGBY UNION FOOTBALL CLUB.

IT is understood that the Committee and Members of the Gloucester Football Club who now hold the majority of the issued Shares of the Football Company, are desirous of acquiring the control of the Ground and in fact the Ground itself and all the other assets of the Company situate at Kingsholm.

Before dealing with the only manner in which this acquisition can be legally carried out, the fact may be recorded here that the Football Company was formed in the year 1891 by the Subscribers to its Memorandum & Articles of Association to acquire the ground and then generally to let and utilize the Ground for the purpose of Athletic Sports of all kinds and particularly to let a portion of the Ground for the use of the Gloucester Rugby Union Football Club for the purposes of Football.

The above mentioned Subscribers paid par value for their shares and for every Share issued by the Company par value has been paid. From the incorporation of the Company to the present time the Shareholders have looked upon their investment as of assistance to Sport generally and not from an income bearing point of view.

If the Football Club are seriously desirous of acquiring the Ground and the Assets of the Company, this can only be carried on proper formal lines and the procedure will be as follows:-

The Assets of the Football Company, according to the audited Balance Sheet dated 4th December 1922 for the year ending 31st August 1922 were as follows:-

Assets

Freehold land, Football & Athletic Ground, Fences, Rollers, Machines, Plant and Effects.   £6640. 4. 7.

Cash at Bank and in hands of Secretary.   241. 13. 1.

£ 6881. 17. 8.

1.

The Liabilities on 31st August are according to the above mentioned account:-

Issued Share Capital.

3150 Shares of £1. each fully paid.	£3150. 0. 0.
Due on Mortgage .	3500. 0. 0.
	6650. 0. 0.
Balance in hand from Revenue Account.	231. 17. 8.
	£ 6881. 17. 8.

The first step is to get an offer in writing from the Football Club, addressed to the Directors of the Football Company, making a definite offer to purchase the Ground and all the Assets of the Company for a certain sum.

The amount of this certain sum must be sufficient to clear off the Mortgage and it should also be sufficient with any cash assets in the hands of the Football Company.

1. Not only to pay the necessary expenses which will have to be incurred by the Football Company in connection with the Transfer of the Ground, etc. to the Football Club and the winding up of the Company but also

2. To enable the Liquidator of the Company out of the balance eventually available for that purpose to pay to each Shareholder par value for his shares.

The Liquidator of the Company will have to deal with fully paid shares in his winding up and he cannot under Company Law in any way differentiate between Shareholders on the basis of what they gave for their shares if they gave less than par, when they acquired them.

The Shares are all £1. fully paid Shares and as I have already stated the Company for each original share issued received £1. and the Liquidator will have to deal with them on the footing that all the issued shares rank equally, when he comes to distribute the assets in his hands amongst the Shareholders of the Football Company.

For these reasons the figures of the offer to be made by the

2.

Football Club to the Football Company require very careful consideration.

When this definite offer is in the hands of the Chairman oft he Directors , he should instruct the Secretary to call an Extraordinary General Meeting of the Shareholders of the Company to consider this offer.

The Notice for this Meeting would be in the following form -

THE GLOUCESTER FOOTBALL & ATHLETIC GROUND COMPANY LTD.

NOTICE IS HEREBY GIVEN that an Extraordinary General Meeting of the Members of the above named Company will be held at

on (Monday) the   day of   1923

for the purpose of considering and if thought fit of passing with or without modification, the following Resolution as an Extraordinary Resolution of the Company, namely:-

That the offer of the Gloucester Football Club to purchase the whole of the Assets of the Company for the sum of £ now before this Meeting be accepted and thatthe Directors be requested to instruct the Company's Solicitors to carry out the sale and to complete the matter as soon as possible.

By Order of the Board

Secretary.

Gloucester.
January 1923.

Assuming this Resolution is passed, the Company's Solicitor will then have to carry through the necessary legal formalities.

The next important point to be considered is in whose names shall the Conveyance of the Freehold Land on behalf of the Football Club be taken.

3

These persons, whoever they are, will simultaneously with the completion of the Conveyance to them have to execute a Deed setting out that they hold the property on behalf of the Football Club and not beneficially.

It has been suggested that Lloyds Bank Ltd. would take over this Trust on behalf of the Football Club.

If this is the wish of the Club, the Bank should be approached on the matter.

The Football Club will have to find the cash for the purchase money and this cash will have to be paid over to the Football Company, who will out of it, pay off the Mortgage and obtain the Deeds of the property in exchange.

Immediately this money is in the hands of the Company another Extraordinayy General Meeting of the Company will have to be held to appoint a Liquidator, who will wind up the Company in Voluntary Liquidation.

He will take possession of the Cash Balance after paying off the Mortgage money and after payment of the expenses of liquidation, he will divide the surplus between the Shareholders of the Company in proportion to the number of shares held by each Shareholder.

The expenses of the sale to the Football Club and of the winding up will have to be considered in fixing the price to be paid for the Assets of the Company and these will all be paid by the Liquidator and he will only divide the net balance between the Shareholders.

Certain expenses will also be payable by the Football Club, they will have to pay the stamp duty on the Conveyance and their part of the costs of the Conveyance and the Trust Deed and for this reason the amount of the purchase money must be very carefully considered.

As to who shall be appointed as Liquidator, that is a matter for the Shareholders of the Football Company to consider and decide. Someone conversant with Company law and who has

3.

stock-in-trade, and any real or personal property of any kind necessary or convenient for the purposes of or in connection with the Company's business or any branch or department thereof.

3.13   To erect, construct, lay down, enlarge, alter, repair and maintain any roads, railways, tramways, sidings, bridges, reservoirs, shops, stores, factories, buildings, works, plant and machinery necessary or convenient for the Company's business, and to contribute to or subsidise the erection, construction and maintenance of any of the above.

3.14   To borrow or raise or secure the payment of money for the purpose of or in connection with the Company's business, and for the purposes of or in connection with the borrowing or raising of money by the Company to become a member of any building society.

3.15   To mortgage and charge the undertaking and all or any of the real and personal property and assets present or future, and all or any of the uncalled capital for the time being of the Company, and to issue at par or at a premium or discount, and for such consideration and with such rights, powers and privileges as may be thought fit, debentures or debenture stock, either permanent or redeemable or repayable, and collaterally or further to secure any securities of the Company by a trust deed or other assurance.

3.16   To make advances to customers and others with or without security, and upon such terms as the Company may approve, and to give indemnity for or to guarantee, support or secure the performance of all or any of the obligations of any person company or organisation whether by personal covenant or by mortgage, charge or lien on the whole or any part of the undertaking property and assets of the Company both present and future, including its uncalled capital, or by all or any of such methods; and in particular but without limiting the generality of the foregoing, to give indemnity for or to guarantee, support or secure whether by personal covenant or by any such mortgage charge or lien, or by all or any of such methods, the performance of all or any of the obligations (including the repayment or payment of the principal and premium of, and interest on any securities) of any company which is for the time being the Company's holding company or subsidiary or another subsidiary of any such holding company.

3.17   To receive money on deposit or loan upon such terms as the Company may approve, and generally to act as bankers for customers and others.

3.18   To remunerate in such manner as the Company shall consider expedient any person, firm, company or organisation rendering services to the Company

3.19   To remunerate persons from time to time serving as officers or employees of the Company and to make severance and termination payments upon the termination of the appointment or employment of any such persons.

3.20   To grant pensions, allowances, gratuities and bonuses to officers or ex-officers, employees or ex-employees of the Company or its predecessors in business or the dependents of such persons; to make payments for or towards all manner of

Page 4

insurance for the benefit of such individuals and their families and dependants and without prejudice to the generality of the foregoing to purchase and maintain for any officer of the Company insurance against any liability which by virtue of any rule of law would otherwise attach to him in respect of any negligence, default, breach of duty or breach of trust of which he may be guilty in relation to the Company and to such extent as may be permitted by Law, to indemnify or to exempt any such person against or from any such liability

3.21   To establish and support or to aid in the establishment and support of any schools and any educational, scientific, literary, religious, or charitable institutions or trade societies, whether such institutions or societies be solely connected with the business carried on by the Company or its predecessors in business or not, and to institute and maintain any club or other establishment or benefit fund or profit-sharing scheme calculated to advance the interests of the Company or of the officers of or persons employed by the Company.

3.22   To draw, make, accept, endorse, negotiate, discount and execute promissory notes, bills of exchange, and other negotiable instruments.

3.23   To invest and deal with the moneys of the Company not immediately required for the purposes of the business of the Company in or upon such investments and in such manner as may from time to time be determined.

3.24   To pay for any property or rights acquired by the Company either in cash or fully or partly paid-up shares, with or without preferred or deferred or special rights or restrictions in respect of dividend, repayment of capital, voting or otherwise, or by any securities which the Company has power to issue, or partly in one mode and partly in another, and generally on such terms as the Company may determine.

3.25   To accept payment for any property or rights sold or otherwise disposed of or dealt with by the Company, either in cash, by instalments or otherwise, or in fully or partly paid-up shares or stock of any company or corporation, with or without preferred or deferred or special rights or restrictions in respect of dividend, repayment of capital, voting or otherwise, or in debentures or mortgage debentures or debenture stock, mortgages or other securities of any company or corporation, or partly in one mode and partly in another, and generally on such terms as the Company may determine, and to hold, dispose of or otherwise deal with any shares, stock or securities so acquired.

3.26   To amalgamate or affiliate with or become a member of or enter into any partnership or arrangement for sharing profits, union of interests, reciprocal concession or co-operation with any company, firm, person or organisation carrying on or proposing to carry on any business within the objects of the Company or which is capable of being carried on so as directly or indirectly to benefit the Company, and to acquire and hold, sell, deal with or dispose of any shares, stock or securities of or other interests in any such company, and to guarantee the contracts or liabilities of, subsidise or otherwise assist, any such company or other firm person or organisation.

3.27 To purchase or otherwise acquire, take over and undertake all or any part of the business, property, liabilities and transactions of any person, firm or company carrying on any business which the Company is authorised to carry on, or the carrying on of which is calculated to benefit the Company or to advance its interests, or which is possessed of property suitable for the purposes of the Company.

3.28 To establish on and subject to such terms as may be considered expedient a scheme or schemes for or in relation to the purchase of or subscription for any full or partly paid shares in the capital of the Company by or by trustees for or otherwise for the benefit of employees of the Company or of its subsidiary or associated companies.

3.29 To the extent permitted by law to give financial assistance for the purpose of the acquisition of shares of the Company for the purpose of reducing or discharging a liability incurred for the purpose of such an acquisition and to give such assistance by means of a gift loan guarantee indemnity the provision of security or otherwise.

3.30 To sell, improve, manage, develop, turn to account, exchange, let on rent, royalty, share of profits or otherwise, grant licences, easements and other rights in or over, and in any other manner deal with or dispose of the undertaking and all or any of the property and assets for the time being of the Company for such consideration (if any) as the Company may think fit.

3.31 To undertake and execute the office of custodian, trustee, executor, administrator, liquidator, receiver, attorney or nominee of, or for, any person, association, scheme, trust fund, charity or governmental or public authority as may seem expedient to the Company and either gratuitously or otherwise.

3.32 To distribute among the members in specie any property of the Company, or any proceeds of sale or disposal of any property of the Company, but so that no distribution amounting to a reduction of capital be made except with such sanction (if any) as shall for the time being required by law.

3.33 To do all or any of the above things in any part of the world, and either as principals, agents, trustees, contractors or otherwise, and either alone or in conjunction with others, and either by or through agents, trustees, sub-contractors or otherwise.

3.34 To do all such other things as are incidental or conducive to the above objects or any of them.

And it is hereby declared that the objects of the Company specified in each of the foregoing paragraphs of this Clause shall be distinct and separate objects of the Company and shall be in no way limited by reference to any other paragraphs hereof or to the order in which the same appear.

4. The liability of the Members is limited.

5. The share capital of the Company is £4,000 divided into shares of One Pound each..

Page 6

Company Number:- 34603

THE COMPANIES ACT 1985
(as amended)

PRIVATE COMPANY LIMITED BY SHARES

NEW
ARTICLES OF ASSOCIATION

- of -

GLOUCESTER RUGBY FOOTBALL CLUB LIMITED

INCORPORATED ON 12 AUGUST 1891
ADOPTED ON   15 MAY 1996

PRELIMINARY

1.

    1.1   In these Articles "Table A" means Table A in the Schedule to the Companies (Tables A to F) Regulations 1985 (SI 1985 No 805) as amended by the Companies (Tables A to F) (Amendment) Regulations 1985 (SI 1985 No1052) and "the Act" means the Companies Act, 1985 including any statutory modification or re-enactment thereof for the time being in force.

    1.2   The Regulations contained in Table A shall apply to the Company save in so far as they are excluded or modified hereby. Regulations 41, 64 to 69 (inclusive), 87, 94 to 99 (inclusive), 101, 110 and 118 shall not apply, but, subject as aforesaid, and in addition to the remaining Regulations of Table A the following shall be the Articles of Association of the Company.

PRIVATE COMPANY

2.   The Company is a private company within the meaning of s.1(3) of the Act.

SHARES

3.   The share capital of the Company is £4,000 divided into 4,000 ordinary shares of £1.00 each.

4.

4.1   The Directors shall have general and unconditional authority to allot, grant options over, offer or otherwise deal with or dispose of any relevant securities of the Company (as defined in Section 80 of the Act) to such persons, at such times and generally on such terms and conditions as the Directors may determine. The authority hereby conferred shall, subject to Section 80(7) of the Act, be for a period expiring on the Fifth anniversary of the adoption of these Articles unless renewed, varied or revoked by the Company in General Meeting, and the maximum amount of relevant securities which may be allotted pursuant to such authority shall be the authorised but as yet unissued share capital of the Company at the date hereof.

4.2   The Directors shall be entitled under the authority conferred by Article 4.1 or under any renewal thereof to make at any time prior to the expiry of such authority any offer or agreement which would or might require relevant securities of the Company to be allotted after the expiry of such authority.

5.   In accordance with Section 91(1) of the Act Sections 89(1) and 90(1) - (6) (inclusive) of the Act shall not apply to the Company.

6.

6.1   The lien conferred by Regulation 8 of Table A shall attach also to fully paid shares and to all shares registered in the name of any person indebted or under liability to the Company whether he be the sole registered holder thereof or one of two or more joint holders and shall extend to all moneys presently payable by him or his estate to the Company. Regulation 8 of Table A shall be modified accordingly.

6.2   The liability of any Member in default in respect of a call shall be increased by the addition at the end of the first sentence in Regulation 18 in Table A of the words "and all expenses that may have been incurred by the Company by reason of such non-payment"

7.

7.1   Subject to the provisions of the Act, any shares in the capital of the Company may be issued on the terms that they are, or at the option of the Company are to be liable, to be redeemed on such terms and in such manner as the Company before the issue of the shares may by Special or Written Resolution determine.

7.2   Subject to Chapter VII of Part V of the Act the Company may purchase its own shares (including redeemable shares) whether out of distributable profits or the proceeds of a fresh issue of shares or otherwise.

SHARE CERTIFICATES